ROH

Mr. Peter Hayes

I love Nautilus

Author Hugo Kein
8 April 2003

KOREAN AMERICANS AND INTER-KOREAN RELATIONS

Hugo W. Kim

East-West Research Institute
Washington, DC, March 2003

Published in the United States of America
by East-West Research, Inc.
407 Sixth Street, S. W., Washington, DC 20024
Internet: www.ewri.org
Published Date: March 15, 2003

The East-West Research Institute (EWRI) was founded by Dr. Hugo Wheegook KIM in May 1990 to promote U.S.-Korea relations and the two-Korea relations for peaceful unification. The EWRI is dedicated to the advancement of East Asian studies particularly in the field of Korean affairs. EWRI provides public policy makers with a strategic perspective on issues relating to international relations, economics and business, and international security affairs pertaining to the two Koreas and the four powers of United States, China, Japan, and Russia.

Cover Page Design: Christopher A. Taggart

Library of Congress Cataloging-in-Publication Data

Kim, Hugo W., 1941-
Korean Americans and Inter-Korean Relations /Hugo W. Kim

ISBN 0-9729021-0-4 (paper, 190 pages)

1. Korean Americans – History and Politics
2. Korea – Inter-Korean Relations
3. Korea – National Unification
4. South Korea – Democracy and Economic Development
5. Asia-Pacific Region – Economic Integration
6. Asian Americans – History and Politics
I. Kim, Hugo W., 1941-

Library of Congress Control Number: 2003090919

Printed in the United States of America

TABLE OF CONTENTS

PREFACE

This book is a collection of my five papers: the first paper has been written recently, but other four papers were published in the academic journals previously. The book title for the collection of five papers was too vague to decide. The title "Korean Americans" represents the first paper, and "Inter-Korean Relations" includes four remaining papers focusing on Korean affairs. The first paper was written as part of the Project of the Korean American Heritage Foundation launched by the Centennial Committee of Korean Immigration to the United States in Washington, DC. This study provides an overview of the history of immigration to the United States and how the different races came to be integrated into America, compares the assimilation process of both European and Asian immigrant groups into the mainstream of America, analyzes political participation of Asian Americans, and suggests how to reorganize the Korean American Association for political empowerment by integrating community resources through an efficient networking system. As a Project Manager, I intended this to provide a theoretical background for the Project team to design a final proposal. The thirteen team members, specialized in various areas, met several times in 2002, which was helpful to develop the last section of this paper.

The second paper investigates development of regional integration, particularly relations between the Asia-Pacific region and the Korean peninsula; and examines problems and remedies of inter-Korean economic cooperation in the long run. It suggests policy recommendations to the related governments including Pyongyang and Seoul. The third paper was on "From Confrontation to Cooperation: A New Paradigm of Inter-Korean Relations." The study includes globalization and regional convergence, evaluation of North Korean survival strategies, ROK engagement policy toward DPRK, and inter-Korean economic cooperation. It suggests that a peace treaty mandating disarmament between the two Koreas is a precondition for inter-Korean economic cooperation. The fourth paper was written after the financial crisis of Asian countries. Economic development facilitates democratization, while democracy is necessary to maintain sustainable growth of capitalistic economies by maximizing efficiency. So the balanced growth between politics and economy reduces the cost generated by the political-economic complex. The fifth and final paper examines whether President Park Jung Hee chose the best growth strategy, whether his authoritarian presidency was necessary for economic development, and whether Chairman Kim Jung Il of North Korea can follow the lesson from the experiences of South Korea. The last paper is closely related to the fourth paper in terms of relations of politics with economy.

I was trained in economics in the school years, but Korean studies required me to engage in inter-disciplinary studies in the last fifteen years because they are closely related to broad subjects including international relations, domestic politics, economics, international security, sociology, and others such as management. Therefore, I may not be specialized in any of those areas, but I fully accept my responsibility for any shortcomings in this book. In publishing this book, I would like to express my gratitude to Dr. Ung Soo Kim from the bottom of my heart, who was one of my graduate professors at the Catholic University of America in Washington, DC, inspiring me to pursue the truth and justice in my life. My thanks are extended to my dear wife EJ who has continuously supported my studies, and my two daughters June and Heji who gave me love and energy. As a first generation immigrant, I am grateful to have given the opportunity to fully pursue my academic endeavors in an advanced supporting system in the United States. In addition, it would not have been possible without the support from the South Korean Army's overseas education program, from which my academic journey began.

Finally, if any reader wants to discuss with the author about issues that appear in this book, please contact me through e-mail at hugo.kim@verizon.net, to which I will respond as soon as possible.

Hugo Wheegook Kim, Author
Washington, DC, March 15, 2003

Chapter I
A Historical Overview of the Immigration to the United States and Political Participation of Asian Americans: A Perspective of Korean Americans[*]

Introduction

1. The history of the United States consists largely of the history of immigration because the land and nature were untouched by external civilization until the first English immigrants settled at Jamestown, Virginia in 1607 and the Dutch settled in Albany, New York in 1618. Since then, western Europeans came to America for economic opportunities, religious freedom, social mobility, and political reasons, importing almost 400,000 African slaves by the end of the Civil War. When the economy began to expand rapidly during the period of industrialization in the mid-nineteenth century, the United States received massive immigrants from eastern and southern Europe, as well as Asian immigrants from China and Japan. But the Chinese Exclusion Act of 1882 and the Immigration Act of 1924 prohibited Asian immigration because of racial prejudice of Americans. However, the Immigration Act of 1965 reopened Asian immigration to the United States. The United States became a country of immigration for all races to pursue their happiness in peace and prosperity under a system of democratic politics and a market economy. However, different interests between races caused social problems in reality. American Indians were assimilated through forced education and acculturation, and the U.S. Congress passed the laws in 1953 and 1975 to abolish reservations and allow them self-determination as U.S. citizens. European old immigrants considered new immigrants from eastern and southern Europe as an "inbetween" class which was above African and Asian but below white Americans, while those newcomers have been assimilated into the mainstream of America. African Americans started as slaves, and the Civil War brought them freedom but without means. Owing to the civil rights movement and the Civil Rights Act of 1964, their social status has improved tremendously. Accordingly, the status of Hispanic and Asian Americans began to improve.

2. European immigrants experienced different processes of assimilation to the American way of life based on ethnic identities. Irish immigrants moved into the large cities, controlled lower position workers in both private and public sectors, and mobilized urban voters, but their early political success diminished when the relative share of Irish population declined. Italians came to America largely in the early twentieth century with the intention of returning home. They attached family interests in wealth, transplanted a Sicilian criminal society to America, and focused less on education so that their social mobility became slower than others until World War II. Jewish immigrants were young and skilled, and engaged in manufacturing and trade.

---

[*] This study is part of the Project of the Korean American Heritage Foundation launched in 2002 by the *Centennial Committee of Korean Immigration to the United States* in Washington, DC. The author intended to provide a theoretical background for this project.

They focused on education with experiences of historical urbanites, socialization, and marginality so that their economic, social, and political mobility became a role model for all immigrants. On the other hand, Asian immigrants had unhappy experiences with discrimination in the past. Chinese immigration was legally prohibited in 1882, which affected Japanese with the same degree although the Gentlemen's Agreement allowed family reunion of Japanese. After the attack on Pearl Harbor, all Japanese residing in the area of Western Defense Command, native-born as well as alien, were separated into the ten War Relocation Centers and contained until December 1944. Aliens of German and Italian nationality were similarly interred, but not native-born, affecting a small part of them, while about 95 percent of Japanese in America were relocated. After the Immigration Act of 1965, the population of Asian Americans increased from 1.4 million in 1970 to 10.0 million in 2000. Asian Americans have been successful in their economic and social mobility, but their political participation lags far behind that of European immigrants.

3. Political participation of Asian Pacific Americans includes electoral engagement, non-electoral political activities for minority group protection, social justice and equal treatment for individuals, friendship development between the United States and their countries of origin, and internal politics within each ethnic community. They have pursued political empowerment by electoral participation, campaign fund raising, publicity promotion, and lobbying activities. However, Asian Americans have not represented themselves in American politics as much as their share of the U.S. population (3.8 percent), while the Jewish Americans represent almost 8 percent of members of the U.S. Congress. What is the problem of Asian Pacific Americans? The majority of Asian immigrants came to America after enactment of the Immigration Act of 1965, so that the first generation of them is the majority of each ethnic community and their children are in college education. They have been busy trying to survive in jobs, as either employees or self-employed in small businesses, while at the same time they face society with a class problem due to language insufficiency, cultural barriers, and discrimination. There have been no aggressive driving forces to organize Asian Americans for political empowerment unlike African Americans, while each ethnic community believes that they are too small in population to influence politics. Recently, the first generation of Asian Americans shows more interest in politics than before, which means that the myth of silent minority of Asian Americans will be gone sooner or later. Since 44 percent of Asian Americans have received a college education in 2000, their political, economic, and social mobility into the mainstream will be inevitable in the future. However, the ethnic diversity of Asian Americans has been a barrier for them to make a united front in politics, but it can be overcome by creating an efficient networking system. If Korean Americans in a city is efficiently organized, for example, this model can be transplanted to the major metropolitan areas where Koreans are intensively concentrated. Those units create an ethnic association for all Koreans in the United States. Each Asian ethnic association in America sends their delegates to the Asian Pacific American Association representing Asian Americans, which can participate in multiracial coalition movements for more political influence if necessary.

4. The purposes of this study is (a) to provide an overview of the history of immigration to the United States and how the different races came to be integrated into America, (b) to compare the assimilation process of both European and Asian immigrant groups into the mainstream of America, and (c) to analyze political participation of Asian Americans and suggest how to reorganize the Korean American Association for political empowerment by integrating community resources through an efficient networking system. This research intends to provide a theoretical background for Korean Americans to restructure the Korean American Association by integrating community resources for political empowerment. The study consists of six sections excluding introduction and conclusion. The first section overviews the history of immigration to the United States by four stages: colonial, industrial, limited immigration, and post industrial periods. The second section investigates the racial integration in the United States which includes immigration theories and practices of five races. The third section examines assimilation of European immigrant groups of Irish, Italian, Jewish, and Polish and the fourth section does the same of Asian immigrant groups of Chinese, Japanese, and Koreans. The fifth section analyzes political participation of Asian Americans and considers an example of Korean Americans as an ethnic minority. The sixth and final section suggests how to create a new form of the Korean American Association of Greater Washington to integrate community resources for political empowerment. This is a proposal to create a representative model for Korean Americans in other regions. In applying this proposal, proper communications between related parties within the community and between communities would be desirable to avoid unnecessary conflicts. The study applied a systems approach for the last section. Please note that this paper incorporates history, politics, economics, sociology, and management where the author is partially specialized, but he fully accepts his responsibility for any shortcomings in this paper.

Historical Overview of Immigration to the United States

5. The land of North America was open to Europeans in the age of mercantilism – nations pursued economic self sufficiency with export surplus by government control of the economy owing to strong military and naval forces.[1] The European immigration to America in the seventeenth century was caused not by demand of American Indians, but by forced supply or conquest of Europeans due to their political, economic, social, and religious desires.[2] The Portuguese reached the coast of Brazil in 1500, settled successfully in Sao Paulo and Pernambuco in the Northeast and created a governorship in 1550, and competed with Spain and France until they were ceded to Spain from 1580 to 1640.[3] Spain conquered the great Aztec and Incan empires for their mercantilist needs through mining, agriculture, and trade.[4] European mining methods produced more silver sent to Spain, but killed many Indians so that the population of Peru fell by one half and that of Mexico declined by one-third a century after the Spanish conquest.[5] The inflow of precious metals into Spain caused inflation for its economy while its government spent more treasure than was supplied for its political and religious ambitions.[6] However, it was a great benefit that food crops

developed by American Indians such as corn, potatoes, and manioc were introduced around the world as a new source of human diet.[7] Contrasted to this, the Jesuits entered Cordoba of Argentina in 1599,[8] and non Spanish Europeans began to acquire Caribbean islands after 1600, such as Jamaica, where the Spanish had not settled. As the Indian population declined rapidly, a new slave trade developed in the Caribbean where the large plantations were established by Europeans demanded cheaper labor forces for sugar exports. Slave traders made high profits by buying slaves from the west coast of Africa and selling them from Brazil to Mexico and later to North America.

6. The European immigration to colonial America began with the Dutch and French pursuing the fur trade with the Indians. The Dutch settled at Fort Orange (Albany, New York) in 1618 and New Amsterdam (New York City) later, but domestic policies discouraged massive settlements so that it was difficult for average citizens to obtain usable land in the colony. In the later period, the expansion of Dutch settlements was restricted by the Yankees moving down from New England. The French settled in the St. Lawrence River valley initially, gained control of the Ohio and Mississippi valleys later, and settled near New Orleans in the eighteenth century, despite the lack of supportive policies from the French government. The French were successful in fur trade in its early stages, and considered Indians as trading partners and potential military allies. The French Huguenots left for the New World in order to get better economic opportunities coupled with religious freedom. They tried to Christianize Indians and treated them as nearly as equals. The desire of acquiring land was another motive for the French to leave their fatherland for America. The population in Europe was 95 million in 1600 but increased to 120 million in 1700, 190 million in 1800, and 400 million in 1900. The rapid growth of population and limited land expedited French and other European immigrants to leave their countries for America. Finally, France had less incentive to hold colony in America, while Britain was concentrating resources on the colonial war by minimizing her efforts in Europe. The British won the Seven Year's War due to her naval superiority, and the Treaty of Paris in 1763 forced France to cede Canada and the lands east of the Mississippi to Britain. Britain also received Florida from Spain, which gained part of the Louisiana territory from France instead.[9]

7. The first English immigrants in America settled at Jamestown, Virginia in 1607 financed by the London Company, and it was organized without women and operated along semi-military lines.[10] Many became seriously ill and died, and their survival was threatened without a continuous supply of tools and manufactured goods from England, although the arrival of women in the later years strengthened the new system because it provides more incentive for the settlers to build families, develop properties, and become permanent immigrants. Since the company failed to finance further, the Crown took over the colony's charter in 1623. As Virginia became successful in producing and exporting tobacco to Europe in huge quantities, more labor was demanded and immigration to the colony was stimulated. The passage cost for an immigrant paid by Virginia planters was the average annual wages of Englishman, and sponsors required three to seven years' labor from the new arrival providing room and

board without wages. Although Europeans had employed African slave labor in the Caribbean islands and South America, Virginia initially imported Africans as indentured servants, not slaves, but slavery was declared to be hereditary in 1664. The proportion of slaves was 11 percent of the colonial population in 1700, but the number increased rapidly. The settlement in New England started from Plymouth in 1620, New Hampshire in 1623, and Massachusetts Bay in 1629 with motives of economic gain, political ambition, and religious colonization.[11] Unlike Virginia, where immigration was pushed by investors, the immigrants who came to New England were recruited by promoters who promised them that they would have a better life in America. They were organized into family groups, who were economically secure and socially educated in England, in which the Puritans were a minority.[12] Massachusetts created the two colonies of Rhode Island and Connecticut and established trading posts inland and on the seacoast of Maine. Maryland was founded by George Calvert in 1634, who desired to colonize the land to be a haven for Catholic believers. It was successful economically through planting tobacco.

Table 1. National or Linguistic Stocks in the United States, 1790 (White only)

National & Linguistic	Proportion %	National & Linguistic	Proportion %
English	60.1	French	2.3
Scotch	8.1	Swedish	0.7
Irish-Ulster	5.9	Spanish	0.8
Irish-Others	3.6	Unassigned	6.8
German	8.6		
Dutch	3.1	Total	100.0

Source: *Annual Report of the American Historical Association for the Year 1931* (Washington, DC: U.S. Government Printing Office, 1932)

Table 2. Estimated Slave Imports into the Americas: Importing Region 1451-1870 (in Thousand)

Region & Country	1451-1600	1601-1700	1701-1810	1811-1870	Total
British North America			348.0	51.0	399.0
Spanish America	75.0	292.5	1401.3		1552.1
British Caribbean		263.7	1401.3		1665.0
French Caribbean		155.8	1348.4	96.0	1600.2
Dutch Caribbean		40.0	460.0		500.0
Danish Caribbean		4.0	24.0		28.0
Brazil	50.0	560.0	1891.4	1145.4	3646.8
Europe and Old World	149.9	25.1			175.0
Total Number (Proportion %)	274.9 (2.87%)	1341.1 (14.02%)	6051.7 (63.26%)	1898.4 (19.85%)	9566.1 (100%)

Source: Philip D. Curtin, *The African Slave Trade: A Census* (Madison, WI, 1969)

8. The first census of the United States in 1790 indicated that three-fifth of white Americans were English as shown in Table 1. The Germans were 8.6 percent, in second place. When 13,000 German refugees from Rhineland immigrated to England during the period of 1703-1713, the British government sent 600 to North Carolina and

3,000 to New York.[13] Some of their descendants moved to Pennsylvania where German immigrants continuously grew. In third place, the Ulster Irish were 5.9 percent, mostly concentrated in Pennsylvania, while the other Irish were 3.6 percent who came to America as indentured servants or well-established Catholic immigrants to New York and Philadelphia.[14] In fourth place, the Scotch was 8.1 percent who settled in New Jersey and South Carolina, while that of Dutch was 3.1 percent, who largely settled in New York. Finally, 9,566,100 African slaves were imported during the period of 1451-1870, with 63.3 percent were traded between the years of 1701-1810, shown in Table 2, ironically when the Enlightenment was blooming in Europe and its colonies. Considering that all Caribbean islands imported 5,345,399 African slaves (55.9 % of all slaves imported into the Americas) and Brazil accounted for another 3,646,800 (38.1%) during the entire period, the number of slave imports into British North America was only 399,000 (4.2%), which was relatively small. The number of blacks in North America totaled 250,000 in 1750, 750,000 in 1790, and 1,772,000 (899,000 male and 873,000 female) in 1820.[15] Meanwhile, most of early settlers considered Native Americans as uncivilized savages to be conquered by the superior culture of Europe. The population of American Indians was five to six million when Columbus discovered the New World but declined to 237,000 by 1900 when they were assimilated into the western civilization.

Table 3. Immigration to the United States, 1820-1924 (in Thousand)

Year	Total	Rate/1000	Irish	German	Scandinav	Italian	Greeks
1820-30	151.8	1.2	54.3	7.7	0.3	0.4	0.02
1831-40	599.1	3.9	207.4	152.5	2.3	2.3	0.05
1841-50	1,713.2	8.4	780.7	434.6	14.4	1.9	0.02
1851-60	2,598.2	9.3	914.1	951.7	24.7	9.2	0.03
1861-70	2,314.8	6.4	435.8	787.5	126.4	11.7	0.07
1871-80	2,812.2	6.2	436.9	718.2	243.0	55.8	0.21
1881-90	5,246.6	9.2	655.5	1,453.0	656.5	307.3	2.31
1891-00	3,687.6	5.3	388.4	505.2	371.5	651.9	15.98
1901-10	8,795.4	10.4	339.1	341.5	505.3	2,045.9	167.52
1911-20	5,735.8	5.7	146.2	144.0	203.5	1,109.5	184.20
1921-24	2,344.6	5.3	71.9	148.1			
Total	35,999.4		4,578.9	5,907.9	2,147.9	4,195.9	370.41

Source: Roger Daniels, *Coming to America: A History of Immigration and Ethnicity in American Life*, New York: Harper Perennial, 1990, pp. 121-238.

9. The second stage of immigration to the United States began in 1820 when the colonial period in America was terminated. The share of European immigrants to America totaled 95 percent in the period of 1820-1860, but declined gradually to 85 percent in the years of 1900-1920, while the Asian immigrants increased from zero to 4 percent in the same period. Table 3 shows that the total number of immigrants to the United States was 35,999,400 in the period of 1820-1924. In the years 1901-1910, immigrants reached a peak of 8,795,400, an average of 10.4 immigrants in a year per one thousand existing Americans. The proportion of foreign-born population was at 9.7 percent in 1850, but rose to 14.7 percent in 1910 and 13.2 percent in 1920. During the

century, 4.6 million Irish moved to the United States to escape from hunger from the famine and to enjoy religious and political freedom. They were able to transform the Roman Catholic Church and politics in America. The 5.9 million Germans migrated to the United States in family groups for economic opportunities, while it was observed that religious and political motivations were much less significant in the nineteenth century. Also, 4.2 million Italians moved to the United States in this century mainly for economic betterment, although significant numbers moved directly to Argentina and Brazil. The eastern Europeans migrated to the United States in this century from among twenty-six ethnic groups. The foreign-born Polish-speaking population was 0.94 million and its second generation was 1.71 million in 1910. Foreign born Yiddish or Hebrew speaking population was 1.05 million and their second generation was 1.68 million in the same year. Finally, Chinese immigration to the United States began with California gold rush in 1849,[16] and 300,000 Chinese entered until passage of the Chinese Exclusion Act in 1882. The Chinese population in America was 63,199 in 1870, rose to 107,488 in 1890, but declined to 74,954 in 1930. Just after the arrival of some political refugees, 150 Japanese immigrants came to Hawaii in 1869 and about 30,000 Japanese were brought there under contract to plantation owners, where a large number of Chinese was already employed. The Japanese population in the United States was 24,326 in 1900 and increased to 138,834 by 1930.

Table 4. Immigration and Emigration by Period, 1921-1945

Period	Number of Immigrants	Number of Emigrants	Net Migration
1921-24	2,344,599	604,699	1,739,930
Annual Average	586,150	151,168	439,982
1925-30	1,762,610	440,377	1,322,233
Annual Average	293,768	73,396	220,372
1931-45	699,283	502,434	196,849
Annual Average	46,619	33,496	13,123
Total	4,806,492	1,547,480	3,259,012
Annual Average	192,260	61,899	130,360

Source: Roger Daniels, *Coming to America: A History of Immigration and Ethnicity in American Life*, New York: Harper Perennial, 1990, p. 289.

Table 5. Immigration by Period and by Region, 1921-1945

Period	Number of Immigrants	Europe %	Americas %	Others %
1921-24	2,344,599	65.7	30.7	3.6
1925-30	1,762,610	53.2	45.2	1.7
1931-45	699,283	57.4	38.8	4.0
Total	4,806,492	59.9	37.2	2.9

Source: Roger Daniels, *Coming to America: A History of Immigration and Ethnicity in American Life*, New York: Harper Perennial, 1990, p. 290.

10. A century of immigration to the United States changed her ethnic composition until 1924 when the U. S. Congress passed the Immigration Act, also known as the National Origins Act, that further reduced quotas for immigrants deemed to be less desirable. Immigrants from northern and western Europe were considered

highly adaptable and more likely to "fit in" with Americans than immigrants from southern and eastern Europe. As a result, immigrants from Great Britain, Germany, and Ireland were assigned generous quotas. Quotas for countries such as Russia, the source of most Jewish immigrants, and Italy were cut back. Practically all Asians were barred from entering the United States.[17] In this century of immigration, American nativism was triumphant in three phases. In the first phase, anti-Catholicism prevailed in America, mainly against the Irish Catholic immigrants, and German Catholic immigrants with a lesser degree during the period between 1830 and 1860. In the second phase, anti-Asian sentiments were triggered by Chinese immigration to the United States from the early 1870s, which forced the U.S. Congress to pass the Chinese Exclusion Act in 1882, banning further immigration from China. In the third phase, a broad anti-immigration movement began in the mid-1880s when restricting the movement of immigration was gaining popularity, resulting in the U.S. Congress passing the Immigration Act of 1924.[18] As a result of the restrictive immigration policies of the U.S. government, the total number of immigrants fell to 4,806,492 during the period from 1921-1945. Subtracting the returning immigrants of 1,547,480, net immigration to the United States totaled 3,259,012 during the same period, or 130,360 per year in average as shown in Table 4. In this period, the proportion of European immigrants was 59.9 percent, that of America was 37.2 percent, and others were 2.9 percent shown in Table 5. Although the annual quota was about 150,000 in a year, actual number of total immigrants circumvented this quota because of family unification and need to import skilled labor. But the Great Depression of the 1930s and World War II changed the pattern of immigration. In the period of 1931-1945, 669,283 immigrants came to the United States, but 502,434 (71.8% of them) returned to their home countries.

11. The Immigration Act of 1965 provided "First, that the quota system be phased out over a five-year period, with the released numbers being put into a pool to be distributed on a new basis. Second, that the natives of no one country receive more than 10 percent of the newly authorized quota numbers. Third, a seven-person immigration board be set up to advise the president... After receiving their recommendations the president would be authorized to reserve up to 50 percent of the unallocated numbers to "persons disadvantaged by the change in the quota system and up to 20 percent to refugees...Otherwise, immigrants would be selected under a first-come, first-admitted procedure...subject to the 10 percent limitation noted above."[19] It provided exemptions from preference requirements and numerical quotas for spouses, unmarried minor children and parents of U.S. citizens. Although the law required a global ceiling of 290,000 annually, recorded legal immigration surpassed it by 88 percent on the average. The Refugee Act of 1980 intended to solve the problem of refugee admissions, while the Immigration Reform Act of 1986 required employers to examine the eligibility of employment by providing amnesty for illegal aliens in the past but imposing sanctions for hiring them in the future. The American economy needs workers, either skilled or unskilled, when the economy is expanded. However, during economic recessions, anti-immigration advocates frequently blame foreign

workers for domestic unemployment. Without proper demand from host countries, self-invited immigration faces resistance from domestic interest groups continuously until the labor market adjusts to it.

Table 6. Immigration to the United States by Region, 1941-2000

Year	America	Europe	Asia	Africa	Oceania	Total
1941-1950	354,804	621,147	37,028	7,367	14,551	1,713,251
1951-1960	996,944	1,325,727	153,249	14,029	12,976	2,515,479
1961-1970	1,716,374	1,123,492	427,642	28,954	25,122	3,321,677
1971-1980	1,982,735	800,368	1,588,178	80,799	41,242	4,493,314
1981-1990	3,615,225	465,642	2,738,157	176,893	45,205	7,338,062
1991-2000	4,486,806	1,359,7.7	2,795,672	354,939	55,845	9,095,419

Source: http://www.ins.usdoj.gov/graphics/aboutins/statistics/IMM00yrbk/IMM2000list.htm
Note: The total numbers of the far right includes all immigrants from the world.

12. The number of immigrants to the United States increased rapidly in the second half of the twentieth century owing to the Immigration Act of 1965.[20] Their total number was 2,515,479 during the period of 1951-1960, but increased to 9,095,419 in the last decade of the century. In the same period, the number of immigrants from Europe declined or remained unchanged, while that from other regions increased. The European immigrants were 1,335,727 in the 1950s, declined to 465,642 in the 1980s, but recovered to the same level of the 1950s in the next decade. Meanwhile, the immigrants from South and Central America increased rapidly from 996,944 in the 1950s to 4,486,806 in the 1990s. The number of Asian immigrants increased from 153,249 in the decade of 1950s to 2,738,157 in the 1980s, but remained unchanged in the last decade of the century. The number of immigrants from Africa and Oceania increased continuously in the second half of the twentieth century. Thus, we have reviewed the history of immigration to the United States in terms of four periods: colonial period (to 1820), industrial period (1820-1925), limited migration period (1925-1965), and the period of postindustrial migration (after 1965). The disappearance of ideology, revolution of information technology, uninterrupted factor mobility, productivity convergence, and trade liberalization expedited globalization[21] overcoming time and space in transportation and communications, continuously forcing the world to be integrated in politics, economy, and society. The flow of population has become easier since 1991 owing to less expensive cost and relaxed government intervention, while globalization brought various issues to the world, particularly the need for the balanced economic growth.[22] But the war against terrorism since September 11, 2001 has temporarily disturbed the trend of globalization, although it is expected to be recovered sooner or later.

13. The population residing in the United States as of November 1, 2000 was 276.06 million, consisting of 82.2 percent White, 12.8 percent Black, 0.9 percent American Indian, and 4.1 percent Asian and Pacific Islander. The proportion of not Hispanic White was 71.3 percent, not Hispanic Black 12.2 percent, not Hispanic American Indian 0.7 percent, and not Hispanic Asian and Pacific Islander 3.8 percent,

and Hispanic origin of all races 11.9 percent as of November 1, 2000 as shown in Table 7. The number of all foreign-born resident population was 25.8 million, consisting of not Hispanic White 25.3 percent, not Hispanic Black 7.0 percent, not Hispanic American Indian 0.2 percent, and not Hispanic Asian and Pacific Islander 24.5 percent, and Hispanic origin of all races 43.0 percent as of July 1, 1999. Notably, the population of not Hispanic Asian and Pacific Islander was 6,333,000, which was only 3.8 percent of the American population. The white population will decline to about one-half of the American population by 2050 due to their lower fertility and high immigration rates of other races.

Table 7. Resident Population (as of November 1, 2000) and Foreign-Born Resident Population (as of July 1, 1999) Estimates of the United States by Race and Hispanic Origin (Thousand)

Classification	Resident Population		Foreign-Born Resident Population	
	Population	Percent	Population	Percent
All Race	276,059	100%	25,831	100%
White Not Hispanic	196,929	71.3%	6,547	25.3%
Black Not Hispanic	33,619	12.2%	1,805	7.0%
American Indian Not Hisp.	2,509	0.7%	43	0.2%
Asian and Pacific Islander	10,620	3.8%	6,333	24.5%
Hispanic Origin Any Race	32,832	11.9%	11,103	43.0%

Source: http://www.census.gov/population/estimates/nation/intfile3-1.txt and http://www.census.gov/population/estimates/nation/nativity/fbtab002.txt

Immigration and Racial Integration in the United States

14. The reasons why international migration occurs are explained by six theories. First, neoclassic economists believe that international immigration is caused by geographic differences in the supply of and demand for labor. Individual actors move from labor-surplus country to the a labor-scarce country, while highly skilled workers (human capital) move from capital-rich to capital–poor countries for high returns on their skills.[23] Migration is decided by not only isolated individual actors, but also families or entire communities to maximize expected income, to upgrade political and social status, and to pursue religious freedom.[24] Second, labor market theorists believe that international migration is caused by a permanent labor demand caused by the structure of advanced economies. This demand-pull theory justifies that the new immigrants take jobs of low wage, unstable hours, and unpleasant working conditions because they begin as target earners until they earn money for a specific goal.[25] Third, structural theorists argue that global capitalism perpetuates income inequality and reinforces a stratified economic order because political power is unequally distributed across nations.[26] This dependency theory prevailed in Latin America in the 1960s and 1970s, which illustrated that international migration inevitably occurs in the process of capitalist development. Fourth, people gain social capital as a system of relationships through membership in networks and social institutions, and then convert it into other forms of capital to improve or maintain their positions in society. Those networks promote international migration.[27] Fifth, "cumulative causation" presumes that international migration tends to sustain itself in ways that make additional movement

progressively in line with the expansion of networks and various economic and social activities.[28] Finally, the role of government is an important element for international migration even in the age of globalization. Since the impact of immigration is wide and deep in both sending and receiving countries, governments change immigration policies from time to time to adjust to environment.[29]

15. The patterns of assimilation vary. Robert Ezra Park formulated the *race relations cycle* to describe the assimilation process of immigrants: contact, competition, accommodation, and eventual assimilation.[30] Milton Gordon introduced *three conceptual models* of assimilation in America: Anglo-conformity, melting pot, and cultural pluralism.[31] Anglo-conformity was a center force of Americanization during and after World War I and ignored other assimilation dimensions. The idea of melting pot came from the view that all the races of Europe were melting and reforming, which became popular in the immediate aftermath of World War II. In his cultural pluralism, "once structural assimilation has occurred, either simultaneously with or subsequent to acculturation, all of the other types of assimilation will naturally follow."[32] Gans and Sandberg thought that generations were the engine for ethnic change by introducing the notion of *straight-line assimilation*: "each new generation represents on average a new stage of adjustments to the host society, that is, a further step away from ethnic ground zero, the community and culture established by the immigrants, and a step closer to more complete assimilation."[33] The *segmented assimilation* explains that immigrants are absorbed by different segments of American society due to external and internal factors of immigrants. The progressive trends of social mobility were observed across generations of immigrants owing to educational attainment, job skills, length of stay, English proficiency, and cultural exposure.[34] Meanwhile, *socioeconomic assimilation* is suggested by measuring social mobility and income growth: the former means occupational mobility of immigrants by participating in social activities of the American mainstream through higher education and career management, while the latter follows accordingly.[35] Glazer and Moynihan introduced *ethnogenesis* theory: ethnicity is not a fixed form handed down by tradition, but a form continuously regenerated and hence transformed in the process of adjustment to American society.[36] Massey and Mullan introduced *spatial assimilation* holding that spatial location of an ethnic group is a crucial variable affecting its socioeconomic position:[37] there is close relationship between housing and jobs, educational opportunities, and income growth in socioeconomic assimilation. Finally, *marital assimilation* or amalgamation is another outcome of the assimilation process, where the minority farther loses its ethnic identity. Intermarriage increased across ethnic lines in America but remained within the three religious communities of Protestants, Catholics, and Jews (triple melting pot)[38] although marriage outside ethnic groups was extensive in later generations.[39]

16. The performance of ethnic groups differs in the process of assimilation due to internal and external causes. Internal causes include intellectual orientation, cultural characteristics, social class, and enclave economy. Hernnstein and Murray insisted that the class structure of contemporary American society reflects the distribution of

intelligence, that races differ in intelligence, and "the lower IQ test performance of blacks and Latinos indicates that they are less intelligent than whites and Asians."[40] Contrary to this, the American Psychological Association asserted that "early educational interventions are effective in raising performance and achievement levels for disadvantaged groups."[41] Others believe that cultural characteristics (values, attitudes, beliefs, customs, and habits learned from family and community) make immigrants successful, such as Asians who characterized as industrious, thrifty, and self-reliant with high motivation for education. The social class of immigrants is also essential for their performance: more than two-thirds of Jewish immigrants were skilled workers, professionals, or merchants, while only one-sixth of southern Italians and one-sixteenth of Polish immigrants belonged to that category. Moreover, the concept of an enclave economy explains that "the immigrant community itself is a major factor influencing the range of opportunities available to individual immigrants." In contrast to internal causes, external causes are opportunity structure of society and cultural characteristics of a minority. Although different language and culture are barriers in the process of assimilation, the main external barrier for immigrants to overcome is the role of prejudice and discrimination in creating and maintaining racial and ethnic inequality. It is unlikely that "racial inequalities would disappear, primarily because racial discrimination and inequalities are perpetuated by the way in which economic and political institutions are structured and organized in American society."[42] But the social class has gradually become more important than race in determining minority access to the privilege and power of the mainstream.

17. The impact of immigrants is broad and deep during their assimilation process. Politically, immigrants can change the composition of voters if a certain race or an ethnic group moves to a certain electoral district. Considering that Hispanic Americans will be 22 percent of the American population by 2050, for example, their concentration in major cities will largely influence future American elections soon after their naturalization. Economically, (a) there is no evidence of significant reduction in native employment,[43] and "the immigration surplus might be larger when the immigration flow is composed exclusively of skilled workers...Immigration also generates a sizable redistribution of wealth in the economy, reducing the incomes of natives who are now competing with immigrant workers in the labor market and increasing the incomes of capitalists and other users of immigrant services."[44] (b) Contrary to public perception, "when all levels of government are considered together, immigrants generate significantly more in taxes paid than they cost in services received."[45] (c) Middle class immigrants in sending countries bring a quite sum of capital to provide a financial foundation in America, which is a kind of capital inflow, while those from the lower class come with empty hands. Moreover, this foreign direct investment contributes to immigration and vice versa. (d) Since self-employed businesses brought more profits and social ascendance, some immigrants became successful in small-scale businesses using their entrepreneurship.[46] In society and culture, international migration improves mutual understanding and friendly relationships between sending and receiving nations, spreads different cultures, and

expedites globalization. The first generation maintains dual lives of *transnationalism*, representing two cultures of their sending and receiving communities.[47] The social mobility of the second generation immigrants is affected by racial stratification, economic opportunities, spatial segregation, and factors intrinsic to the group such as financial and human capital, family structure, community organization, and cultural patterns of social relations.[48] Later generations return to *symbolic ethnicity*, which is a nostalgic allegiance to the mother culture, although it usually does not remain permanent.[49] With regard to religious affiliation, intermarriages between different religions are an increasing trend in America, and immigrants are less predisposed in religious matters than previous centuries. The United States will have new immigrants continuously, who will create more competitive and diversified ethnic communities.

18. Let's investigate the process of assimilation of five ethnic groups: American Indians, European, African, Hispanic, and Asian Americans. The U.S. government dealt with American Indians or Native Americans in five major historical stages: removal, assimilation, the Indian New Deal, termination and relocation, and self-determination.[50] The U.S. Congress passed the Indian Removal Act in 1830 which forced them to move west of the Mississippi River to the Indian Territory (later to become the state of Oklahoma). The General Allotment Act of 1887 provided tribal lands to be allotted to individual American Indians and additional legislation created American Indian boarding schools: "many were forcibly taken from their families and enrolled in boarding schools, where they were compelled to adopt white styles of dress and were punished for speaking their own native languages."[51] The Indian Reorganization Act of 1934 was a New Deal program for American Indians, offering some relief from the Great Depression, in which the U.S. government repudiated the allotment policy and acknowledged American Indians to be detribalized. The government created the Indian Claims Commission in 1946 and dissolved in 1978, while the Congress passed the House Concurrent Resolution 108 in 1953 and abolished all reservations although only two were actually terminated because the Indian advocacy groups opposed to take action. The American Indian Self-Determination and Education Assistance Act of 1975 allowed tribal governments to do a larger role in reservation administration of various programs. The social Darwinism of the "survival of fittest" was applied to the American Indians who survived from forced assimilation and became American citizens despite the painful process of assimilation.[52] The 2000 census estimated the resident population of American Indians to be 2,509,000 or 0.7% of the entire population of the United States. Their average household income became less than two-thirds of that of white Americans until recent years. The Indians were the first Americans in the United States but were forcibly assimilated into European culture and religion, gradually but progressively. Sometimes the history of civilization was too cruel to be praised although civilization itself provides generous benefits to us.

19. Europeans came to the United States almost exclusively from northern and western Europe, consisting of Irish, Germans, and Scandinavians until the 1880s (the old immigration). But the wave of immigration shifted to eastern Europe of Italians,

Greeks, and Armenians as well as southern Europe of Poles, Jews, and Hungarians since 1890 (the new immigration). The change in ethnic composition caused nativist whites to fear the cultural impact of new immigrants on American institutions. The ideology of scientific racism that prevailed in period of the turn of the century endorsed Caucasians as nation's social and intellectual elites (the best and brightest) and consequently the U.S. Congress passed the National Origins Quota Act in 1929 giving the highest quotas to nations of northern and western Europe.[53] The old immigrants considered the newcomers as an "inbetween" class: above African and Asian Americans but below white Americans. However, the mixture of blood and their voting power pushed them to join the whites.[54] In the job market, new immigrants competed largely with African Americans, and they suffered from employment discrimination at least in the defense industry until late World War II. The new immigrants and their descendants had been culturally assimilated into the mainstream of American life, but they were not structurally assimilated by maintaining their ethnic identity in generations. Among the old immigrants, Irish Americans adapted to and changed American urban politics with the Democratic Party. Among the new immigrants, Italian Americans founded relatively few ethnic organizations due to individualism and intense attachment to family, but Jewish Americans from eastern Europe were successful in politics such as by sending six Jewish Representatives to the U.S. House in 1917 from New York, New Jersey, and Chicago. As intermarriage between different ethnic groups of whites prevailed into succeeding generations, the significance of race between the old and the new immigrants was rapidly declined after World War II, while white-black relations were getting worse, particularly after the late 1950s. The United States classifies race by five categories in census as shown in Table 7.

20. African Americans were shaped by the production system with the laws and policies of the state.[55] First, during the plantation period, although blacks initially possessed a similar legal status with white indentured servants, they fell to slave status by the 1660s to supply free lifetime labor to plantations. The status of slavery forced blacks to be lower-caste members of the American society. Second, former slaves were formally given liberty by passage of the 13th Amendment abolishing slavery, the 14th Amendment providing equal protection under the law, and 15th Amendment guaranteeing the right to vote, but no means were given to realize it. In addition, lack of social mobility meant that 89 percent of emancipated blacks remained in the South as late as 1910. Many southern states enforced racial separation and excluded African Americans from political, economic, social, and educational opportunities available to most other Americans. Third, blacks began to move to urban areas for employment largely after World War II so that 86 percent of its population lived in cities by 1996. For example, the population of blacks in 1990 was 75.7 percent in Detroit, 39.9 percent in Philadelphia, 39.1 percent in Chicago, 28.7 percent in New York, and 29.5 percent in Dallas.[56] Finally, the urbanization of black population facilitated the civil rights movement during the late 1950s and the 1960s, led by middle class African Americans. Resultingly, the U.S. Congress passed the Civil Rights Act of 1964 and the Voting Rights Act of 1965. In 1967, President Lyndon Johnson created the National

Commission on Civil Disorders (Kerner Commission) to investigate the causes of urban riots. The Commission reported that American institutions were the primary source of the racism that permeates the society. The rise in African American voters increased their representation in politics, and their education and employment opportunities improved tremendously in the next thirty years. As the social status of blacks improved, some lawmakers argued in 2000 that affirmative action to protect minority interests was no longer necessary although it did not attract political support.[57] This implies that over a generation of affirmative action was enough for disadvantaged races to stand by themselves without blaming others.

21. Hispanic Americans (or Latinos) are fast growing ethnic categories, projected to be 22 percent of the U.S. population by 2050, with great diversity of cultural background. Fully three-fourths of Hispanic Americans are of Mexican, Puerto Rican, and Cuban origins. Initially Mexicans coexisted with Anglos in California, Texas, Arizona, New Mexico, and Colorado.[58] As the United States annexed these areas under the Treaty of Guadalupe-Hidalgo in 1848, most Mexicans fell to a lower-class status of landless laborers and were politically and economically impotent. In the 1920s, Mexican immigrants filled agricultural jobs in southern states when blacks moved to urban areas in the 1920s. During World War II and the Korean War, Mexicans filled American labor shortages as guest workers, and the legal immigration increased after World War II. Some of them remained illegally, and others crossed the border without proper documents. Mexicans were once involved in agricultural labor but the majority moved to urban areas. Urbanization of the Mexican population expedited their assimilation into Anglo society, gradually shifting away from Spanish language and culture for the next generations to become middle class. Puerto Rico was annexed to America in 1898 and its people became American nationals in 1917. Due to unrestricted migration between the mainland and the island, the majority moved to the New York City area. Puerto Ricans have maintained strong ethnic communities with low intermarriage rates. Cuban immigrants were primarily political refugees for whom President Kennedy provided the Cuban Refugee Program to take care of escapees from a neighboring communist dictatorship. The program provided job training, professional recertification, assistance for employment, subsidization of education costs, and funds for research and teaching opportunities. The early exodus included educated professionals having better socioeconomic background, but successive waves were younger and less educated. The Cuban enclave economy with their cohesiveness facilitated initial adjustment and success of Cuban Americans in Miami and New York. Hispanic Americans, in sum, differ from others in terms of race mixture (blacks, Amerindians, and whites) and different history of entrance from various regions having different culture.

22. The major ethnic groups of Asian Americans are Chinese, Japanese, Filipino, Korean, Asian Indian, and Vietnamese as shown in Table 8. The Chinese entered the country as laborers of agriculture, mining, and railroad construction, and their immigration reached its peak from 1873 to 1882 when the U.S. Congress passed

the Chinese Exclusion Act. The Japanese began to enter the country in the mid-1880s and its government won the Gentleman's Agreement with the United States in 1907 to end discrimination against Japanese living in America.[59] After Japan attacked Hawaii, President Franklin Roosevelt sent Japanese Americans, two-thirds of them native-born American citizens, to ten hurriedly built relocation camps, where some of them remained for almost four years.[60] In 1988, the U.S. Congress passed and President Ronald Reagan signed a bill providing reparations and a formal apology to Japanese Americans. The Philippines became U.S. territory after the Spanish-American War in 1898, so that Filipinos could enter the country easily, and they replaced the Chinese and Japanese workers after 1924. The major waves of other Asian immigration including Koreans and Asian Indians came after the Immigration Act of 1965.[61] Asian immigration to America has two negative memories: the Chinese Exclusion Act of 1882 and the relocation of Japanese Americans in 1942, which have been viewed as a symbol of institutional discrimination against Asian Americans. Because of their yellow skin and almond eyes, they cannot escape from the distinction of race and they are not fully integrated into the mainstream. Since the Confucian culture highly respects scholars, Asian American parents emphasize the importance of education and their descendants prepare for high education with achievement motivation. Asian Americans are described as the Model Minority – a hard working, thrifty, goal-oriented, and self-reliant people. The household income in Asian American families has been higher than in the general population. They have been adjusting constructively to American culture, while they maintain their ethnic identity with cohesiveness of their communities. Their socioeconomic mobility was progressive although their political participation has been slow and less desirable.[62]

Table 8. Asian American Population by Major Ethnic Group, 1940-2000

Year	Chinese	Japanese	Filipino	Korean	As. Indian	Vietnam	Total
1940	106,334	285,115	98,535				489,984
1950	150,005	326,379	122,707				599,091
1960	237,292	464,332	176,310				877,934
1970	436,062	591,290	343,060	69,150			1,439,561
1980	812,178	716,331	781,894	357,393	387,223	245,025	3,466,421
1990	1,645,472	847,562	1,406,770	798,849	815,447	614,547	7,273,662
2000	2,314,537	796,700	1,850,314	1,076,872	1,678,765	1,122,528	10,019,405

Source: http://factfinder.census.gov/servlet/DTTable?_ts=46704393041 for 1990. U.S. Census Bureau, *The Asian Population 2000: Census 2000 Brief*, Washington, DC: U.S. Department of Commerce, February 2000, p. 9. For the period from 1940-1980, see Roger Daniels, *Coming to America: A History of Immigration and Ethnicity in American Life*, New York: Harper Perennial, 1990, pp. 351, 359, 363. "Total" means all Asian American population.

Assimilation of European Immigrant Groups

23. The ethnic history of immigration to the United States differs from each other due to their intrinsic and extrinsic conditions. This section investigates economic, social, and political mobility of four ethnic immigrant groups into the mainstream of the United States including Irish, Italian, Jewish, and Polish to learn lessons in the process

of assimilation. Approximately, 4.58 million Irish immigrated to the United States (12.7 percent of total immigrants) during the period of 1820-1924 as shown in Table 3. Being oppressed by the British rule, they were trained as a disciplined army to fight underground political warfare, and impoverished by the increasing number of landless people in the absence of domestic industries. The emigration was the sole source of relief to escape from the potato famine. The number of Irish immigrants to the United States totaled 780,719 (45.6 percent of total immigrants) during the 1840s and 914,119 (35.2 percent) in the next decade. They were largely unskilled or uneducated workers without capital, and willing to do almost anything to survive. They flocked into the coal mines, the steel mills, and the construction industry competing with blacks for employment. However, they quickly learned skills and gradually moved into skilled blue-collar occupations as the economy rapidly industrialized in the second half of the nineteenth century. Irish immigrants moved into metropolitan areas because the big cities provided easy-to-get dirty jobs and cheap lodgings for survival. Since the early gangsters were Irish, urban police departments recruited their police forces from the Irish to control gangs, and city fire departments did the same since fire stations were related to Irish gangs. As a result, the Irish people gradually became to control urban police forces and fire fighters as new immigrants increased and the cities were urbanized. Meanwhile, the Irish Americans could control lower position workers in both private and public sectors, which became a power base for political mobilization of the major cities such as Boston, New York, and Chicago in the coming decades.[63] Meanwhile, massive migration of Irish Catholics was fearful to America's Protestant majority who wanted to ban aid to Catholic schools.[64]

24. The Irish Americans were easily organized in politics as they were homogeneous in language, religion, land, history, and social structure, and able to maintain ethnic cohesiveness owing to long oppression by external forces. The Irish Immigrant Society and Catholic churches helped immigrants newly coming into the wards, creating an Irish networking system. As the number of Irish immigrants to America rapidly increased and became concentrated in urban areas, they created voting power in local and regional politics. Since the industrialists controlling the GOP were interested in keeping low wages after the Civil War, the Irish as urban proletariat controlled labor unions and joined the Democratic Party. The industrialization and urbanization brought many new opportunities in politics, economy, and society for Irish immigrants to shift upward to the middle class of the mainstream. In fact, "the Irish used a political strategy to move from the working class into the middle class in the late nineteenth and early twentieth centuries."[65] They mobilized urban voters, participated in party politics, and held municipal offices, so that the share of public sector resources was disproportionately distributed to Irish Americans, which accelerates the development of an Irish middle class in America. Adult males registered to vote were 70 percent for the Irish, compared to 37 percent for other ethnics in San Francisco in 1900. The proportion of their public employees climbed from 11 percent in 1870 to 30 percent in 1900 for nation's fourteen largest cities, while that of the overall Irish labor forces in those cities remained at 20 percent. The political power generates economic

power which regenerates political power, which cycle continues until the system collapses. Since politics only could not make the poor be rich for the Irish working class and the liberal political party could not maintain radical forms of working class politics, early success of the rainbow theory of Irish urban politics became less powerful when the share of Irish population declined, and their next generations were gradually absorbed into white Protestant society through intermarriage.[66]

25. A surprising number of Italian intellectuals came to America in the late seventeenth and early nineteenth centuries, and formed a regular exile community in New York after 1849. In the Civil War, Italian immigrants organized a "Garibaldi Guard" that fought in the Union Army as an International Brigade. As the agricultural conditions of southern Italy became worse, four million migrated from Mezzogiorno and Sicily to America in the years 1880-1924, among which more than three million arrived in the years 1900-1914. The first generation lived in the years 1900-1930, which characteristics were different from other ethnic groups. First of all, the Mezzogiorno society was a society of family, not individuals. The supremacy of family interests was in the economic value attached to children, and marriage was treated as between families rather than between individuals. Families connected one another to strengthen their position through the institution of godparentship. Italian Americans founded relatively few communal and fraternal organizations, and regarded themselves as citizens of a village or a town, not of a nation. Second, there was a secret criminal society of ancient origins in Sicily to combat external invaders, and its members lived by violence and extortion as its purposes had been corrupted. Members of the Mafia were among the immigrants and transplanted its criminal society in large cities of the United States. Sometimes, crime had served as a means of upward social mobility for a minority of young immigrants.[67] Third, southern Italian peasants came to abraod with the intention to work and make enough money to purchase land when they returned home, which made them accept unskilled manual positions for a longer period. They were "birds of passage" or a rootless population that would not able to assimilate successfully. As a result, Italians did not have a great propensity to be naturalized, their political participation was low, and few Italian Americans won or were appointed to high political office. Despite visible improvement, Italian immigrants remained over 40 percent as non-citizens by 1930, which was the highest proportion among immigrant groups. In addition, they kept the highest percentage of adults who could not speak English. The effect of this trend remained for a while until World War II.

26. Despite their rural origins,[68] more Italian immigrants moved into large cities such as New York, Boston, Chicago, and Philadelphia. The Italian areas were built by so called "chain migration" where the men came first and their wives and children followed, and that immigrants from the same towns and provinces settled near one another to provide a buffer against the shock of new environment and thereby to arrange their gradual adjustment. As a result, their housing and sanitatary conditions with a dense population made the immigrant ghettoes horrible, although around a half of Italian immigrant families owned homes by 1930. In New York City in 1905, nearly

60 percent of Italians were unskilled or semiskilled manual laborers, over 20 percent of them were skilled blue-collar workers, 18 percent were low white-collar workers, and only a tiny percentage were in the upper white-collar category. In education, some Italian parents ignored compulsory attendance laws, withdrew their children from school, and sent them to work as soon as the law allowed.[69] Thus, their ultimate educational attainment was quite low. By 1930, only 11 percent of Italian Americans who entered New York City high schools graduated from them, while 40 percent of other ethnic students who entered the same received diplomas. Their lower educational achievement restricted the occupational mobility of their second generation. Like other ethnics, Italian immigrants experienced prejudice and discrimination from northern and western European Americans who doubted that Italians were whites. This nativism strengthened the restrictionist movement by passing the immigration laws of 1921, 1924, and 1929, limiting the quota of immigration from eastern and southern Europe. However, their political, economic, and social mobility into the mainstream of America became visible since the World War II owing to more education, career management in white-collar occupations, residential integration and suburbanization, and intermarriage with different ethnics and religions.[70] Italian Catholicism differs from the Irish one that dominates Ameircan Catholic churches. The Italian American held 15 percent of American Catholic population, but held the positions of 12 percent of priests, 5 of 253 bishops, and 1 of 34 archbishops. A considerable number of Italian immigrants fell away from the Church, and some even converted to Prostentantism.

27. The American Jewish population was about 150,000 in 1860. A few of them were descended from Jews who came to America as indentured immigrants during the colonial period, but most of them were German Jews and their descendants. The former had settled largely in a few cities but the latter scattered over the frontier for trade. The German Jewish immigrants between 1860 and 1900 were engaged successfully in trade, and the number of Jewish firms worthy of commercial rating rose from 374 to over 2000 in various sectors. Meanwhile, Russian Jews crossed borders illegally to come to the United States seeking economic opportunity and civil liberty based on religious freedom. The number of American Jews increased to about 4 million by 1924, more than 3 million of them were eastern Europeans and their descendants among which 2.16 million were Russia Jews. They were young and skilled: about 70 percent of them were between ages of fourteen and forty, and two-third of them with previous experience in skilled jobs. They showed the greatest propensity to stay in the United States and their proportion of females was 45 percent. The first generation of Russian Jews lived in the years 1900-1930 and about 60 percent of them scattered in the region from Boston through New York to Philadelphia and Baltimore. They largely engaged in the garment industry and retail trade, owned over 95 percent of the clothing manufacturers in New York, with 20 percent of them were employed in retail trade in the 1910s. Their working conditions were miserable and living conditions were not better: the population density rate in the lower East Side of New York was 730 persons per acre in 1910, exceeded only by Bombay, India.[71] The established uptown German Jewish community, supporting capitalism and anti-Zionist movement, created the

American Jewish Committee in 1906 to fight a growing the anti-Semitism in America. By contrast, the downtown Russian Jewish workers, supporting socialism and the Zionist movement, created the American Jewish Congress in 1915.[72] The uptown Jewish factory owners were disturbed by downtown Jewish workers who initially had socialist ideas but eventually adjusted to a reformist track.

28. The economic success of American Jews came from rationality, hard work, savings, and a strong achievement drive. "The sources of this so-called Jewish achievement drive have been attributed to: (1) a religiously inspired emphasis on education, which, secularized, has been linked to disproportionate intellectual preoccupations since the early Middle Ages; (2) a history as urbanites par excellence, which has given Jews an advantage in the centers of business, professional, and intellectual life; (3) a greater socialization in middle-class norms and habits, and a greater capacity to defer gratification; and (4) long-term experience with marginality, which has taught them how to form new social relations in different class envirronments."[73] In 1908, more than 8 percent American Jews received higher education compared to 2 percent of Americans. By 1930 in New York City, although Jews comprised one-fourth of the city's population, they were 55 percent of city's physicians, 64 percent of its dentists, and 65 percent of its lawyers. In the early 1990s, 87 percent of college-aged American Jews were enrolled in higher education compared to 40 percent of Americans, and per capita Jewish income was almost double that of non-Jews due to accumulated wealth and professional jobs. They were particularly successful in investment banking. During the last three decades, Jews (3 percent of population) are 20 percent of professors in the leading universities, 21 percent of civil servants, 40 percent of partners in the leading law firms in New York and Washington, 26 percent of reporters, editors, and executives of the major print and broadcast media, 59 percent of directors, writers, and producers of the fifty top-grossing motion pictures from 1965 to 1982.[74] The U.S. Congress had 10 Jewish Senators and 33 Representatives by the 1994 election, comprising 8 percent of the seats. President Clinton appointed five Jewish Cabinet Secretaries, and nominated two Supreme Court Justices who were confirmed.[75] The political influence of Jews is linked to their financial situations, opinion-making professions such as journalism and academia, activism and voting, networking of organizations, and sizable blocks of Jewish voters in key states.[76] The Democratic Party has been receptive to Jewish voters favoring political liberalism and defending themselves against anti-Semitism.[77]

29. The Jewish ethnic identity has been diminished by intermarriage, low birthrate, and the trend of liberalism in political activism. First, more than half of Jews were marrying outside the faith in the 1990s, and 7 percent of their children were enrolled in formal Jewish education. The proportion of Jewish intermarrage will increase and the next generations of mixed families will largely lose their Jewish identity. Second, the fertility rate of Jewish women is 20 percent below that of all American white women and 10 percent less than the level needed for death replacement, which will reduce the Jewish population to 2 percent by 2050 despite a continuous

inflow of Jewish immigrants.[78] The decline of population means reduced voting power with fewer numbers of activists. Third, the United States has remained safe and hospitable for Jews since the end of World War II. The Jewish political and economic success and integration into American society will lessened group defensiveness, cohesion, and identity. On the other hand, religious Judaism of the synagogue is central to the tribal durability, while the Jewish community center is a place for social life of children and adults. Jewish education and religious life provide "the strongest deterrent" to dissolution of Jewish identity although the erosion of ethnicity is a natual course of assimilation into the American society. Jewish institutions are "more dedicated to safeguarding the Jewish race than to teaching Juadaism."[79] But Jewish culture no longer provides the glue that keeps the Jewish community together as much as in previous decades. Finally, the dream of Jewish state became a reality by the declaration of Istael's statehood in 1948.[80] The Six Day War in 1967 reminded American Jews the fear of another Holocaust for Israelis, which strengthened their tribal identity.[81] As the economy of Israel grows not to be dependent on American Jewish funds of half billion dollars per year now, the Israel connections lose much of the strength sustaining its identity. While the cultural distance between Israeli and American Jews becomes wider, the state of Israel is not the core of tribal identity for most American Jews, who believe that the criticism of Israel contributes to the anti-Semitism.[82]

30. Poland was absorbed by Prussia, Russia, and Austria with three partitions in 1772, 1793, and 1795 until the Treaty of Versailles restored its statehood in 1919. Except for a handful of Poles who immigrated during the colonial period, the first group of about a hundred Poles with military experience came to America to participate in a fight for freedom during the American Revolution.[83] Political refugees, after a failed rebellion in 1830 and unsuccessful insurrection in 1863, were exiled to America in later years. The waves of imigration began in the 1870s with German Poles, followed by Russian and Austrian Poles between 1890 and 1914. Although they came from three parts of Poland, common language and religion made them cohessive as Polish Americans, just like German and Russian Jews. By 1910, the population claiming Polish as their mother tongue was 2,651,621 (foreign born was 36.4 percent), among which Russian Poles were 40.9 percent, Austrian Poles 30.1 percent, and German Poles 26.5 percent. By 1920, Polish immigrants numbered about 400,000 in Chicago, 200,000 in New York, 125,000 in Pittsburgh, and about 100,000 in Buffalo or Milwaukee or Detroit.[84] The majority of Polish immigrants were landless peasants or small peasant landholders who could no longer make a living from the soil. In Chicago in 1911, about two-thirds of Polish were unskilled laborers, 22 percent were skilled traders, and the remainder were equally divided among small businessmen (including 3 percent of saloonkeepers) and the unemployed. They faced the similar problems to other ethinc groups from eastern and southern Europe working in steel mills, coal mines, stockyards, and farms: prejudice and discrimination, hard labor with low wages and long hours, and poor housing. The Polish immigrant community was divided among two forces: (a) the religionists who established the Polish Roman Catholic Union (PRCU) in 1873 to preserve the Catholic faith and Polish heritage, and focused upon

immediate religious and educational needs for Polish Americans to elevate the immigrants' intellectual and material existence; (b) the nationalists, who established the Polish National Alliance (PNA) in 1880, believing that it was the community's primary goal to restore Polish independence, and welcomed other religions by separating nationality from faith.[85] While the conflict between them divided their community, other fraternal organizations attempted to link Polish Americans by offering various programs compromising the two differences.

31. The American Poles involved themselves in three politics of Poland, Polonia, and America. First, the political refugees considered themselves temporary residents of the United States and seldom lived among the mass of Polish immigrants. Some of political refugees was connected with the Polish Socialist Party in Poland, and played a large role in the resurrection of the Polish state during the First World War, after which 96,000 of Polish immigrants returned to an independent Poland. Second, the politics of Polonia was that between PRCU and PNA. Father Vicent Barzynski directed the St. Stanislaus Kostka parish from 1874 to 1899. As a rerurrectionist priest, he organized twenty-five other parishes in Chicago; founded a Polish orphanage, hospital, and secondary school, an order of American-born nuns, a parish savings and loan association, and a Polish publishing company. Participating in PRCU, he considered the "spiritual-cultural unity of all American Poles as a more immediate and attainable goal than the liberation of Poland" and pointed that "the principles guiding us shall be ... to regard highly the Constitution of the United States, as citizens of the country. We must participate actively in the public life of our country ... Specifically, we Poles must not consider ourselves as visitors but as an integral part of this country."[86] But the independent church movement demanded that "the owners and administrators of the church's wealth in America should be the Polish people, and the bishops and priests are custodians of the curhches and schools as delegates of the people," which was opposed by PNA. Third, participation in American politics marked a significant step in the Americanization of Polish community by facilitating economic and social mobility into the mainstream. However, Polish Amreicans have not been successful in local, state, and national politics. As of 1970, nine congressional districts were represented by Polish Americans, but few political positions went to them since Polish-American leaders were unable to capitalize ethnic on voting power.

Assimilation of Asian Immigrant Groups

32. This section investigates the assimilation process of the three Asian immigrant groups to the United States including Chinese, Japanese, and Korean Americans. The first wave of Chinese immigration began with the California gold rush in 1849 and ended with the passage of the Chinese Exclusion Act of 1882. During that period, near 300,000 Chinese, mostly adult males (the male to female ratio of Chinese population in the United States was 21 to 1 in 1880), entered the United States. Many Chinese borrowed money on a credit ticket system that the loan would be paid back with high interest after employment. Immigration was profitable for both western ship

owners and Chinese intermediaries. The majority of Chinese who came to America were sojourners, and many actually returned home. The Chinese population in the United States in 1880 was 105,465, among which 102,102 (96.8%) lived in the West Coast: 72,472 (67.4%) in California, 9,510 in Oregon, 3,186 in Washington, 3,379 in Idaho, and 1,965 in Montana. In 1890, the Chinese population in San Francisco was 21,745, Oakland 1,794, Sacramento 1,781, and Portland 1,668.[87] The majority were hired in both unskilled and semiskilled jobs difficult for the host society to fill because of physical labor, low wages, irregular hours, and low status. The minority provided services within their community such as labor contracts, restaurant, laundry, and retail services. The Central Pacific Railroad hired up to 10,000 Chinese workers, but most of them were laid off when the railroad was completed in 1869. A census about 75 percent of California's male Chinese in 1880 showed that one-fifth were miners, one-fifth were common laborers, one-seventh were in agriculture, one-seventh were in labor-intensive manufacturing such as textiles, shoe-making, and cigar-making, one-seventh were domestic servants, and one-tenth were engaged in laundering.[88] Since most newcomers wanted to live among their own kind like others, Chinese immigrants formed their ethnic immigrant community in a shabby urban area, Chinatown, which later became attractive to tourists.

33. From the 1850s, both racism and nativism became endemic in the United States, and sudden increase in Chinese immigrants brought anti-Chinese fears of a Yellow Peril. The U.S. Congress passed the Chinese Exclusion Act in 1882, which prohibited Chinese immigration, although employers welcomed the Chinese as cheap and dependable labor. The Geary Act of 1892 required registration of Chinese in the United States, and about 105,000 Chinese registered in 1894. Many Chinese were murdered and brutalized by anti-Chinese rioters, but many criminals were not found or if they were, they were released without proper punishment. Most Chinese immigrants belonged to associations, which were created for self-protection. A family association or a clan system consisted of families with the same last name, which meant that they had the same ancestors. A district association was created by geographic districts such as those from the home province of Guangdong. Those district associations joined the Chinese Consolidated Benevolent Association (CCBA) aligning with merchant groups. The CCBA, also known as Chinese Six Companies headquartered in San Francisco, was a representative organization having two functions: to provide an immigrant mutual protective association and to maintain social and economic control within the Chinese community. The General Chinese Chamber of Commerce was another organization joined by the American Chinatown elite. Outside these legitimate organizations, tongs were secret societies in China, which became criminal organizations linking Chinese Americans to provide prostitution, gambling, and drugs, although they also contributed to patriotic fundraisers for China. In the 1910s, three major Chinese newspapers existed for immigrants concerned about China's future. *Chinese World* kept conservative views favoring reform of the absolute monarchy into a constitutional monarchy for a modern and strong China. *Young China* maintained revolutionary views favoring a radical revolution for China to be a republic towards a modern nation.

Chung Sai Yat Po held neutral and capitalistic views favoring that the way to build a modern and strong China was to develop its industry and commerce.[89]

34. Shehong Chen views an ideological foundation of the Chinese American identity in the 1920s as follows.[90] First, the Chinese in the United States had faith in republicanism as a suitable political system for a modern China. The CCBA wrote a letter to President Wilson, on behalf of all Chinese in the United States, asking him to advise Yuan Shikai not to restore monarchism in China[91] Second, they believed that Confucianism and traditional Chinese cultural values provided rich and harmonious life, which should be preserved although intellectuals saw conflicts between democracy and Confucianism, such as in liberation of women. Third, diasporic life in the United States made the Christian church an inevitable part of their emergent identity for Chinese Americans. The Chinatown Young Men's Christian Association (YMCA) was established in San Francisco in 1912, New York City in 1916, Oakland in 1921, and Seattle in 1923. The YMCA was a meeting place for the growing second generation, and sponsored lectures and talks on various subjects to educate and broaden visions of the Chinese American community, which facilitated their social mobility into the mainstream. Fourth, Chinese Americans believed that capitalism was the best economic system for a modern and prosperous China, but were alienated by Sun Yat-sen's alliance and cooperation with communists. Meanwhile, the Immigration Act of 1924 prevented Chinese from bringing their families to the United States. But the Chinese Americans won equal treatment in 1930 allowing that the Chinese wives of American citizens who got married before May 26, 1924 to enter the United States. A California bill to control Chinese herbal medicine was withdrawn from the California legislative agenda in 1925 by efforts of the herb dealers. As Sino-American relations became closer in World War II, a disproportionately large number of Chinese Americans served as liaison officers or interpreters in the U.S. Army or on diplomatic missions in China. The U.S. Congress repealed the Chinese Exclusion Act, and the new law in 1943 provided the token of immigration quota of 100 a year for China owing to extensive lobbying by the Citizens Committee.

35. Chinese Americans are a highly divergent group in terms of places of origin, social and economic status, and political affiliations related to China. The rise of the People's Republic of China in 1949 divided Chinese Americans into two camps supporting either Taiwan or the Mainland, while the Immigration Law of 1965 revitalized Chinese immigration to the United States. The positive development of Sino-American relations since 1972 resulted in the growth of the Chinese American community. First, the increasing number of Chinese immigrants to the United States, particularly from Hong Kong and Taiwan in the last three decades, included many entrepreneurs with capital, so that they could open domestic and transnational businesses creating jobs in both America and China. Second, the Chinese government sent tens of thousands students a year to America since Deng's choosing of the open policy in 1978 for its modernization, which has expedited economic, social, scientific, and cultural exchanges between two countries and contributed to democratization of

China. After the 1989 Tiananmen incident, President George Bush allowed over 60,000 Mainland Chinese in the United States between 5 June 1989 and 11 April 1990 to remain legally in the United States. Third, the Chinese government joined the World Trade Organization in 2001 making Chinese markets more attractive to foreigners, so that Chinese Americans benefit by having better opportunities for trans-Pacific business and employment. Fourth, increasing trade and investment between the United States and China expanded transportation and communications for efficient transactions in goods and services as well as money markets, which has formed a Sino-American networking system that expedites globalization. Fifth, the rising number of educated intellectuals and an efficient networking system between trans-Pacific nations made Chinese Americans play a more influential role in shaping U.S. policy toward China and China's policy toward the United States.[92] Finally, Chinese Americans have contributed to modernization of China particularly in science and technology. Unfortunately, the Clinton Administration inappropriately handled the case of Dr. Wen Ho Lee, reminding Asian Americans of historic racial discrimination in the past.[93]

36. The large-scale Japanese immigration to Hawaii through labor contracts began in 1884, although about 150 Japanese came to Hawaii to work on sugarcane plantations in 1869. It was an initial step for Japan to send its people to the new world, and Hawaii was a staging point for Japanese to migrate to the United States and Canada. The white Americans in Hawaii wanted to counterbalance the large number of Chinese workers (18,000 in 1884) by partially replacing newcomers from Japan. The Hawaiian authorities reported that 771 Japanese former laborers left for America as of the end of 1894. The Japanese population in the United States was 24,326 in 1900, rising 138,834 by 1930, when 70.2 percent of them lived in California. They competed with Chinese laborers in West Coast farms, but the decline of Chinese work forces from the early 1900s caused employers to raise wages. Anti-Japanese sentiment prevailed on the West Coast, where the American Federation of Labor insisted that "the Pacific coast and inter-mountain states" were suffered from "Chinese and Japanese cheap coolie labor." The San Francisco School Board ordered on October 11, 1906 all Japanese pupils to attend the Chinese school, which was reported by newspapers in Tokyo and Washington. Thus, a local discrimination became an international incident that violated the 1894 treaty between the two countries, guaranteeing reciprocal "most favored nation" rights of residence to nationals in each country. President Theodore Roosevelt thought that it might cause "the gravest consequences to the nation" so he promised that the Japanese would be treated just like other civilized peoples and authorized the states to use armed forces to protect Japanese if they were menaced by mobs.[94] The case settled by the Gentlemen's Agreement consisted of six notes exchanged between two countries in late 1907 and early 1908. Tokyo agreed not to issue passports to laborers in the future, but to issue passports to the parents, wives, and children of laborers already residing in the United States. Since Japanese immigrants could bring their spouses to America, its population doubled in less than twenty years, and their female ratio became balanced to 46.3 percent by 1930.[95]

37. The Japanese Association of America (JAA) was founded by Japanese-born residents (Issei) in the United States in 1909.[96] Through its local chapters, the Japanese consulate issued certificates required by the Gentlemen's Agreement relating to its immigrants traveling outside the country with the right to return and the ability to bring wives, parents, and other relatives into the United States. The associations were not only self-help and protection groups, but "organs of Japanese propaganda" as an invisible government. The JAA established a rule of thumb that anyone who could show a bank account or other assets of $800 would be eligible to bring his wife. If a local office of JAA certified one's eligibility to the consulate, a necessary passport and travel documents were issued, which gave controlling power to JAA. The Japanese were gradually moving to farm operators from laborers throughout the west. Japanese labor was crucial in the establishment of sugar beets in Idaho, Colorado, and Utah, but grew other corps in other states. California passed the Alien Land Act in 1913, prohibiting Japanese Americans from owning property, but Japanese land tenure continued to expand. Japanese owned 74,769 acres and leased 383,387 acres of agricultural land in California in 1919. They opened up new lands and introduced new high-yield crops, which supplemented rather than competed with other western producers. As anti-Japanese tide peaked in American in 1921, Tokyo announced that its government would not issue further passports to picture brides. The U.S. Congress passed the Immigration Act of 1924 that did not exclude Japan, despite prevalent anti-Japanese sentiment in America, although it was successful in reducing the Japanese quota to 100 persons per year. California was the heart of Japanese America, and its population increased to 36,866 in Los Angeles County, 5,000 in San Francisco, and 7,000 in Seattle by 1940. In the same year, Japanese males in California, Oregon, and Washington were employed as follows: 51.4 percent in agriculture, forestry, and fishing; 23.6 percent in wholesale and retail trade; and 17.1 percent in personal services; while 33.4 percent of Japanese females worked for payments. Second generation professionals (Nisei) founded the Japanese American Citizens League (JACL) in 1930, which stressed Americanization and the exercise of civil rights.[97]

38. After Japan attacked Pearl Harbor on December 7, 1941, President Franklin D. Roosevelt signed Executive Order No. 9066 empowering the U.S. Army to designated areas from which "any or all persons may be excluded." One of the key players was Lt. General John L. DeWitt, the commander of the Western Defense Command and the U.S. 4th Army, who stated that "the Japanese race is an enemy race" and "the very fact that no sabotage has taken place to date is a disturbing and confirming indication that such action will be taken." It was announced on March 2, 1942, that "Japanese, German, and Italian" aliens and "any person of Japanese ancestry" would be excluded from Military Area No.1 which was a starting point for the removal of all Japanese, native-born as well as alien, from the entire area lying west of the Sierra Nevada and Cascade Mountains based on military necessity. After reporting to collection points near their homes, each group moved to assembly centers and then to relocation centers. The War Department constructed ten relocation centers in seven states, and created the War Relocation Authority (WRA) as a civilian

organization on March 19, 1942. The barracks were designed by standard plans with different-sized apartments to accommodate various families and groups of single people, and empty barracks were used for community activities. Each relocation center operated agricultural enterprises despite standard rationing, and ran war-related industries such as making camouflage nets. The people contained in centers were 120,313, 95 percent of Japanese in America, two-third of whom were native-born. About 1,200 volunteers from relocation centers and later draftees created the 442nd Regimental Combat Team. The combined 442nd and 100th Infantry Battalion of Hawaii National Guard both fought in Italy and France, and became the most decorated unit of its size in American history.[98] In addition, more than 16,000 Nisei served in the Pacific and in Asia, mainly in intelligence and translation. On December 17, 1944, the War Department lifted relocation, but the Japanese Americans had lost homes and businesses of 4 to 5 billion dollars in 1999 values, and suffered from physical and mental difficulties.

39. The rise of People's Republic of China in 1949 and the break out of the Korean War in 1950 made Americans recognize the strategic importance of Japan for U.S. national security, and the U.S.-Japanese relations became warmer in the Cold War period. However, anti-Japanese sentiment continued in America after the war, and equal opportunity under the law and presented in public speeches remained as lip service. The JACL joined the civil rights coalition with others by participating in the National Leadership Conference on Civil Rights. Later the U.S. Congress passed the Japanese American Claims Act in 1948, allowing only for "damage to or loss of real or personal property" but not for economic, legal, and moral shortcomings (which was compensated eventually by the U.S. Congress in 1988) although the Claims Act was a symbol of the improved image of Japanese Americans. In 1950, the Japanese American population was at 141,768, which was dispersed in California 84,956 (59.6%), Illinois 11,646 (8.2%), Washington 9,694, Colorado 5,412 (3.8%), and Utah 4,452 (3.1%). As a result of decentralization, most Japanese Americans were employed in large corporations, although 20.9 percent of those in California were still employed in agriculture. The day of the Issei had passed and the new communities were largely Nisei and Sansei (third generation). "Economically, there was no longer an ethnic economy to shelter Japanese Americans; culturally there were no longer established ethnic institutions to shape their lives. There were neighborhood clusters of Japanese, but no real Japantowns."[99] Japanese Americans gradually increased to 847,562 peaked in 1990 and fell to 796,700 in 2000. The image of Japanese Americans positively improved because of followings: ethnic revival of the 1960s and 1970s and increased number of Asian immigrants, the civil rights movement and changing values of equality, increased perception and awareness by the majority society of other ethnic groups, economic and social development and its status, and increased American cosmopolitanism. The 1970 census indicated that 51.5 percent of 25 years and older Japanese Americans received secondary education, and 29.5 percent received college education. Expanded education contributed to their economic and social mobility into the mainstream of America.

40. The first Koreans came to Hawaii in 1903 through labor contracts with sugar planters owing to efforts of Horace Allen, U.S. Ambassador to Korea at the time when plantation owners had labor problems with Chinese and Japanese workers. However, Japan forced Korea to become its protectorate in 1905, and issued a law in the following year that prohibited its immigration permanently. Between 1903 and 1905, about 7,226 Korean immigrants came to Hawaii, among which 2,000 returned home. Most of the Korean immigrants stayed in Hawaii but moved to cities for better jobs or to open small businesses. About 1,000 of them went to California, Oregon, and Washington to be hired in agriculture and to work on railroads. The Koreans in Hawaii formed three types of community organizations: a council based on the traditional Korean village headed by a mayor, church groups, and a self-help financial association or "kye."[100] The Korean nationalist immigrants formed the Korean National Association (KNA) in 1909 in San Francisco, but its movement faced many problems because of lack of cooperation from quarrels and disputes toward the common goal to free Korea from Japanese rule. An Chang-ho organized the Corps for the Advancement of Individuals in 1913 in San Francisco. He thought that education promoted virtue, intellect, and health, raising the consciousness of all Korean Americans, which would be essential to achieve Korean independence.[101] Pak Yong-man believed that Korean independence could be achieved by defeating Japan militarily. He recruited 300 ex-soldiers of the Korean Army from immigrants in Hawaii and organized them into a military corps in 1914. Syngman Rhee understood that Korean independence could be achieved by diplomatic efforts of turning America and world opinions to the Korean side. He established the Comrade Society in Honolulu in 1920 to compete with the KNA.[102] From the beginning of World War II, Koreans in the United States were very supportive in the fight against Japan for Korea's independence, but they had a difficult time, although they were not contained separately, since Korea was officially part of the Japanese empire. Some even put a little sign of "I'm no Jap" on their clothing.

41. The second wave of Korean immigrants arrived from 1950 to 1965, which consisted of three groups. One group was Korean wives of American servicemen, which number rose to 1,340 in 1964 and 3,000 in 1971. The total immigrants in this category were 53,629 by the end of 1980. Many of them suffered from cultural shock and a language barrier and were isolated from both the American and Korean communities. It has been reported that there were many cases of physical abuse, alcohol abuse, suicide, and a high divorce rate. The second group was Korean orphans adopted by American couples in the United States, which were about 6,203 in the period from 1955 to 1966. Among them, 41 percent were fully Koreans, 46 percent had white fathers, and the rest were Afro-Koreans.[103] Most adoptive parents were white protestant families living in the rural and small communities. Many adoptees faced the problem of dual identity as they grew older and became conscious: "The older I get, the more I realize I can't avoid being Korean."[104] The third group consisted of students, visitors, businessmen, and others engaged in commerce, whose number exceeded 27,000 in this period. Many of them pursued professional career such as medical doctors, lawyers, and college professors accepted by the white community. They were

concerned more about American society than immigrant communities, but now have reached the age of retirement. The third and final wave of Korean immigration came as a result of the Immigration Act of 1965, which removed national origins and allowed 170,000 for each Asian nation a year. Over 30,000 Koreans on average immigrated annually to the United States over the last three decades, and the population of Korean Americans increased from 69,150 in 1970 to 1,076,872 in 2000 shown in Table 8.[105] The population of Korean Americans is only 0.39 percent of the American population, and 10.8 percent of the not-Hispanic Asian and Pacific Islander population in the United States, but their status remains a small ethnic minority. The Census 2000 indicated that Korean Americans lived in large cities divided among several metropolitan areas: Los Angeles (24.0 percent), New York (15.8 percent), Washington (6.9 percent), San Francisco (4.3 percent), and Chicago (4.3 percent) shown in Table 9.

Table 9. Korean American Population in the Selected Areas, 2000

Metropolitan Area	Population	Percent
Korean Population in the United States	*1,076,872*	*100%*
Los Angeles Metropolitan Area	257,975	24.0
New York Metropolitan Area	170,509	15.8
Washington Metropolitan Area	74,454	6.9
San Francisco Metropolitan Area	57,386	5.3
Chicago Metropolitan Area	46,256	4.3
Seattle Metropolitan Area	41,189	3.8
Total of above Six Metropolitan Areas	*647,769*	*60.15*

Source: Eui-Young Yu, "Korean Population in the United States," *International Journal of Korean Studies,* VI (1) (Spring/Summer 2002), p. 87.

42. The Korean immigrants in the last three decades were young, married, and relatively well educated, while those who came through family reunification were in lower socio-economic status than the general population of Korean immigrants during the same period.[106] Fully 49.2 percent of Korean Americans (KAs) received a BA or BS or higher degree of education according to Census 2000, which was higher than 28.4 percent of white Americans for the same year. The average income of KAs was $32,807 in 2000, being lower than $36,754 of white Americans.[107] The proportion of managerial jobs for KAs in 1990 was 15 percent for male and 9 percent for female as shown in Table 10. The KA male proportion in managerial jobs was 2 percent higher than that of all Americans, but 5 percent lower than that of Japanese American male workers; while KA female workers in this category were much lower than the proportion of all Americans as well as that of Japanese and Chinese. The proportion of professional jobs for KAs was 16 percent for male and 11 percent for female. It was 4 percent higher than that of all Americans, but 8 and 4 percent lower than that of both Chinese and Japanese male workers. In technical and sales jobs, the proportion of KAs was 29 percent for male and 25 percent for female in the same year. Considering that the proportion for all Americans on technical and sales jobs was 15 percent for male and 16 percent for female (versus 8 and 17 for Chinese, and 17 and 16 for Japanese), the KA proportion was unusually high due to the increasing number self-employed to

small business owners. In service jobs, KA male workers had a similar proportion to all Americans. In sum, a large proportion of Koreans Americans resides in urban areas, and engages largely in small businesses as well as managerial and professional jobs. In jobs of production and craft and operators, the proportions of KA male workers were relatively lower than that of all Americans although Chinese and Japanese male workers showed the same low percentages. The occupational data for 2000 will more explain the social mobility of Korean Americans.

Table 10. Occupational Distribution by Sex:
Selected Asian Americans Compared to All U.S. Workers, 1990
Left Male, Right Female in Percent

Occupation Male and Female	All USA		Chinese		Japanese		Filipino		Koreans		Vietnam	
Managerial	13	11	15	15	20	14	10	10	15	9	5	7
Professional	12	17	24	17	20	19	12	20	16	11	13	9
Technical and Sales	15	16	18	17	17	16	15	16	29	25	18	17
Administrative Support	7	28	8	21	9	28	16	25	6	14	8	18
Service	10	17	19	14	9	14	16	17	10	20	12	19
Fish and Forest	4	1	1	1	4	1	2	1	1	1	2	1
Production and Craft	19	2	8	3	12	3	12	3	12	6	19	10
Operators	20	8	9	13	2	5	15	7	12	14	22	20

Sources: U.S. Bureau of Census, *Asian and Pacific Islanders in the United States*, CP-3-5, August 1993 in Norman R. Yetman, *Majority and Minority*, pp. 224 for 1990 data.

43. The number of business firms owned by Korean Americans was 135,571 in 1997 with 339,000 dollars of average sales per firm and 2.46 average employees (for Chinese Americans, 252,577 firms, 420,000 dollars, and 2.74 persons respectively). The total sales by KA firms were over 45.9 billion dollars in the same year, which was 0.25 percent of business sales by all U.S. firms.[108] The Los Angeles Riot in 1992 damaged small businesses owned by Korean Americans. The conflict between Korean business owners and black customers was rooted from expansion of Korean businesses into black communities. First, in the 1940s and 1950s when racial segregation was enforced in America, black entrepreneurs maintained various businesses in their residential areas. But in the 1970s and 1980s when racial integration became a reality, their marginal businesses could not survive in the new environment, so other ethnic groups, particularly Korean Americans gradually took over black neighborhood businesses in free competition. Second, large and well capitalized firms did not want to take risks in the black communities, but new Korean immigrants dared to open businesses in the black areas as middlemen minorities. Third, the newcomers from Korea could not choose attractive and expensive commercial centers for their startup businesses because of lack of language capability and capital availability. They were able to take over small businesses with little capital by taking risks in unattractive areas.[109] The black peoples in the riot area claimed that Korean Americans took over black-owned businesses, and made profits with high prices and took money away from but never returned it to their black communities; and Korean store owners were exploiters with discourteous and rude behavior. But the Korean American community

explained that the cause of conflict was a misunderstanding due to the language barrier and cultural differences.[110] Increasing communication and cooperative activities between two communities have recently improved relationships. Meanwhile, Korean Americans created various organizations to protect their political and economic interests, to pursue social values with recognition, and to enjoy personal interests, hobbies, and beliefs.[111]

Asian Pacific Americans and Political Participation

44. As reviewed in previous sections, the legal status of Asian Pacific Americans (APAs) has changed through American history. (a) In 1870 the U.S. Congress amended the Naturalization Law of 1790 (granting the right to naturalize only to free white) extending this right to naturalize to "aliens of African nativity or persons of African descent" but forcing Chinese immigrants to remain "aliens ineligible for citizenship." That Law discriminated against Chinese in America by prohibiting their naturalization although business owners needed their productive labor. (b) The U.S. Congress passed the Chinese Exclusion Act in 1882, which prohibited Chinese immigration to the United States. As a result, the family reunion of adult males (the male to female ratio was 21:1 in 1880) became impossible, so that the population of Chinese Americans began to decline. (c) Japanese immigrants filled the shortage of Chinese labor after 1882, but were classified as Mongolians like Chinese. Anti-Japanese sentiment was similar to anti-Chinese one. But under protest, the Japanese government signed the Gentlemen's Agreement with the U.S. government in 1907, which agreed that Japan would not issue passports further to laborers, but would issue them for family unification. (d) The U.S. Congress passed the Immigration Act of 1924, which prohibited Asian immigration to the United States. Since then, the Asian labor shortage was filled by Filipinos after the Spanish-American War in 1898. (e) After Japan's attack on Pearl Harbor, all Japanese Americans were removed from the region under the control of the Western Defense Command to the ten War Relocation Centers separated in the seven states and released by December 1944. On the other hand, the U.S. Congress repealed the Chinese Exclusion Act of 1882 and passed the new law of 1943 allowing China to have 100 of annual immigration quota. (f) The U.S. Congress passed the Immigration Act of 1965, which removed the old quota system of 1924 and reopened immigration to Asian countries extensively. As a result, the population of Asian Pacific Americans became politically significant in some areas.

45. The rapid mixture of the melting-pot after World War II, the new development of the Cold War, the human rights movement in 1950s and 1960s, and the recognition of economic and strategic importance of Asian countries contributed to this change. As a result, the population of Asian Americans increased from 878,000 in 1960 to over 10.0 million in 2000, which was still only 3.8 percent of all Americans.[112] Meanwhile, legal protection for minorities against discrimination was provided, but Asian Americans have remained in a silent minority in politics. Claire Jean Kim argues the racial position of Asian Americans by triangulation of white-Asians-black with

relative valorization and civic ostracism. First, the Model Minority myth "exaggerates Asian American prosperity, homogenizes this extremely diverse population, and obscures discriminatory treatment against it…conservatives embraced formal colorblindness in a strategic effort to delegitimate the emergent Black Power movement and arrest the growth of race-conscious social programs." Second, she alleges that Affirmative Action intends "to level the playing field between the unfairly advantaged and the unfairly disadvantaged," but it has discriminated against a small population of Asian Americans by restricting social rewards to competition on the basis of merit. Third, in the Afro-Korean conflict in Los Angeles in 1992, "the media depoliticized the event and used Asian Americans and the norms of colorblindness to protect white privilege from a Black Power challenge." Finally, although the bar on naturalization was lifted in 1950, she holds that "white opinion makers continue to police the boundary between whites and Asian Americans by imputing permanent foreignness to the latter" as shown in the reports on Kristi Yamaguchi in 1992, the campaign finance scandal with John Hwang in 1996, and the U.S.-Japan trade tensions of the 1980s and early 1990s. In sum, Kim views that the racial triangulation of Asian Americans continues "to protect white privileges from both black and Asian American encroachment today" and Asian Americans have been accepted provisionally for this purpose, but "they have never been embraced as true Americans."[113]

Table 11. Young Population, Education, Income, and Intermarriage by Race, 2000

Classification	U.S. Total	White (N-H)	Asian	Korean
Population Age 20-49	43.99 %	43.26 %	51.33 %	51.71 %
Sex Ratio Age 20-49: Male/Female	97.38 %	101.31 %	93.28 %	91.53 %
Education: BA/BS or Higher	26.8 %	28.4 %	44.06 %	49.2 %
Household Income /Median	$43,162	$46,896	$57,313	$42,010
Household Income /Mean	$58,730	$62,761	$74,829	$62,798
Marital Status				
Married, Spouse Present	56.0 %	59.7 %	57.4 %	59.3 %
Divorced	09.8 %	10.1 %	04.6 %	05.3 %
Never Married	23.9 %	20.6 %	28.5 %	31.1 %
Race of Couples 1990				
Same Race Couples %	97.1 %	97.0 %	70.0 %	
Specified Group and White	02.7 %	03.0 %	28.7 %	NA
Specified Race and other Race	00.2 %	NA	01.3 %	

Source: U.S. Census 2000 and related years.
http://landview.census.gov/hhes/income/histinc/h05.html
http://www.census.gov/population/socdemo/hh-fam/p20-537/2000/tabA1.txt
http://www.census.gov/population/socdemo/race/interractab2.txt

46. The number of Asian Americans has increased rapidly since 1965, and will increase from 3.8 percent in 2000 to about 8.0 percent in 2050, while their ethnic range diversifies widely. Asians came to America overwhelmingly from working-class origins before 1965, but in the later period, they came from the white-collar class with educated backgrounds. As shown in Table 11, they are much younger than the U.S. population: the population share of age from 20 to 49 for Asian Americans was 51.7

percent in 2000, while that for whites was 43.4 percent in the same year. The education attainment of Asian Americans is much higher than that of the U.S. population: 44.1 percent of Asian Americans received the bachelor's degree or higher in 2000, while 28.4 percent of white Americans received the same in that year. The household median income of Asian Americans was $57,313 in 2000 while that of the white was $46,896 in the same year.[114] The ratio of professional and managerial jobs for Asian Americans was 16 percent of their population in 1990, which surpassed the American average of 12 percent. Asian Americans reside largely in the white suburban areas, and their proportion who married white Americans was 28.7 percent of Asian American couples in 1990. Though their performance has been that of a Model Minority and many of them have participated in the dominant society, they feel themselves marginalized as forever foreigners regardless of their nativity and socioeconomic achievement.[115] This feeling of foreignness has following roots. Asian Americans experienced discrimination by white Americans, particularly in California, until 1965. The parents of Asian Americans taught their children to ignore American racism rather than to challenge it, which was their way of survival in foreign countries by hiding their ethnic pride (Confucian passiveness). Asian Americans trained their children to work hard at schools and in jobs, to carry their shares of responsibilities in society, and not to miss coming opportunities for success toward the American dream. The physical distinctions of Asian Americans, which are different from whites, have largely caused them to feel alienated. The population of Asian Americans is too small to influence U.S. politics so that the feeling of minority status remains unchanged. Since the majority of Asian Americans are in first generation of immigration-age with transnationalism, it is too early to be an American mainstream in feeling as well as reality. However, their mobility into the mainstream in the future would be significantly different from that of previous decades.

47. Asian Americans are gradually increasing their political participations in domestic and non-domestic as well as electoral and non-electoral affairs.[116] Despite ethnic diversification, they have created an extensive network of pan-Asian associations as a meaningful means for political empowerment and mobilization into the mainstream of America. First, APAs have tried to increase electoral participation of the naturalized citizens as the number of immigrants has risen since 1965. The various ethnic political organizations have helped qualified residents to apply for naturalization, enhanced electoral registration, and encouraged participation of voters in their immigrant communities.[117] This is a starting point of electoral politics from the grass-roots of voters linked to either the Democratic or Republican Party in elections. Second, APAs have engaged in non-electoral political activities to advance or protect their group interests. They have joined group activities by organizing either the working class for labor interests[118] or small business owners for their business interests. For example, the Korean Immigrant Workers Advocates is for the former,[119] but the Korean Drycleaners Association is for the latter. Third, APAs have sought "social justice and equal treatment by engaging in legal challenges against discriminatory laws and practices in education, employment, housing, land ownership, immigration, and other significant

public policy areas."[120] The civil rights organizations have been supportive for those challenges. Fourth, like other ethnic groups, APAs have supported political and economic development and friendship relations between the United States and their countries of origin. Chinese Americans, for example, have supported modernization and democratization in China by funding such as for its 1911 revolution or pushing the U.S. foreign policy such as for the democracy movement in 1989. Korean Americans have supported peaceful reunification of the two Koreas and arranged humanitarian aid to the North, and promoted U.S.–Korea friendship relations through organized activities. Finally, APAs have engaged in politics of their internal ethnic communities by joining one or more organizations such as ethnic immigrant associations, small business associations, socio-cultural service groups, religious organizations, and others. The role of ethnic news and media has been essential to improve communications within their communities, particularly for the first generation of immigrants.

Table 12. Citizen Voting-Age Population and Number Voted in 2000 (Thousand)

Classification	18 & Over Citizens		Registered Voters	Number Voted
U.S. Total	202,609	186,366	129,549 (69.5%)	110,826 (59.5%)
White Non-Hispanic	148,035	144,732	103,588 (71.6%)	89,469 (61.8%)
Black	24,132	22,753	15,348 (67.5%)	12,917 (56.8%)
Asian Pacific	8,041	4,718	2,470 (52.4%)	2,045 (43.3%)
Hispanic	21,595	13,158	7,546 (57.3%)	5,934 (45.1%)

Source: http://landview.census.gov/prod/2002pubs/p20-542.pdf

Note: (a) White non-Hispanics top citizen voting-age population, (b) women, older people, and married people are more likely to vote, (c) people with more education, higher incomes, and jobs are more likely to vote, (d) home owners and long time residents are more likely to vote, and (e) people in the mid west are most likely to vote.

48. In electoral politics, APAs are "a genuine swing group" unbounded by strong partisan identifications. They are the emerging immigrant majority as a heterogeneous and progressive group in composition and political orientation but without an effective strategy to incorporate their voting power into a specific camp.[121] As shown in Table 12, the number of APA citizens was 4,718,000 or 58.7 percent of their eligible voting-age population in 2000 (compared to 92.0 percent for the U.S. total). The proportion of registered voters of APAs to their eligible voting-age citizens was 52.4 percent (compared to 69.5 percent for the U.S. total), and the proportion of APA voters who actually voted to their voting-age citizens was 43.3 percent (compared to 59.5 percent for the U.S. total). The voting registration and turnout rates of Asians, Blacks, Latinos, and American Indians are all lower than those of whites in 2000 and in previous elections.[122] APAs should continuously promote naturalization and election participation to increase their influence in American politics. A study showed that California's Asian American community has relatively positive perceptions of other racial and ethnic groups as neighbors, and it is believed that the problems of discrimination are real and the needs for affirmative action still exist.[123]

49. The APA communities can achieve political empowerment through electoral votes, campaign funds, publicity, and lobbying. First, APAs can elect their own ethnic representatives to federal, state, and local offices by mobilizing their voters. Since representatives include elected officials and political appointees, APAs can gain a similar effect by supporting representatives from other races who will protect their interests and appoint APAs to available political positions. Because APAs comprise only 2.4 percent of voting-age American citizens, multiracial political coalitions are necessary to win elections, particularly in electoral districts where APAs are concentrated.[124] But the problems lie in ethnic differences between APAs themselves although campaign efforts for more votes may increase the share of actual votes. Second, APAs can raise campaign funds for electoral candidates at all levels. The more money APAs raise, the larger their political influence will be as long as the supporting candidates are elected. Though money power is not equally transferred to votes, APAs can support elections indirectly. The fundraising activities are helpful in organizing more manpower and mobilizing voters to support designated candidates because real contacts with networking are involved in collecting campaign funds. Advertising expands the visibility of candidates widely and may reach undecided voters at critical moments. Third, APAs can provide publicity to support their ethnic candidates or to convey ethnic interests. The purchase of ownership or domination of management for some news and media companies is also helpful to improve publicity. It is beneficial for increasing numbers of APAs to join the news and media community as professional journalists or policy contributors from the outside. Ethnic news and media improve communications between the first-generation immigrants and attract ethnic voters. Fourth, lobbying activities are another way to maintain interests of APAs by setting clear objectives in a specific time period. APAs seek out politicians representing their interests in "the corridors of power" in the three levels of governments. Then, policy proposals are provided by think tanks, letters, telephone calls, and visits may follow.[125]

50. The Asian American communities are so diversified that integration for political empowerment will be a long, burdensome process. Therefore, each ethnic group should integrate itself at first, and then send its representatives to an APA Association for pan-Asian American coalition. Korean Americans can be used as a sample case to integrate community resources for political empowerment. Considering that the population of Korean Americans rose from less than 70,000 in 1970 to over 1 million by 2000, the year of 2003 is the immigration age of thirty for their majority, which is more than two generations behind Italian or Jewish Americans in assimilation. The reality of Korean Americans is similar to European immigrants in the 1930s in several respects: (a) The first generation of Korean Americans lives in transnationalism, where they put one leg in America while the other leg remains in Korea, and the weight of life gradually moves from Korea to America as time passes. (b) The assimilation process was slow and painful due to insufficient language abilities and cultural differences with foreignness of the ethnic minority, prejudice and discrimination, and distorted public perceptions. (c) Owing to economic and social development in South Korea, families of Korean immigrants were able to bring capital with entrepreneurship

to open small businesses, which expedited them to settle rapidly and secure their economic lives in America. (d) As shown in early Jewish immigration, parents of Korean Americans have emphasized education for their children. As of 2000, almost a half of them received bachelor's degree in either America or Korea, which secured better jobs and incomes. (e) The majority of the second generation is in college and alternates lifestyles between Korean and American ways of life or to blend the two ways of life. Despite the conflict between cultural differences, they want to work with the first-generation who has dominated community resources. (f) The majority of Korean Americans are Protestants and some are Catholic, and few believe in Buddhism. Religion in addition to benefits from ethnic lifestyle with some racial distinctiveness has largely contributed to maintain ethnic connections for Koreans.[126]

51. The political participation of Korean Americans can be explained by as follows. (a) In electoral politics, the Korean American (KA) community in the Washington metropolitan area has maintained the KA Republicans or Democrats of Virginia or Maryland. The KA Coalition and the League of KAs have been organized and run by youth groups for political participation. They have worked for naturalization, registration, and voting participation of KAs continuously, and participated in campaign fundraising for both parties. But their activities were not successful due to lack of KA participation and non-existence of an efficient networking system. (b) In business politics, KAs have created associations to protect their business interests, such as the KA Chamber of Commerce, KA Food Business Association, KA Grocery Association, KA Retail Liquor Association, KA Drycleaners Association, and others. The KA business community has tried to widen the market potential not limited to KA customers but to broader customers of the population, transform the business structure toward medium-sized one for better opportunities, maximize its strength and minimize its weakness in business such as trade with and investment in Korea and other Asian countries, and protect KA business interests such as the case against business rezoning for dry cleaning stores in Fairfax County in 2000. (c) In politics of society and culture, KAs have created various organizations such as KA Associations of Korean Home Provinces, Alumni Associations of Korean Schools, Korean Language Schools, KA Scholarship Foundation, Korean Cultural Foundation of USA, Korean Amateur Sports Association, Korean Taekwondo Master's Association, Association of KA Doctors-Lawyers-Professors, Association of KA Political Scientists-Economists-Sociologists, and Council of Korean Churches. They have pursued professional values and provided services to members and their community, but depended on voluntary services and annual fundraisers. Since no organizations can survive without proper funds, it is necessary to integrate community resources, which will provide proper sources of money and manpower for planning and executing their programs.

52. Like other ethnic Americans, (d) KAs are still concerned about Korean affairs. In politics concerning the Korean peninsula, KAs can contribute to the reunification of the two Koreas as well as promotion of friendly relations between the United States and the two Koreas (or a unified Korea in the future), both of which are

mutually supportive. First, we have expected that the two Koreas will be unified under democratic politics with free-market economy. KAs can make policy inputs into the political process of America or Korea. It is desirable for North Korea to liberalize domestic politics and expedite market openness, followed by dismantling of weapons of mass destruction. It is desirable for the two Koreas to sign a peace treaty mandating disarmament, through which a significant portion of defense expenditures in both sides can be converted into non-defense sectors. As a result, the new investment can absorb manpower released by disarmament. Second, KAs can promote U.S.-Korea relations by increasing mutual understanding through proper communications. KAs speak two languages and understand two different cultures, so that they are familiar with their spheres of interests. (e) KAs have involved in politics within the KA community. The Korean American Association of each region (KAA) has symbolically represented the KA community. But KAA cannot claim represent Korean Americans because of insufficient participation in election. KAA does not have proper fund sources and manpower to pursue its goals and manage community affairs. Major decisions of KAA are made by its Board of Directors, not by voters. KAA cannot integrate community resources because of no power to control conflicts of interest between different organizations of the community. KAA has no capability to pursue pan-Asian Americanism with APA Association as well as multiracial coalition movements. In sum, KAA is unable to lead politics within the KA community because of non-existence of an efficient networking system led by a dominant power in the community providing fund and manpower. Thus, it is necessary for the KA community to create an efficient networking system or to restructure the existing KAA system to order to integrate their limited resources for political empowerment of Korean Americans.

Korean Americans and Integration of Community Resources

53. We examined political participation of Asian Americans and analyzed that of Korean Americans in the previous section. It is desirable that a representative organization of Korean Americans such as KAA leads their ethnic political empowerment, but most KA organizations in politics, economy, society, culture, and religion are not capable to support organized activities with proper money and manpower. Unlike Jewish Americans, Korean Americans in the past century had no leadership of driving forces to integrate community resources toward political empowerment although the number of KA organizations has increased. It is time to create a new KA Association having an efficient networking system with a representative congress, supportive administration, and research institute as a think tank. This author suggests that Korean Americans in the Washington metropolitan area organize a new system with the KA Association of Greater Washington, DC (KAA-GW) as a regional model, to be transplanted into other KA communities such Los Angeles, New York, and San Francisco. The newly created KAA of each region send their delegates, based on the share of KA population of each region, to the KA Association headquartered in Washington, DC. KAA represents all Korean Americans in the United States, and its organizational structure is similar to the proposed KAA-

GW having the above three functions. Similarly, a representative organization of each ethnic Asian Pacific Americans sends proper delegates, based on the population share, to the Asian Pacific American Association (APAA) to integrate their political power. Asian Americans also can join coalition movements with Blacks and Hispanics, if necessary, by sending their delegates to multiracial organizations to strengthen their influence in American politics because they are the minority. Figure 1 shows a line of command from a model unit of KAA-GW upward to KAA to APAA to multiracial coalitions, and downward to its three branches of KA Congress, KA Administration, and KA Research Institute (a think tank).

Figure 1. From Korean Americans to Asian Americans to Multiracial Coalition

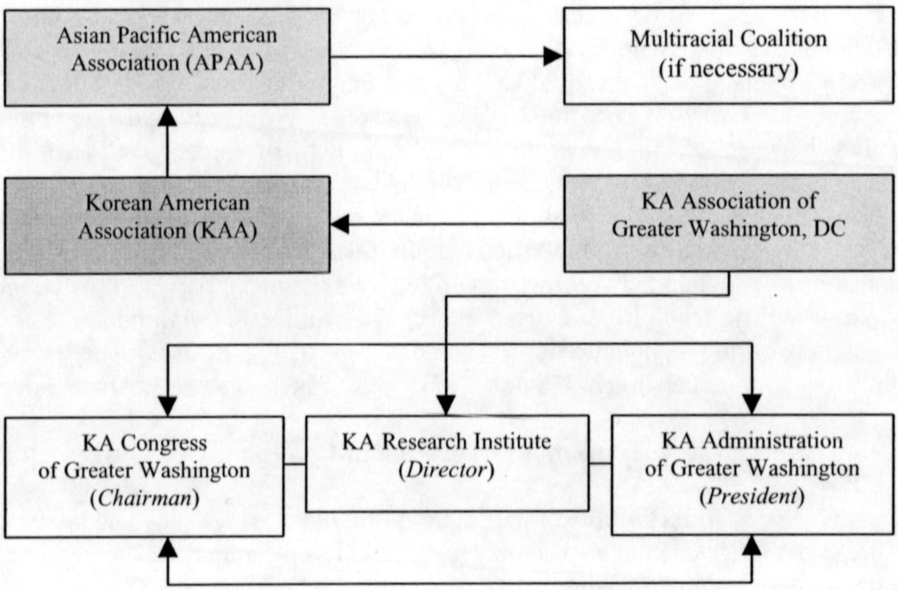

Note: The KA Association of Greater Washington, DC (KAA-GW) as a model unit is transplanted to LA, NY and other regions. The representatives of each unit create a KA Association (KAA), which delegates form an Asian Pacific American Association (APAA). APAA joins the Multiracial Coalition for more political influence. KAA-GW has three functions: KA Congress (Chairman), KA Administration (President), and KA Research Institute (Director).

54. In fact, the weaknesses of the current KAA-GW is significant. First, the President of KAA-GW is directly elected by Korean Americans who register for the election. However, the number of participants is too small to represent the entire Korean American community. Since the election campaigns need a significant amount of financial support, presidential candidates are limited to wealthy self-funded candidates, which force the exclusion of qualified candidates. Second, major decisions of the KA Association are made by the Board of Directors, whose members are not elected by voters. To run for office is one thing, and to run the system is another, which is the other reason for its lack of representativeness. Third, the KAA-GW has no

manpower and financial resources to run the system properly. Presidential candidates announce their plans and projects during the campaign period, but they cannot keep the promises because of lack of resources once elected. Fourth, KAA-GW does not have an administrative line of command. The KAA-VA or MD or others do not belong to the KAA-GW so that the activities of the President are limited to ceremonial participation. Finally, the current KAA-GW has no capabilities to integrate organizations in the KA community and to link Korean Americans to the APAA and multiracial or multiethnic coalitions. Those are the reasons to restructure the existing KAA-GW. This can be analyzed by *the systems approach* shown in Figure 2. The proposed system of KAA-GW has six subsystems including goals and values, organizational structure, personnel, finance, technology, and control and coordination. The system interacts with suprasystem of local, regional, national, and global environments, which are usually more powerful than the system, although the system itself can maintain a leadership in some cases. The subsystems also interact with each other within the system according to external stimulation such as environmental changes or various inputs. A new input enters the system and produces an output, which reenters the system by feedback operations. This process continues until the output satisfies the goals and objectives of the system. It is essential to set specific objectives based on general goals and values although those objectives are modified from time to time according to changes of system's capability and external environment.[127]

Figure 2. A Systems Approach to Create the Korean American Association

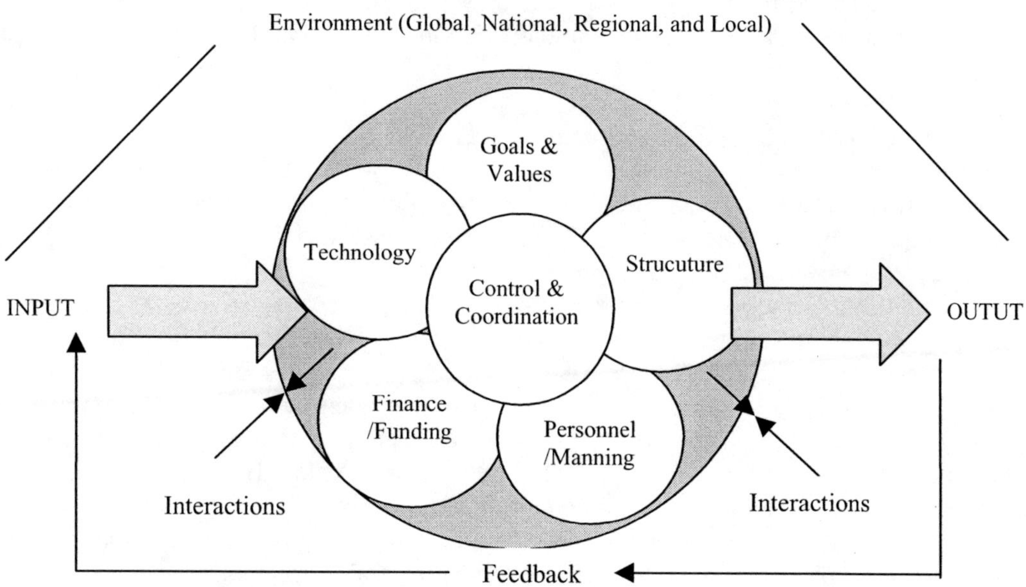

Note: (a) The system is the KA Association of Greater Washington which is the largest circle. (b) The subsystems include six smaller circles within the largest circle, which includes goals and values, organizational structure, personnel, finance, technology, and control and coordination. (c) The suprasystem is global, national, regional, and local environments, which interact with the system.

55. The KA ethnic identity lies in a distinct color line which Korean Americans and their descendants will face continuously in America. Thus, their ethnic interests need to be protected from disadvantages of the minority, while KAs contribute positively to advancement of American civilization. The KAA-GW enables KAs to enjoy happiness by helping themselves to participate actively in politics, economy, society, culture, and religion into the mainstream of America through integration of community resources with an efficient networking system. The goals of KAA-GW include followings: (a) In politics and government, it helps Korean Americans to participate in American politics for their political empowerment through electoral participation, campaign fund raise, publicity supports, and lobbying activities. (b) In economy and business, it helps KA businesses profitable through attraction of more customers, structural transformation, coordination between KA business associations and government regulations, and others. (c) In society and labor, it helps KA workers to receive equal and fair treatment in employment as well as their daily lives by pursuing social justice: watching law enforcement practices or proposing new laws if necessary. (d) In education and training, it helps KA children to receive higher education in prominent schools based on their capabilities, while it provides job training and English courses for newcomers, and Korean courses for the native-born. (e) In culture and sports, it helps Korean American to join cultural and sport activities in American lives based on individual tastes and to buildup friendships through group activities. (f) In religion, it helps Korean Americans to be harmonious between different religions by supporting interreligious activities between protestant, catholic, and Buddhism. (g) With the Korean peninsula, it helps Korean Americans to contribute to reunification of the two Koreas under a system of democratic politics and market economy, while it helps them to promote friendly U.S.-Korea relations which is also beneficial for Korean Americans themselves.

56. The organizational structure of KAA-GW consists of three branches as suggested in Figure 1. First, the KA Congress is formed by KA Congressmen elected by qualified voters, over 18 years old, residing in Virginia, Maryland, and DC, and paying annual dues. The electoral districts are divided into fsix categories: region or politics and government, economy and business, society and labor, education and sciences, culture and sports, and religion. As shown in Figure 3, the KA Congress forms six standing Committees of political, economic, social, educational, cultural, and America-Korea relations affairs, and creates some subcommittees for a certain period of time if necessary. The number of the KA Congressmen depends on the number of participants in KAA elections. If 25,000 voters participate in the first election, the inaugural KA Congress will have 250 Congressmen. The KA Congress elects its Chairman who has an authority to appoint the Committee Chairman of each standing committee and subcommittee. Second, the KA Administration consists of six departments: planning and budget, information and communications, personnel, finance, supply and logistics, and operations as shown in Figure 4. The Director of the Operations Department is not only an administrative staff member, but a commander controlling and coordinating with regional offices: Washington, Virginia, Richmond,

Figure 3. The Korean American Congress: Organizational Structure

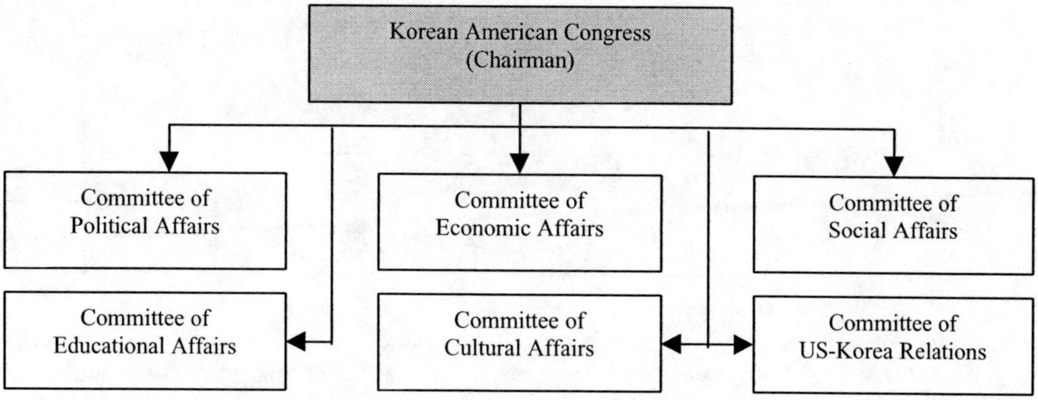

Note: The electoral districts are divided by six categories: politics and government, economy and business, society and labor, education and sciences, culture and sports, and religion.

Figure 4. The Korean American Administration: Organizational Structure

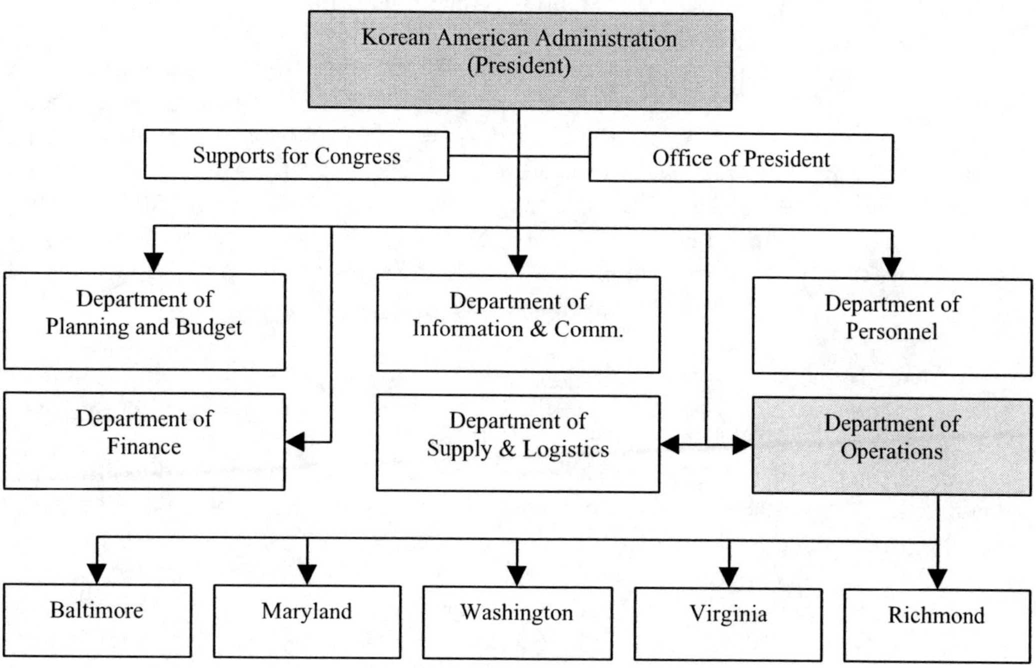

Note: The Director of the Department of Operations is a staff for President of KAA-GW as well as the only commander of its operations by communicating with local offices daily basis.

Figure 5. The Korean American Research Institute: Organizational Structure

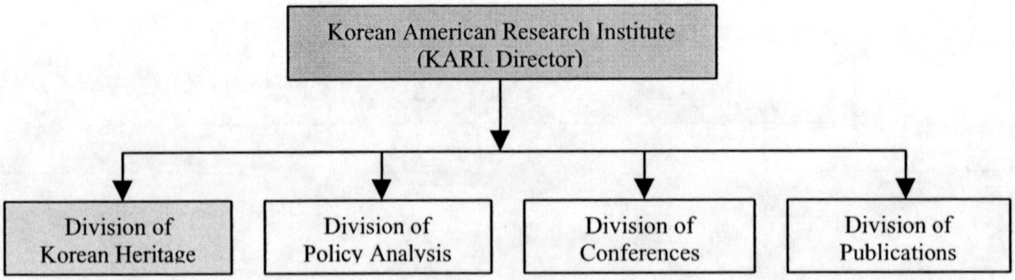

Maryland, Baltimore, and some others. The President of the KA Administration is elected by the KA Congress and represents the association externally, while the departmental directors are appointed by the President and confirmed by the Congress. The president of KA local offices are elected under their own rules and work with their local governments, but KAA coordinates their local budget and programs with KAA's annual planning and budget to promote efficiency of KA activities. The KA Administration submits an annual budget with plans to the KA Congress for approval, and budget performance is evaluated by the KA Congress once a year. Third, the KA Research Institute (KARI) provides policy recommendations for KA interests and increase publicity for various KA affairs. KARI consists of four departments of Korean Heritage, Policy Analysis, Conferences, and Publications as shown in Figure 5. The Korean Heritage Division maintains and promotes Korean heritage as a source of Korean American culture, while the Policy Analysis Division forms research teams according to annual projects to reduce the cost of research. The Conference Division prepares conferences, and the Publications Division is in charge of journal and other publications. The Director of KARI is appointed by the President and confirmed by the KA Congress. All positions within the KA Congress, Administration, and Research Institute serve on a voluntary basis except a few secretarial positions.

57. Both personnel and finance for the KA administration is essential to strengthen its capability because qualified manpower provides productive services, which can be continued with proper financial support. The first step in the electoral process is that each candidate must persuade KA voters to join KAA with annual membership fee of a check (the amount is decided by the KA Congress) in a given campaign period. Any Korean Americans who gained 100 votes or more from any category of districts submit the list of voters with collected annual membership fees with his or her candidate fee to be a Congressman in a specified term. The electoral districts are divided by six categories: geography or politics and government, economy and business, society and labor, education and sciences, culture and sports, and religion. The list of voters should included the full name, U.S. social security number, date of birth, home address, telephone number, fax number (option), and e-mail address (option). The election committee checks the accuracy of the list by cross examination

to avoid double voting by participants. When the list is cleared, the election committee announces him or her to be a KA Congressman. The *Election Committee* is a standing committee of KAA-GW to administrate all elections. It consisted of nine members including Chairperson of the Committee, who is nominated by the KA President and confirmed by the KA Congress. In the beginning, the Ad Hoc Committee has the both rights of nomination and confirmation until a new KA Congress is formed and functioning. All decisions regarding elections of KAA-GW are made by the majority votes of the Committee. Any Korean Americans aged 18 or over can vote for a KA Congressman (one person has one vote) by paying a defined membership fee. And any Korean Americans aged 25 or over who has no criminal records are qualified to be a candidate of the KA Congressman by paying a defined amount of the candidate fee. Let's assume that John Kim lives in the County of Fairfax (region or politics and government), runs a restaurant business in DC (economy and business), joins the Home of Seoul Club (society and labor), teaches Korean language on Sunday (education and sciences), joins the Mountain Climbing Club (culture and sports), and attends to the Catholic Church of Virginia (religion). He can vote, according to his preference, for any candidate of six categories with his one vote by paying the membership fee with his personal check which can be substituted by his family members. In the second step, being formed by elected representatives, the KA Congress elects both Chairman of the KA Congress and President of KA Administration, and confirms all Department Heads of the KA Administration and the Director of the KA Research Institute based on recommendations of the KA President. The Division chiefs of the KARI are appointed by its Director without confirmation. Finally, followings need to be considered in manning. First, the KA community has been diversified so rapidly that the problems of classes between white and blue collar workers became deeper and wider, which has been an obstacle to disturb harmony of the community. The KAA-GW leaders should consider this problem seriously in appointing qualified individuals to various positions and working with them in daily operations in terms of efficiency with harmonious participation. Second, the KAA-GW depends largely on voluntary services without material compensation. If the leadership cannot attract personal interest, it is not easy to maintain voluntary services with ethnic cohesiveness. Third, the leadership of the KA should recognize that the generation gap will remain problematic as long as new immigrants come continuously. Thus, the role of the next generations should be increased in the community.

58. The major sources of finance for KAA include followings: (a) a defined amount of annual membership fee from all voters to be collected by each Congressman whom they voted, (b) a defined candidate free from KA Congressmen, (c) personal contributions largely from Korean Americans, (d) contributions by KA profit and non-profit organizations in the region, (e) contributions by Korean businesses in America and American businesses in Korea, (f) matching funds from all levels of governments in America and the Korean government, (g) fundraising banquets and activities, (h) revenues from self generating activities, and (i) others such as contributions of appointees to major positions of KAA-GW. It is necessary to increase the endowment

fund of KAA continuously by saving at least a half of annual revenue each year. The annual membership fee is mandatory for each voter, but should not be a burden to KA voters because it is not desirable if the fee prevents electoral participation. It is a good idea to raise the endowment fund from prominent individuals and successful companies in America. If the existing KA organizations join KAA as its subsystem, the economies of scale for KAA will be improved. For example, the International Council on Korean Studies (ICKS) has held annual conferences since 1996 and published the International Journal of Korean Studies for several years. If KAA is able to include ICKS as its subsystem, it can function as KARI without much change. If the KA Scholarship Foundation joins KAA as its subsystem, KAA will provide administrative supports for KASF, which will improve its efficiency. However, KAA-GW should not centralize all of KA activities because it is not necessary and possible. It is better for KAA-GW to help and encourage each organization to function properly through coordination.

Table 13. Asian and Korean Americans in VA, MD, and DC by County (Census 2000)

Regional Classification		Total Population	Asian Alone	Korean Alone	% to Population	
					Asians	Koreans
VA	***Virginia Total***	***7,078,515***	***261,025***	***45,273***	***3.69***	***0.64***
	Arlington County	189,453	16,327	1,572	8.62	0.83
	Chesterfield County	259,903	6,154	1,237	2.37	0.48
	Fairfax County	969,747	126,038	28,028	13.00	2.89
	Henrico County	262,300	9,451	850	3.60	0.32
	Loudon County	169,599	9,067	883	5.35	0.52
	Montgomery County	83,629	3,320	683	3.97	0.82
	Prince William County	280,813	10,701	1,694	3.81	0.60
	York County	56,297	1,829	540	3.25	0.96
	Alexandria City	128,283	7,249	1,335	5.65	1.04
	Fairfax City	21,498	2,617	615	12.17	2.86
	Newport News City	180,150	4,195	1,210	2.33	0.67
	Richmond City	197,790	2,471	439	1.25	0.22
	Virginia Beach City	425,257	20,869	924	4.91	0.22
	Other Areas	3,853,796	40,737	5,263	1.06	0.14
MD	***Maryland Total***	***5,296,486***	***210,929***	***39,155***	***3.98***	***0.74***
	Anne Arundel County	489,658	11,225	3,603	2.29	0.74
	Baltimore County	754,292	23,947	5,249	3.17	0.70
	Frederick County	195,277	3,269	564	1.67	0.29
	Harford County	218,590	3,313	801	1.52	0.37
	Howard County	247,842	19,037	6,188	7.68	2.50
	Montgomery County	873,341	98,651	15,130	11.30	1.73
	Prince George's County	801,515	31,032	3,843	3.87	0.48
	Wicomico County	84,644	1,478	524	1.75	0.62
	Baltimore City	651,154	9,985	1,826	1.53	0.28
	Other Areas	980,173	8,992	1,427	0.92	0.15
DC	***Washington***	***572,059***	***15,189***	***1,095***	***2.66***	***0.19***
Total Population		12,947,060	487,143	85,523	3.76	0.66

Source: http://factfinder.census.gov/servlet/DTTable? ts=59386420997
http://factfinder.census.gov/servlet/DTTable? ts=59389308560
http://factfinder.census.gov/servlet/DTTable? ts=59386652716

59. The subsystem of technology contributes to communications in operating KAA in the age of globalization. An efficient computer system reduces secretarial work, and expedites their communications for all levels of organizational activities of KAA, so that a handful of qualified workers can support all of KAA's administration. For example, if all members of KAA provide their e-mail addresses, most messages can be delivered instantly by the e-mail system in both English and Korean. Additionally, the general information about KAA can be posted on its website so that many internal and external telephone calls will be reduced. Finally, the subsystem of control and coordination maximizes the system's efficiency and minimizes operational costs. Control is a function of commanding within the system, while coordination is that of adjustment between subsystems as well as between the system and external forces. KAA controls subsystems and coordinates with them within the system by linking them to each other with proper interactions. For example, when the objectives are set more or less than the system's capability, the system either reduces objectives or expands its capacity, or does both together. This is the function of control and coordination of the system as a result of internal and external interactions. The annual audit evaluates the performance of the system whether KAA achieved the objectives set by the KA Congress. As an example of feedback, suppose that Korean Americans participate in votes by 45 percent of voting-age citizens while the American population participates in votes by 60 percent of the same in average. Setting the objective 60 percent for KA voting-age citizens to go to elections, KAA helps naturalization for more KA citizens, registration for more available voters, and actual voting participation. Those efforts continue until the KA electoral participation reaches at the level of American population. As an example of interactions, KAs were active for humanitarian aid to North Korea during the period of Clinton administration, but became inactive in the Bush's since President Bush declared "axis of evil" in January 2001. This is a result of interactions between the KA community and the changing environment of the United States. If external forces are stronger than internal ones, the system will follow the wind. But the system will not be disturbed by external forces if the case is opposite.

60. Table 13 shows the population of Asian Americans as well as Korean Americans in major counties and cities in Virginia, Maryland, and District of Columbia in 2000. Korean Americans numbered 45,273 in Virginia (0.64 percent) and 39,155 in Maryland (0.74 percent), which was higher than the Koreans' share of the U.S. population (0.39 percent), although those living in Washington, DC (0.19 percent) are far below the national average. The shares of Asian and Korean Americans residing in Fairfax County in Virginia show 13.00 and 2.89 percent respectively, and those in Fairfax City are similar to Fairfax County. Meanwhile, the shares of Asian and Korean Americans in Montgomery County, Maryland were 11.30 and 1.73 percent respectively, and those in Howard County in the same state were 7.68 and 2.50 respectively in the same year. Therefore, the Asian and Korean Americans residing in those counties and city have more voting power than other areas if they are naturalized as citizens, fully register to vote, and vote on the election day. If Asian Americans organize a multiracial coalition with African and Hispanic Americans, their political influence would be

amplified. The statistics shown above are useful to mobilize electoral participation and to restructure the Korean American Association in those three states. This type of population statistics would be useful in the other metropolitan areas in mobilizing voters for political empowerment if their share of the ethnic population is considerably higher than their share of the U.S. population nationwide.

Summary and Conclusion

61. *In summary*, this study overviewed the history of immigration to America, racial integration, and the assimilation of European and Asian immigrant groups, and examined political participation of Asian Americans and the integration of Korean Americans. The industrial expansion of the U.S. economy demanded labor forces continually from external sources of Europe, Africa, Asia, and others. Since the late 1960s, when America opened the immigration door, young and skilled immigrants have flown into America, particularly through overseas education and training programs in the United States.[128] The massive inflow of young educated immigrants made America younger and progressive, which became part of valuable sources for American prosperity. The massive immigration to America in the industrialization period often created racial problems. American Indians were conquered and assimilated by force, while European immigrants struggled but became successful in joining the white mainstream. African Americans were freed by the Civil War, and their status has improved after the civil rights movement. Hispanic and Asian immigrants were considered as "low class" but their economic and social mobility became more visible over the last three decades. Despite continuous efforts toward integration, racial conflicts remain in reality in America.[129] In the process of assimilation, distinct differences between ethnic groups were observed in the first half of the twentieth century. Irish immigrants were successful in politics, while Italian immigrants were interested in immediate wealth rather than education for the future. Jewish immigrants engaged in various businesses while emphasizing education for the next generation, while Polish immigrants were initially involved in the independence movement in Poland. Meanwhile, Asian immigrants were treated differently by white Americans from the beginning because of racial prejudice against Asians, particularly in the states on West Coast. However, the public perception about Asians in America has been positively changed because of the prevailing reality of the melting-pot in the post-war period, the multiculturalism of the civil rights movement in the 1950s and 1960s, the new development of international relations in the Cold War period, the rising economic and strategic importance of Asian countries, the impact of globalization in the post Cold War period, and the socio-economic success of Asian Americans.

62. The population of Asian Americans was 3.8 percent of the U.S. in 2000, which projected to increase to 8.0 percent by 2050. Asian immigrants after 1965 came from established families with high education in their home countries, and they are much younger than the American population: 51.7 percent of Asian Americans were in the age range from 20 to 49 by 2000, while 43.3 percent of white Americans were in the

same. Asian Americans received bachelor's degrees or higher by 44.1 percent, while white Americans did the same by 28.4 percent in 2000. They are in managerial and professional jobs more than the American average, and their incomes are approaching whites although most of them remain in disadvantaged positions in jobs with exceptions in highly specialized professional jobs. Many Asian Americans reside in suburban areas, and 28.7 percent married white Americans as of March, 2000. However, many Asian Americans feel themselves marginalized and remain as foreigners. Recently, they are gradually participating in electoral politics, non-electoral politics for protection of ethnic groups, activities for social justice and equal treatment of ethnic individuals, politics related to the United States with countries of origin, and politics within their ethnic communities. Their ways of political participation includes mobilization of votes, fundraising, promotion of publicity, and lobbying activities. But the integration of Asian Americans is not simple because of ethnic diversification. For example, eastern Asian Americans such as Chinese, Japanese, and Koreans have commonalities in history, culture, and religion, but southern Asian Americans such as Asian Indians or Indonesians are different from them, particularly in culture and religion. As a result, the pan-Asianization of Asian Americans is less cohesive for political empowerment. Therefore, the integration of each ethnic group is desirable in the first stage before the integration of Asian Americans. An ethnic group integrates themselves within its ethnic community, and sends a proper number of representatives to an Asian Pacific American Association. The existing pan-Asian organizations will help the integration of Asian Americans. This APA Association can form a multiracial coalition for more influence in American politics, if necessary.

63. It is questionable how to integrate an ethnic community. This study used the Korean American community as an example. The majority of Korean Americans reside in metropolitan areas of large cities such as Los Angeles, New York, and Washington, DC. The study proposes a restructure of the Korean American Association of Greater Washington, DC as an experiment towards the first step. If the experiment is successful, the KAA-GW can be transplanted to other cities, which will restructure the existing KAA of each region. The KAA of each region sends their delegates to the Korean American Association (a new form of federation) to create a representative organization for Korean Americans in the United States. Then, a new KAA-GW will be formed as a model unit in terms of goals and objectives, organizational structure, manning and funding, technological support, and control and coordination. The purposes of the KA Association are to promote KA interests in politics, economy, and society; protect Korean Americans from disadvantages of the ethnic minority; guide them to enhance their roles for American civilization; and promote U.S.-Korea friendship relations. The structure of KAA-GW consists of the KA Congress, Administration, and Research Institute. The KA Congress has six standing committees formed by KA Congressmen who are elected by five categories of electoral districts by gathering 100 votes or more per Congressman. The KA Administration consists of six departments and five regional offices maintaining daily contacts with individuals of Korean Americans in the region. The KA Research Institute consists of four divisions:

Korean heritage, policy analysis, conferences, and publications. Manning and funding with technological supports are essential to run the system efficiently. It is important to control subsystems properly and coordinate them to avoid unnecessary conflict each other. An efficient networking system is able to integrate community resources for political empowerment of Korean Americans.

64. *In conclusion*, American civilization has been constructed by immigrants. The early- comers forced later immigrants to assimilate to their culture and system, but the massive inflow of new immigrants until the outbreak of World War I made America a melting-pot of different races and ethnicities.[130] Since the perfect mixture of different cultures was impossible, the multiculturalism has been accepted since the civil rights movement. Currently, the United States pursues equality in politics, efficiency in economy, and diversification in society and culture. The majority respects interests of the minority in theory, but the power politics dominate the decision making process of all levels of governments in America in reality. Therefore, the political empowerment of the minority is necessary to promote their ethnic interests and protect themselves from possible injustice and inequality in the changing environment.

In this sense, first, all citizens of Asian or Korean Americans should have confidence in American democracy to be part of American power politics. The political empowerment comes from active participation of individual citizens as grass-roots of political power. A political inclination is solely a matter of personal belief. However, a new Korean American Association is worth while to join because it can help Korean Americans to move into the mainstream.

Second, an efficient networking system is important to integrate resources of each ethnic community, which is a basic component of the Asian Pacific American Association leading their communities for political empowerment. The bottom line of political empowerment is to achieve proportional representation of the Asian Pacific American population in local, state, and federal governments of the United States. For example, the proportional share of Asian Americans in the U.S. Congress should be at least 4 Senators and 18 Representatives in the year 2000 when its population share reached near 4 percent of the American population.

Third, the mobility of Asian Americans into the mainstream in politics is not simply limited to the political community. Political affairs require public supports with electoral votes, financial contribution, and social recognition so that the Asian American community should expand and strengthen their potential capabilities in business and finance and overall society. To expand capacity is one thing, and to integrate resources is another.

Fourth, demographic changes can affect domestic politics gradually, while the power of conservative forces remains strong. The appearance of Asian Americans in politics is not as an Asian in America but as an American citizen. Anyone who is ambitious in politics should be qualified to attract general American voters by receiving outstanding education and managing an excellent career with honorable public mind. Asian Americans support Asian candidates not because of one's ethnicity but because of one's qualification to represent themselves.

Finally, Asians or Koreans in America should keep in mind that they are part of America contributing to her civilization. The goals of political empowerment is not only to pursue interests of their racial or ethnic minority but also to make a larger pie for all Americans, who have led the world with great responsibilities in the age of globalization. In other words, it is desirable for Asian Americans or any other ethnic minority groups to think whether their demand and actions for their interests are fair and beneficial to all Americans.

Endnotes

---

1 Glenn J. Ames, *Colbert, Mercantilism, and the French Quest for Asian Trade*, DeKalb, IL: Northern Illinois University Press, 1996. Henry William Spiegel, *The Growth of Economic Thought*, Durham, NC: Duke University Press, 1971.

2 Charles Wilson, *The Transformation of Europe: 1558-1648*, Berkeley, CA: University of California Press, 1976. G. V. Scammell, *The First Imperial Age: European Overseas Expansion c. 1400-1715*, London: Routledge, 1992. J. H. Parry, *The Age of Reconnaissance*, Berkeley, CA: Univ. of California Press, 1981.

3 Thomas E. Skidmore, *Brazil: Five Centuries of Change*, New York: Oxford University Press, 1999, pp. 10-4. Peter Russell, *Prince Henry 'the Navigator': A Life*, New Heaven, NJ: Yale University Press, 2000.

4 William H. Prescott, *History of the Conquest of Mexico*, New York: The Modern Library, 1998. Jose Lopez Portillo y Pacheco, *They Are Coming: The Conquest of Mexico*, trans. Beatrice Berler, Denton, TX: University of North Texas Press, 1992. Rafael Varon Gabai, *Francisco Pizarro and His Brothers: The Illusion of Power in Sixteenth-Century Peru*, Norman, OK: University of Oklahoma Press, 1997.

5 The University of California, Berkeley estimated that the central Mexican population was 25,200,000 in 1519, but declined to 1,075,000 in 1605.

6 J. H. Elliott, *Imperial Spain, 1469-1716*, New York: Penguin Books, 1999. Henry Kamen, *Spain 1469-1714: A Society of conflict*, 2nd ed., New York: Addison Wesley Longman, 1999.

7 Robert C. Puth, *American Economic History*, New York: The Dryden Press, 1982, pp. 25-8.

8 Richolas P. Cushner, *Jesuit Ranches and the Agrarian Development of Colonial Argentina, 1650-1767*, Albany, NY: State University of New York Press, 1983.

9 M. S. Anderson, *Europe in the Eighteenth Century, 1713-1783*, New York: Holt, Rinehart and Winston, Inc., 1961, pp. 238-264. Robin Reilly, *William Pitt the Younger*, New York: G. P. Putnam's Sons, 1979.

10 Ray Allen Billington, Bert James Leowenberg, and Samuel Hugh Brockunier, ed., *The Making of American Democracy: Readings and Documents*, New York: Rinehart and Company, Inc., 1952, p. 2 & 4. "To the rising merchant class overseas colonies spelled economic opportunity; to

zealous Protestants they offered a bulwark against Catholic Spain and France; to the poor masses they promised salvation – salvation from overcrowded farms, from oppressive political institutions, from burdensome church duties, and from starvation. The plight of the common people in that day when the enclosure of fields for sheep growing converted thousands of peasants into beggars and vagabonds was movingly portrayed by..." "The upper classes hoped that these conditions could be remedied by draining away the excess population, for without such a palliative a dangerous social upheaval might occur."

[11] *Ibid.*, p. 10. "That the forces driving Puritans overseas were not exclusively religious was clearly demonstrated by John Winthrop, the middle-class Englishman who became the leader and first governor of the Massachusetts Bay colony. His reasons for leaving the homeland resembled those of countless other Britons in their emphasis on economic and imperialistic as well as religious motives."

[12] Roger Daniels, *Coming to America: A History of Immigration and Ethnicity in American Life*, New York: Harper Perennial, 1990, pp. 45-52.

[13] Louis XIV attacked Germany, which allied with Britain, devastating much of the Rhineland. The British government established a kind of refugee camps around London for Protestants, while sending 3,500 Catholics back to Germany and 3,800 to Ireland, in addition to sending some of them to America. See Roger Daniels, *Coming to America*, pp. 70-71.

[14] Billington, Leowenberg, and Brockunier, ed., *The Making of American Democracy*, pp. 25-29.

[15] Roger Daniels, *Coming to America*, pp. 53-65.

[16] U. S. Congress, House, *Coolie Trade*, Washington, DC: Government Printing Office, 1856, quoted by Roger Daniels, *Coming to America*, p. 241: "the 'Chinese coolie trade'… a servitude in no respect practically different from … African slave trade [and the flow to] California, a Chinese emigration which has been voluntary and profitable to the contracting parties. The discovery of gold in Australia divided the migration, which hastened to both places at the option of immigrants themselves." For gold rush, see H. W. Brands, *The Age of Gold: the California Gold Rush and the Birth of Modern America*, New York: Doubleday, 2002. For railroad construction, see Stephen E. Ambrose, *Nothing Like It in the World: The Men Who Built the Transcontinental Railroad*, 1863-1869, New York: Simon & Schuster, Inc., 2000.

[17] Microsoft® Encarta® Encyclopedia 2002. © 1993-2001 Microsoft Corporation (CD).

[18] Elliott Robert Barkan, *And Still They Come: Immigrants and American Society 1920 to the 1990s*, Wheeling, IL: Harlan Davidson, Inc., 1996.

[19] Roger Daniels, *Coming to America*, pp. 338-9.

[20] Reed Ueda, *Postwar Immigrant America: A Social History*, New York: Bedford/St. Martin's, 1994 and Louis DeSipio and Rodolfo O. de la Garza, *Making Americans, Remaking America: Immigration and Immigrant Policy*, Boulder, CO: Westview Press, 1998.

[21] Wheegook Kim, "From Confrontation to Cooperation: A New Paradigm for Inter-Korean Relations," *The Korean Journal of Defense Analysis*, Vol. XI, No. 2 (Winter 1999): 35-77.

[22] Stephen Castles, *Ethnicity and Globalization: From Migrant Worker to Transnational Citizen*, Thousand Oak, CA: Sage Publications Ltd., 2000, pp. 79-132.

[23] Gustav Ranis and John C. H. Fei, "A Theory of Economic Development," *American Economic Review* 51 (1961): 533-65. W. Arthur Lewis, "Economic Development with Unlimited Supplies of Labour," *Manchester School of Economic and Social Studies* 22 (1954): 139-91.

[24] Oded Stark and David E. Bloom, "The New Economics of Labor Migration," *Demography* 26 (1985): 1-14. Oded Stark, *The Migration of Labor*, Cambridge: Basil Blackwell, 1991.

[25] Michael Piore, *Birds of Passage: Migrant Labor in Industrial Societies*, New York: Cambridge University Press, 1979.

[26] Paul A. Baran, *The Political Economy of Growth*, Berkeley, CA: University of California Press, 1957.
[27] Pierre Bourdieu, "The Forms of Capital" in *Handbook of Theory and Research for the Sociology of Education*, edited by John G. Richardson, New York: Greenwood, 1986, pp. 241-58. James S. Coleman, *Foundations of Social Theory*, Cambridge, MA: Belknap Press of Harvard University Press, 1990.
[28] Gunnar Myrdal, *Rich Lands and Poor*, New York: Harper and Row, 1957. Douglas S. Massey, "Social Structure, Household Strategies and the Causation of Migration," *Population Index* 56 (1990): 3-26.
[29] Aristide R. Zolberg, "Matters of State: Theorizing Immigration Policy," in *The Handbook of International Migration: The American Experience*, edited by Charles Hirschman, Philip Kasinitz, and Josh DeWind, New York: Russell Sage Foundation, 1999, pp. 71-93.
[30] Robert Ezra Park, *Race and Culture: Essays in the Sociology of Contemporary Man*, New York: The Free Press of Glencoe, 1950, p. 150.
[31] Milton Gordon, *Assimilation in American Life: The Role of Race, Religion, and National Origins*, New York: Oxford University Press, 1964.
[32] *Ibid*., p. 32. See p. 159. "In our view, then, a more accurate term for the American situation is structural pluralism rather than cultural pluralism, although some the latter also remains." For multiculturalism, see Nathan Glazer, *We Are All Multiculturalists Now*, Cambridge, MA: Harvard University Press, 1997.
[33] Herbert J. Gans, "Introduction," in *Ethnic Identity and Assimilation: The Polish Community*, edited by Neil Sandberg, New York: Praeger, 1973, pp. vii-xii.
[34] Min Zhou, "Segmented Assimilation: Issues, Congroversies, and Recent Research on the New Second Generation," in *The Handbook of International Migration: The American Experience*, pp. 196-211.
[35] Lisa J. Neidert and Reynolds Farley, "Assimilation in the United States: Ethnic and Generational Differences in Status and Achievement," *American Sociological Review* 50 (6) (1985): 840-50.
[36] Nathan Glazer and Daniel Patrick Moynihan, *Beyond the Melting Pot*, 2nd ed., Cambridge, MA: MIT Press, 1970.
[37] Douglas S. Massey and Brendan P. Mullan, "Processes of Hispanic and Black Spatial Assimilation," *American Journal of Sociology* 89(4) (1984), and Douglas S. Massey and Nancy A. Denton, "The Construction of the Ghetto," in *American Apartheid*, Cambridge, MA: Harvard University Press, 1993, reprinted, Norman Yetman, ed., *Majority and Minority: The Dynamics of Race and Ethnicity in American Life,* 6th ed., Boston, MA: Allyn and Bacon, 1999, pp. 178-202.
[38] Rubby Jo Reeves Kennedy, "Single or Triple Melting Pot?: Intermarriage Trends in New Haven, 1870-1940," *American Journal of Sociology* 49 (1944): 331-39.
[39] U.S. Bureau of the Census, *Statistical Abstract of the United States: 1995*, Washington, DC: Government Printing Office, 1996, p. 57. Among 54,937 thousand couples in 1995, black and white couples were 328, white and other race 988, black and other race 76, and Hispanic and other origin (not Hispanic) 1,434.
[40] Richard J. Herrnstein and Charles Murray, *The Bell Curve: Intelligence and Class Structure in American Life*, New York: Free Press, 1994, and Arthur A. Jensen, "How Can We Boost I.Q. and Scholastic Achievement?" *Harvard Educational Review* 39 (1969).
[41] Robert M. Hauser, "Review of The Bell Curve," *Contemporary Sociology* 24 (2) (March 1995).

[42] Norman R. Yetman, ed., *Majority and Minority: The Dynamics of Race and Ethnicity in American Life*, sixth ed., Needham Heights, MA: Allyn and Bacon, 1999, p. 269.
[43] Rachel M. Friedberg and Jennifer Hunt, "The Impact of Immigrants on Host Country Wages, Employment and Growth," *The Journal of Economic Perspectives*, Vol. 9 No.2 (Spring 1995): 23-44. For further, see Rachel M. Friedberg and Jennifer Hunt, "Immigration and the Receiving Economy," in *The Handbook of International Migration: The American Experience*, pp. 342-59. Thomas J. Espenshade and Gregory A. Huber, "Fiscal Impacts of Immigrants and the Shrinking Welfare State," in *The Handbook of International Migration*, pp. 360-70.
[44] George J. Borjas, "The Economic Benefits from Immigration," *The Journal of Economic Perspectives*, Vol. 9 No.2 (Spring 1995): 3-22.
[45] Michael Fix and Jeffrey S. Passel, *Immigration and Immigrants: Setting the Record Strait*, Washington, DC: The Urban Insittute, 1994, p. 57.
[46] Ivan Light, "Immigrant Entrepreneurs in America: Koreans in Los Angeles," in *The Immigration Reader: America in a Multidisciplinary Perspective,* edited by David Jacobson, 1998, pp. 265-82.
[47] Alejandro Portes, "Immigration Theory for a New Century: Problems and Opportunities," in *The Handbook of International Migration: The American Experience*, pp. 22-33.
[48] Min Zhou, "Segmented Assimilation," p. 210.
[49] Herbert J. Gans, "Symbolic Ethnicity: The Future of Ethnic Groups and Cultures in America," in *The Handbook of International Migration: The American Experience*, pp. 417-29. See Marcus Lee Hansen, *The Problem of the Third Generation Immigrant*, Rock Island, IL: Augustana Historical Society, 1938, pp. 9-10. "What the son wishes to forget, the grandson wishes to remember."
[50] C. Matthew Snipp, "The First Americans: American Indians," in Silvia Pedraza and Ruben G. Rumbaut, eds., *Origins and Destinies: Immigration, Race, and Ethnicity in America*, New York: Wadsworth Publishing Co., 1996, reprinted in Yetman, ed., *Majority and Minority*, pp. 131-43.
[51] David Wallace Adams, "Fundamental Considerations: The Deep Meaning of Native American Schooling, 1880-1900," *Harvard Education Review* 58 (1988), quoted in Yetman, ed., *Majority and Minority*, p. 92.
[52] Herbert Spencer, *Social Statics: The Conditions Essential to Human Happiness Specified, and the First of Them Developed*, New York: Robert Schalkenbach Foundation, 1995.
[53] The First Quota Act of 1921 and the Second Quota Act of 1924 were transitional measures for the National Origins Quota Act of 1929. The law limited total immigration to 150,000 annually: Great Britain 65,000, Italy 6,000, Hungary 1,000, and Greece 310.
[54] James R. Barrett and David Roediger, "Inbetween Peoples: Race, Nationality, and the 'New Immigrants' Working Class," *Journal of American Ethnic History*, 16(3) (1997), reprinted in Norman R. Yetman, ed., *Majority and Minority*, pp. 145-59.
[55] William Julius Wilson, "The Declining Significance of Race," *Society*, Jan/Feb 1978, reprinted in Yetman, ed., *Majority and Minority*, pp. 160-67.
[56] U.S. Department of Commerce, *Statistical Abstract of the United States, 1996*, Washington, DC: U.S. Government Printing Office, 1996, pp. 44-6. For discrimination, see Douglas S. Massey and Nancy A. Denton, *American Apartheid*, Cambridge, MA: Harvard University Press, 1993, reprinted in Norman R. Yetman, ed., *Majority and Minority*, pp. 179-202.
[57] Neil A. Lewis, "President Faults Race Preferences as Admission Tool," *The New York Times*, January 16, 2003. Is the affirmative action of admission policies at the University of Michigan unconstitutional?

[58] Frank D. Bean and Marta Tienda, "The Structuring of Hispanic Ethnicity: Theoretical and Historical Considerations," *The Hispanic Population of the United States*, New York: Russell Sage Foundation, 1987, reprinted in Norman R. Yetman, ed., *Majority and Minority*, pp. 202-17.
[59] Roger Daniels, *Asian America: Chinese and Japanese in the United States since 1850*, Seattle, WA: University of Washington Press, 1995.
[60] Jeffery F. Burton, Mary M. Farrell, Florence B. Lord, and Richard W. Lord, *Confinement and Ethnicity: An Overview of World War II Japanese American Relocation Sites*, Seattle, WA: University of Washington Press, 2002.
[61] Don Mar and Marlene Kim, "Asian Pacific Americans: Historical Trends," *The State of Asian Pacific America: Ecnomic Diversity, Issues and Policies*, New York: Leadership Education for Asian Pacifics, Inc., 1994, reprinted in Yetman, ed., *Majority and Minority*, pp. 217-25.
[62] Bill Ong Hing, "Asian Immigrants: Social Forces Unleashed after 1965," *The Immigration Reader: America in a Multidisciplinary Perspective*, edited by David Jacobson, Malden, MA: Blackwell Publishers, 1998, pp. 144-82.
[63] Noel Ignatiev, *How the Irish Became White*, New York: Routledge, 1995 and George E. Reedy, *From the Ward to the White House: The Irish in American Politics*, New York: Charles Scribner's Sons, 1991.
[64] George F. Will, "School Choice: The Ugly Opposition," *The Washington Post*, November 25, 2002, p. A25. The fear of Catholic immigrants was pervasive in 1850s when America's Protestant majority wanted the public school to be "a nursery of piety" dispensing "judicious religious instruction." In 1875, the U.S. House of Representatives passed a constitutional amendment bill stipulating that no public money shall go to schools "under the control of any religious sect" targeted Catholics, that was rejected by the U.S. Senate.
[65] Steven P. Erie, *Rainbow's End: Irish-Americans and the Dilemma of Urban Machine Politics, 1840-1985*, Berkeley, CA: University of California Press, 1988, p. 5.
[66] Thomas H. O'Connor, *The Boston Irish: A Political History*, Boston, MA: Northeastern University, 1995. The Irish maintained a powerful role through a half-century of conflict, with the forces of Irish-Catholic Democrats in the neighborhoods pitted against the established influence of Yankee-Protestant Republicans in the downtown wards. By the early part of the twentieth century the Irish were moving into the major centers of political power in Boston. However, due to demographic changes, the Irish can no longer hold on to all the political power they once monopolized.
[67] Richard D. Alba, *Italian Americans into the Twilight of Ethnicity*, Englewood Cliffs, NJ: Prentice-Hall, Inc., 1985, pp. 20-43. Roger Daniels, *Coming to America*, p. 199.
[68] *Ibid.*, p. 51. Among the 1,768,281 Italian immigrants to the United States in the years 1899-1910, their previous jobs of farm laborers were 563,200 (31.85%) and that of other laborers were 767,811 (43.42%).
[69] Leonard Covello, *The Social Background of the Italo-American School Child*, Totowa, NJ: Rowman & Littlefield, 1972, pp. 288-311.
[70] Richard D. Alba, *Italian Americans*, p. 146, The first generation of Italian immigrants married non-Italian wives by 21.9% and non-Italian husbands by 16.9%, the second generation of them married by 51.4% and 47.8% respectively for unmixed and 81.8% and 77.4% respectively for mixed Italians in 1979. Once intermarriage rates reach sufficient high levels, ethnic solidarity cannot be put back together again.
[71] Seymour Martin Lipset and Earl Raab, *Jews and the New American Scene*, Cambridge, MA: Harvard University Press, 1995, p. 20.
[72] *Ibid.*, pp. 23-25. Despite political differences, they were unified for helping overseas Jews, particularly in Russia and Eastern Europe, as well as Israel since 1948.

[73] Seymour Martin Lipset and Earl Raab, *Jews and the New American Scene*, p. 14.
[74] *Ibid*., p. 27.
[75] L. Sandy Maisel, ed., *Jews in American Politics*, New York: Rowman & Littlefield Publishers, Inc., 2001, Part III. Rosters of Jewish Leadership and Voting.
[76] *Ibid*., pp. 145-6.
[77] *Ibid*., p. 102. Louis Farrakhan has accused Jews of controlling the media and financial institutions that oppress African Americans.
[78] Jeong Kwang Hoon, "The Jewish population of the world declines by 50,000 a year," *Yonhap News* (Cario=Yonhap), December 4, 2002. The world Jewish population is now 12,900,000 including 5 million in Israel. The American Jewish population declined from 5.5 million in 1990 to 5.2 million in 2002.
[79] Doug Rushkoff, "Judging Judaism by the Numbers," *The New York Times*, November 20, 2002, Op-Ed.
[80] Theodor Herzl, *The Jewish State*, Norwalk, CT: The Easton Press, 1996. Jacob Katz, *From Prejudice to Destruction: Anti-Semitism, 1700-1933*, Cambridge, MA: Harvard University Press, 1980.
[81] Matthew Frye Jacobson, *Special Sorrows: The Diasporic Imagination of Irish, Polish, and Jewish Immigrants in the United States*, Berkeley, CA: University of California Press, 2002. "A generation later, in the wake of the Six Day War, Jewish Americans from across the country volunteered for Israeli military service – over 2,000 in New York City alone."
[82] J. J. Goldberg, *Jewish Power: Inside the American Jewish Establishment*, Reading, MA: Perseus Books, 1996, pp. 337-67. "Separated by a Common Faith: American Jewry's One-Way Love Affair with Israel"
[83] W. S. Kuniczak, *My Name Is Million: An Illustrated History of the Poles in America*, New York: Hippocrene Books, Inc., 2000, p. 28. In 1777, Benjamin Franklin recruited Casimir Pulaski to be "The Father of the American Cavalry" whose soldiers adhered to him as a brother.
[84] Roger Daniels, *Coming to America*, pp. 214-23.
[85] Stanislaus A. Blejwas, "Polonia and Politics" in *Polish Americans and Their History: Community, Culture, and Politics*, ed., John J. Bukowczyk, Pittsburgh, PA: Univ. of Pittsburgh Press, 1996, pp. 121-50.
[86] *Ibid*. p. 33. Also see p. 40. "For sometime neither Catholic nor Poles existed in America, but only Unionists or Alliancists; who was not a member of the alliance, him the PNA did not regard as a Pole; while whoever was not a member of the PRCU, the PRCU did not regard as a Catholic."
[87] Roger Daniels, *Coming to America*, p. 240; and Roger Daniels, *Asian America: Chinese and Japanese in the United States since 1850*, Seattle, WA: University of Washington Press, 1995, pp. 71-3.
[88] Roger Daniels, *Asian America*, p. 19 and 21.
[89] Shehong Chen, *Being Chinese, Becoming Chinese American*, Chicago, IL: University of Illinois Press, 2002, pp. 19-27.
[90] *Ibid*., pp. 113-145.
[91] In 1912, the National Council in Nanjing elected Yan Shikai provisional president. In 1915, he declared 1916 the first year of the Hong Xian Empire and prepared himself to be enthroned in 1916.
[92] Peter H. Hoehn and Xiao-huang Yin, ed., *The Expanding Role of Chinese Americans in U.S.-China Relations: Transnational Networks and Trans-Pacific Interactions*, New York: M. E. Sharpe, 2002.

[93] David Johnston, "Clinton Criticizes Officials' Actions against Scientist" and Gish Jen, "For Wen Ho Lee, a Tarnished Freedom," *New York Times*, 15 September 2002, p. A1 & A25; James Glanz, "Asian-American Scholars Call for Boycott of Labs," *New York Times*, 31 May 2000, p. A23.

[94] The Japanese government signed the Anglo-Japanese Alliance in 1902, and won the Russo-Japanese War in 1905 ten years after the victory of the Sino-Japanese War. The Japanese were proud of themselves to be a first class world power, which was the reason why Washington treated Japan differently from China.

[95] Roger Daniels, *Coming to America*, pp. 250-8; and Roger Daniels, *Asian America*, pp. 100-28.

[96] The Japanese created other organizations such as the prefectural associations (ken-jin), which were based on the home prefecture in Japan. They were a kind of village and neighborhood associations.

[97] Roger Daniels, *Asian America*, pp. 155-85; and Burton and et al, *Confinement and Ethnicity*, p. 27. "I am proud that I am an American citizen of Japanese ancestry, for my very background makes me appreciate more fully the wonderful advantages of this nation...Because I believe in America, and I trust she believes in me, I pledge myself to do honor to her at all times and all places...to defend her against enemies, foreign and domestic..." which was a JACL creed written by Mike Masaoka in 1940.

[98] Burton and et al, *Confinement and Ethnicity*, p. 54.

[99] Roger Daniels, *Asian America*, p. 286.

[100] For the early period of Korean immigration to Hawaii, see Wayne Patterson and Hyung-Chan Kim, *The Koreans in America*, Minneapolis, MN: Lerner Publications Company, 1977.

[101] Han-Kyo Kim, "The Korean Independence Movement in the United States," International Journal of Korean Studies VI(1) (Spring/Summer 2002): 1-27. "It is tempting to speculate what the Koreans in America could have accomplished with a more united leadership at the top: Could they have secured a better hearing for their cause in the capitals of the allied powers in World War II and altered the course of history for their homeland after 1954?" Jacqueline Pak, "The An Ch'angho Controversy – Gradualist-Pacifism, Cultural Nationalism, or Revolutionary-Democracy," *International Journal of Korean Studies* VI (1) (Spring/Summer 2002): 109-35. Pak challenged previous conceptions of An Ch'angho as a gradualist-pacifist or cultural nationalist, and viewed him as a militarist strategist and revolutionary.

[102] Sucheng Chan, "European and Asian Immigration into the United States in Comparative Perspective, 1820s-1920s," in *Immigration Reconsidered*, ed., Virginia Yans-McLaughlin, New York: Oxford University Press, 1990, p. 48. Korean immigrants donated their savings for nationalist movement so much that only a small number of them could open business because of lack of accumulated capital.

[103] Won Moo Hurh, "Marginal Children of War: An Exploratory Study of American-Korean Children," *International Journal of Sociology of the Family 2* (1972): 10-20.

[104] For an adoptee's story, see Katy Robinson, *A Single Square Picture: A Korean Adoptee's Search for Her Roots*, New York: Berkley Books, 2002.

[105] Won Moo Hur, *The Korea Americans*, Westport, CT: Greenwood Press, 1998, p. 33. The number of Korean immigrants to the United States increased to over 35,000 in the 1980s but declined to below 20,000 in the 1990s, while their returning migration rose to near 6,500 in 1992.

[106] Moon H. Jo, *Korean Immigrants and the Challenge of Adjustment*, Westport, CT: Greenwood Press, 1999, p. 13-18.

[107] Eui-Young Yu, "Korean Population in the United States," *International Journal of Korean Studies,* VI (1) (Spring/Summer 2002), p. 104.

[108] *Ibid.*, p. 98.
[109] Moon H. Jo, *Korean Immigrants and the Challenge of Adjustment*, pp. 70-75.
[110] For the Los Angeles Riot in 1992, see Kwang Chung Kim, ed., *Koreans in the Hood: Conflict with African Americans*, Baltimore, MD: The Johns Hopkins University Press, 1999. Molefi Kete Asante and Eungjun Min, ed., *Socio-Cultural Conflict between African American and Korean American*, New York: Oxford University Press, 2000. Nancy Abelmann and John Lie, *Blue Dreams: Korean Americans and the Los Angeles Riots*, Cambridge, MA: Harvard University Press, 1995. Claire Jean Kim, Bitter Fruit: The Politics of Black-Korean Conflict in New York City, New Haven, CT: Yale University Press, 2000.
[111] For religions of Korean Americans, see Ho-Youn Kwon, Kwang Chung Kim, and S. Stephen Warner, *Korean Americans and their Religions: Pilgrims and Missionaries from a Different Shore*, University Park, PA: The Pennsylvania State University Press, 2001.
[112] The population of Asian alone and Asians in combination with one or more other races was 11,898,828, while that for Koreans was 1,288,427 shown in census 2000. See U.*S. Census Bureau, The Asian Population: Census 2000 Brief*, Washington, DC: GPO, 2001, p. 9.
[113] Claire Jean Kim, "The Racial Triangulation of Asian Americans," *Politics and Society* 27 (1) (March 1999): 105-38, in*, Asian Americans and Politics: Perspectives, Experiences, Prospects*, ed., Gordon H. Chang, Washington, DC: Woodrow Wilson Center Press, 2001, pp. 39-78.
[114] An Asian household includes more workers than a white American household does.
[115] Nazli Kibria, *Becoming Asian American: Second Generation of Chinese and Korean American Identities*, Baltimore, MD: Johns Hopkins University, 2002, pp. 12-3.
[116] Don T. Nakanishi, "Beyond Electoral Politics: Renewing a Search for a Paradigm of Asian Pacific American Politics" in *Asian Americans and Politics*, ed., Gordon H. Chang, pp. 102-29.
[117] Pei-te Lien, *The Making of Asian America through Political Participation*, Philadelphia, PA: Temple University Press, 2001.
[118] Kent Wong, "Building an Asian Pacific Labor Alliance: A New Chapter in Our History," in *The State of Asian America: Activism and Resistance in the 1990s*, Karin Aguilar-San Juan, ed., Boston, MA: South End Press, 1994, pp. 335-49.
[119] Don T. Nakanishi in *Asian Americans and Politics*, ed., Gordon H. Chang, p. 121.
[120] Ibid., p. 122. For laws, see Frank Chuman, *The Bamboo People: Japanese Americans and the Law*, Del Mar, CA: Publisher's Inc., 1976.
[121] Paul M. Ong and David E. Lee, "Changing of the Guard? The Emerging Immigrant Majority in Asian American Politics," in *Asian Americans and Politics*, Chang, p. 170.
[122] Pei-Te Lien, "Voting Participation: Race, Gender, and the Comparative Status of Asian American Women," in *Asian Americans and Politics*, Chang, p. 187.
[123] Wendy K. Tam Cho and Bruce E. Cain, "Asian Americans as the Median Voters: An Exploration of Attitudes and Voting Patterns on Ballot Initiatives," in *Asian Americans and Politics*, Chang, p. 149.
[124] Leland T Saito, "Asian Americans and Multiracial Political Coalitions: New York City's Chinatown and Redistricting, 1990-1991," in *Asian Americans and Politics*, Chang, p. 383-408.
[125] Young Whan Kihl, "Korean-American Participation in U.S. Politics: A Contrast in Success and Failure," presented Joint Conference 2002 hosted by *the International Council on Korean Studies and the Centennial Committee of Korean Immigration to the United States* at Fairview Park Marriott Hotel, Falls Church, VA on August 16-18, 2002. For a public policy institute for an ethnic community, Mark L. Keam, "Korean American Empowerment," presented to the same conference as above.

[126] Kwang Chung Kim and Shin Kim, "Looking at the Future of Korean Americans through Life Experiences of Korean Immigrants and their Children," presented at Joint Conference 2002 above.

[127] Hugo Wheegook Kim, "A Korean American Heritage Foundation," *The Korea Times* (a Korean version of daily newspaper in Washington, DC), July 21-26, 2001, a four-day series.

[128] Jagdish Bhagwati, "Borders Beyond Control," *Foreign Affairs* 82 (1) (January/February 2003): 98-104. For example, 62 percent of engineering doctorates and 54 percent doctorates in economics in the United States were given to foreign-born students, mainly Asians in 1990. It has been estimated that more than 70 percent of foreign-born doctorates produced by U.S. educational institutions have remained in America.

[129] Bob Herbert, "The Other Trent Lotts," *The New York Times*, December 23, 2002, A25. "The Republican Party: Mississippi Burning," *The Economist*, December 21st 2002, pp. 25-6. Recently, Americans having ancestry of the Middle Eastern origin have faced difficulties after September 11, 2001.

[130] The concept of melting-pot meant the mixture of ethnic Europeans before World War I, but since then, its meaning became changed to the mixture of all races in America, particularly after World War II.

Chapter II
Regional Integration and Inter-Korean Economic Cooperation: A Perspective of International Political Economy*

Introduction

1. Regional integration is a significant trend in contemporary international relations and political economy. Regionalism was an important strategy to achieve national security and economic development in the cold war period, particularly in Europe. However, a new wave of regionalism has emerged under the Single European Act of 1987, combined with structural changes of the global system. The major driving forces are "the move from bipolarity towards a multipolar or perhaps tripolar structure, centered around the EU, NAFTA and the Asia-Pacific, with a new division of power and new division of labor; the relative decline of American hegemony in combination with a more permissive attitude on the part of the United States towards regionalism; the restructuring of the nation-state and the growth of interdependence, transnationalization and globalization; recurrent fears over the stability of the multilateral trading order, hand in hand with the growing importance of non-tariff barriers to trade; and the changed attitudes towards (neoliberal) economic development and political systems in the developing countries as well as in the post-communist countries."[1] This renewed trend has been formed by a mixed process of changes by global, regional, national and local interactions, simultaneously involving actors of politics and government, economy and business, and society and labor. As a subsystem, regional economic integration is a main driving force for regional integration through a linear progress of free trade area, customs union, common market and political union.

2. Theoretically, regionalism is based on the neoclassical theory in economics and neoliberalism in international relations. On the one hand, the contemporary trade theories explain gains from trade by taking comparative advantage, expanding the production possibility frontier and generate welfare gains to trading partners. On the other hand, disappearance of immediate enemies makes realists disappointed, but liberalists and constructivists encouraged. The driving forces of the new wave of regionalism have expedited globalization, which influences the entire system of the world. Regional integration pursues economic efficiency in the market and political equality in nation-states through acceptable compromise. However, a dilemma arises from tradeoff relations between politics and economy, so that policy choices of the people are cyclical rather than dialectic by changing the national leadership from an efficiency-oriented party to an equality-oriented one or vise versa.[2] The regionalization as a horizontal force is associated with economic development as a vertical force,[3] and

---

* The two sections of this paper was published by *The Korea Journal of Defense Analysis* XIV(1) (Spring 2002): 277-304. Reprinted by the permission of the publisher. A draft paper was presented to the International Conference of the *Korean Association of International Studies* held on September 21-22, 2001 at the Capital Hotel in Yongsan, Seoul, Korea.

both forces introduce four types of regions: developed (core) region, high intermediate region, low intermediate region, and developing (peripheral) region. In the core region, politics are stable, the economy is dynamic, and national security is strengthened; while the peripheral region is in the opposite. Open regionalism such as in East Asia contributes positively to globalization and convergence.

3. The Asia Pacific Economic Cooperation (APEC) was created in 1989 with the new trend of regional integration, pursuing trade and investment liberalization, business facilitation, and economic and technological cooperation. In fact, APEC has extended to five subregions of Northeast Asia, Southeast Asia, Australia, North America, and South America. The recent development of subregional trade arrangements in the Asia Pacific region such as a Korea-Japan-China free trade area (FTA) has been a concern of Europe and America. It is in question whether subregionalization within the Asia-Pacific region is constructive in terms of welfare gains without hurting non-member countries. As a member state of APEC, South Korea has been diversified its intratrade relations with the United States, Japan, China and others. South Korea tries to balance economic and strategic interests in the long run by creating close relations with the United States as well as China. However, if gradual emergence of an East Asian trade bloc creates negative relations with EU and NAFTA, the world economy may move toward trilateral competition. "EU Competition Commissioner Mario Monti bury GE-Honeywell; and German Chancellor Gerhard Schroeder raise the specter of worker consultation in mergers and acquisitions. As a result, Europe is fast becoming one gigantic poison pill for foreign investors."[4]

Figure 1. Regionalization and the Korean Peninsula

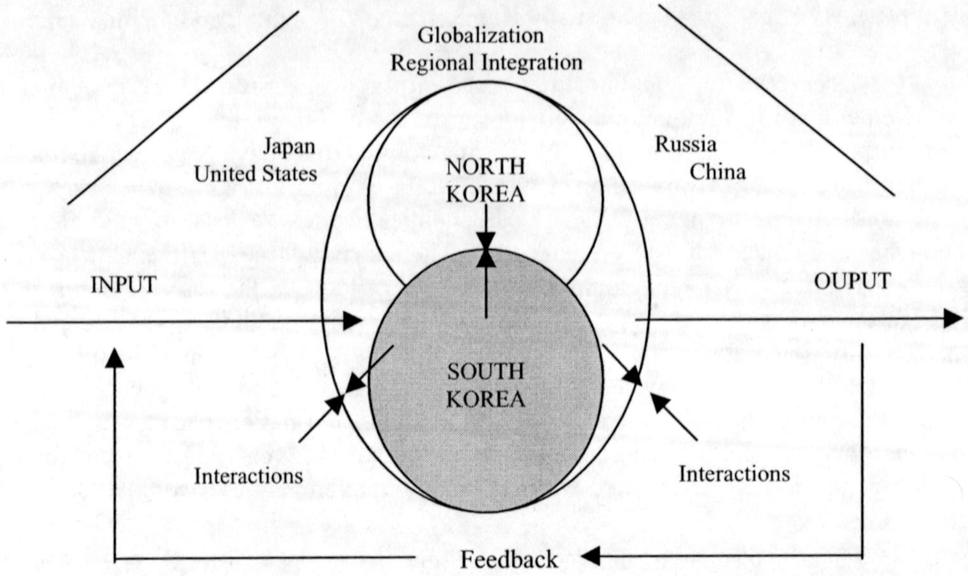

Note: The system is the Korean peninsula, the subsystems are North and South Koreas, and the suprasystem is the Asia Pacific region.

4. It is still unclear whether regional economic integration is beneficial to inter-Korean economic cooperation because the supply side does not know the impact of welfare gains from creation of subregional FTAs, and the demand side is still in the closed and isolated economy, which is unable to capitalize external aid toward sustainable growth. Therefore, we have to see what we have to do in order to link regional integration to Korean peninsular and inter-Korean economic cooperation. First, if North Korea stays away from transformation of its political and economic system, inter-Korean economic cooperation would be bottomless. Second, South Korea is too small and too weak to be a proper supplier because of its current capabilities. However, the leaders of both sides have been eager to give and to receive without reciprocity, which is not sustainable. The first thing to be done by the two Koreas is to find and fix their own problems such as openness and democratization for the North and continuous reforms of subsystems for the South. Particularly, there would be a definite limit of any kind of economic cooperation without resolving problems of military confrontation between North and South. It is common sense to believe that North Korea will build up military capabilities if it recovers economic strength. This is the main reason why South Korean people do not want to go further with the Sunshine Policy of the Kim Dae Jung administration as shown in recent actions of the South Korean Parliament.[5]

5. The purpose of this study lies in to investigate development of regional integration, particularly relations between the Asia-Pacific region and the Korean peninsula; and to examine problems and remedies of inter-Korean economic cooperation in the long run. The study suggests policy recommendations to the related governments including Pyongyang and Seoul. A system's approach is applied to analyze "regional integration and the Korean peninsula." Figure 1 indicates that the system is the Korean peninsula, the subsystems are the two Koreas, and the suprasystem is the environment such as the Asia-Pacific region and the world. Regional changes affect the Korean peninsula while the two Koreas interact with each other. A policy flows into the system, and North and South interact with each other while the system interacts with the environment, producing the first output. Through a feedback process, the first output is associated with external forces and reenters into the system as a second input. This process will continue until the final output becomes a desired result, which must be acceptable by North and South. I applied two recent studies published by the Institute for International Economics in Washington, DC to derive welfare gains from South Korea-initiated FTAs. This study consists of five main sections, excluding the Introduction and Conclusion. The first section reviews the history of regional integration by the region such as Europe, America, Asia-Pacific, Latin America, and others (Arab, Africa, and Eastern Europe). The second section analyzes the theoretical background of regional integration in terms of neoclassical trade theories and four basic theories of international relations including realism, neoliberalism, constructivism, and globalizaiton. The third section considers economic integration of the Asia-Pacific region by country and subregion including the United States, Japan, China, ASEAN, and NAFTA. The fourth section covers relations between regional economic integration and the Korean peninsula applied under the four

mentioned theories. This section also discusses two FTAs, including a Korea-Japan-China FTA and a Korea-United States FTA. The fifth and final section investigates problems and remedies of inter-Korean economic cooperation in the long run. This study is too broad to analyze details of each section, which could be independent research projects for further development. The study teaches us lessons about "importance of interactions" between various subsystems within the system, and those between the system and suprasystem.

Historical Review of Regional Integration

6. A theory of international economics teaches us that foreign trade is mutually beneficial (gains from trade) by expanding the production possibility frontier of trading partners if each nation takes its own comparative advantage in it. However, world history shows that some other elements such as politics or national security nets interrupt foreign trade and investment, so that the world economy suffers from their induced effects. "As John Maynard Keynes pointed out in his prophetic *The Economic Consequences of the Peace*, Germany on the eve of World War I had become the core of a highly interdependent European economy. After the war, although a revival of the European and world economy would be impossible without full German participation, the victors (led by France) decided to punish and isolate defeated Germany rather than reintegrate it into the European economy. As Keynes predicted, this proved to be an important cause of the failure to revive the world economy and thus of its subsequent collapse in the Great Depression of the 1930s."[6] The European leaders could not realize the importance of economic interdependence between the major powers at that time. The economic difficulties after the World War I helped totalitarian fascism and Nazism to rise and be popular among masses while the socialism strengthened and expanded its power base in Europe. Additionally, American isolationism and the withdrawal of the Soviet Union from world affairs created a political vacuum in Europe, which was filled by revived German power. Therefore, it was possible for Germany to build up its military power again in order to ready itself for World War II. Thus, history gives us a good lesson of the expensive cost arising from ignoring economic interdependence.

7. After World War II, the leadership of the United States established a new world order under the principles of the United Nations in cooperation with the victorious powers. The new order pursued an open and multilateral world economy with the participation of Germany and the other defeated powers, which was in contrast to the Treaty of Versailles in 1919. The Bretton Woods Conference in 1944 chose the fixed foreign exchange rates with the gold standard of the world monetary system. It created two institutions under the United Nations: the International Monetary Fund (IMF) for currency management, and the International Bank for Reconstruction and Development (IBRD or the World Bank) for development lending, both which opened for business in 1946. The General Agreement on Tariffs and Trade (GATT) was signed in Geneva in 1947 for multilateral tariff reductions.[7] Meanwhile, communist expansionism by the Soviet Union became so evident that President Harry S. Truman

proclaimed the Truman Doctrine by requesting aid to Greece and Turkey from the U.S. Congress on March 12, 1947. Subsequently, the Marshall Plan was launched to protect Western Europe from communist expansion by creating the Committee of European Economic Cooperation (CEEC) with sixteen nations, later converted into the Organization for European Economic Cooperation (OEEC). The OEEC inaugurated the European Payments Union (EPU) for free multilateral trade within the OEEC. The Marshall Plan came to an end in 1952, and in 1961 the OEEC became the Organization for Economic Cooperation and Development (OECD) by including the United States and Canada, and later Japan and Australia.[8] After the Berlin blockade in 1948, the United States formed the North Atlantic Treaty Organization (NATO) in 1949. The Soviet Union formed the Council for Mutual Economic Assistance (COMECON) in 1949 and Warsaw Pact in 1955.[9]

8. The cold war confrontation forced severe competition between capitalism pursuing efficiency and communism pursuing equality. On the one hand, in the capitalist world, the OECD countries began to recover their economies from the war, and achieved high economic growth owing to American economic aid, proper role of governments and intergovernmental cooperation, and high quality of human capital such as in Germany and Japan.[10] The Bretton Woods system was replaced by the floating exchange rates system in 1973 because of the shortage of world gold reserves and change of the currency values. GATT became ineffective because it was unable to provide a set of rules and procedures as well as a forum for dispute settlement and negotiations. In order to overcome its weaknesses, GATT was replaced by the World Trade Organization (WTO) in 1995. Meanwhile, the six member states of France, Germany, the Benelux countries, and Italy created the European Coal and Steel Community (ECSC) in 1952, and the European Economic Community (EEC) and the European Atomic Energy Community (EAEC) in 1958. As an alternative to the EEC, Great Britain pushed for the creation of the European Free Trade Association (EFTA), which was established in 1959. These four organizations were merged into the European Community (EC) in 1973, which was actually the merger of the EEC with the EFTA. The EC has been gradually deepened and widened, and the Treaty on European Union (or the Maastricht Treaty) in 1992 provides for an Economic and Monetary Union and for more social protection. Finally, the European Community became the European Union (EU) on January 1, 1994. The Treaty of Amsterdam in 1997 reinforced the integration process into a number of non-economic fields including foreign policy, national defense, social justice, and European citizenship. The European Union will continuously pursue further integration toward resource allocation, economic stabilization, income redistribution, and external relations.[11]

9. On the other hand, in the communist world, the Soviet Union expanded its domain and spread the socialist economic system to the Eastern Europe. In its early stage, a series of economic development plans forced intensive mobilization of labor and capital inputs into planned industries, which was relatively successful. But the Soviet Union fell down along with its satellite states in 1991 by its own weight because

its economic capability could not maintain its political-military system. In fact, the centrally planned economy distorted resource allocation; heavy military expenditures reduced investment in the private sector; lack of information flow from censorship jeopardized research and development for advanced science and technology; non-existence of property rights reduced workers' motivation to accumulate wealth; personal compensation based on political loyalty rather than job performance expelled gold for silver due to lack of competition; strategic sanctions against the communist states by the capitalist side isolated the Soviet Union from the world market; and the authoritarian decision-making process by the one-party political system ruined self-adjustment function in running its own system.[12] However, the Chinese system could survive by transforming its system gradually toward the market economy. After the death of Chairman Mao Te Tung, the visionary leader Deng Xiaopeng took power in 1978 and adopted the open policy aggressively to attract foreign direct investment to five special economic zones as free trade areas. Deng sent tens of thousands of young students annually to graduate schools in North America and Europe for advanced education, which became a source of human capital for China's modernization. The rise of China, despite the Tienanmen incident in 1989, became a symbol of the rise of Asian power in the twenty-first century.[13] Thus, the future of China became a concern of major powers.

10. Meanwhile, the three largest countries in North America (the United States, Canada, and Mexico) recognized that their competitiveness is gradually declining in the world market *vis-à-vis* major European and Asian economies. There was a growing consensus among them that their economic integration provides clearer rules of the game with respect to foreign trade and investment. Both Canada and Mexico wanted to access the large and prosperous U.S. market at the time when the United States was in serious trade conflicts with Japan and the European Union both of which were developing inward-oriented policies in the process of economic integration. In addition to this, GATT was not promising in trade negotiations, and regional economic integration in Europe and Asia caused an unsafe feeling against protectionism of regional trading blocs. In this background, the United States signed the Framework Agreement on Bilateral Trade (FABT) with Mexico in 1987, and began to implement the Canada-U.S. Free Trade Agreement (KFTA) in 1989. After Mexican President Carlos de Salinas proposed a U.S.-Mexico trade agreement in 1990, Washington began to negotiate the North American Free Trade Agreement (NAFTA) with Canada and Mexico. NAFTA was implemented on January 1, 1994, when the EC became the European Union. The Miami Summit in December 1994 supported creation of a Free Trade Area of the Americas (FTAA) by 2005. In fact, economic integration brings more benefit for all participants from competition of freer trade by taking comparative advantage: capital and technology in the United States, natural resources in Canada, and labor in Mexico. The three countries have been geographically natural trading partners benefiting from lower transportation costs with shared borders without significant natural barriers. However, the problems lie in the enormous disparities of economic development between the United States and Canada as well as Mexico. The criticism

comes from labor groups, environmentalists, human rights groups, and sentimentalists for the loss of cultural identity, sovereignty and political autonomy. The Agreement does not provide for the free movement of workers between member countries just like the European Union. Canada and Chile agreed on free trade and Mexico revised its free trade agreement with Chile in 1997, but the U.S. Congress refused Chile membership in NAFTA.[14]

11. In Asia, the United States reconstructed Japan by the Dodge Plan and Korea by economic and military aid after the Korean War. The communist government in Indochina was exporting their revolution to the neighboring states during the Vietnam War. To counter the political influence of communist countries such as China and North Vietnam, the Association of Southeast Asian Nations (ASEAN) was created in 1967 by five member states including Indonesia, Malaysia, the Philippines, Singapore, and Thailand (ASEAN-5). ASEAN shifted its emphasis to economic cooperation as the external threat faded. In 1999 ASEAN accepted five additional member states including Brunei, Vietnam, Cambodia, Laos, and Myanmar (ASEAN-10).[15] The ASEAN Region Forum (ARF) first convened in Bangkok in 1994 with eighteen founding members to discuss security issues in a systematic manner. Cambodia, Myanmar, and India joined ARF in 1997, Mongolia in 1998, North Korea in 2000. The total number of ARF member states became twenty-three in July 2000, including the EU, Russia, and China.[16] In January 1989, Australian Prime Minister Robert Hawke proposed the creation of a multilateral forum to enhance Asia-Pacific economic cooperation (APEC) by engaging in its vision with ASEAN. In November 1989 APEC held its first ministerial meeting in Canberra, Australia with twelve founding member states including Australia, Brunei, Canada, Indonesia, Japan, Korea, Malaysia, New Zealand, the Philippines, Singapore, Thailand, and the United States. APEC accepted three additional member states including China, Hong Kong, and Taiwan in 1991 and issued the Seoul APEC Declaration by setting its boundary of objectives and operations. In 1993 APEC accepted Mexico and Papua New Guinea as members, and invited Chile to join in 1994. In 1998, APEC was joined by additional three economies of Peru, Russia and Vietnam.[17] The East Asian Economic Caucus (EAEC) was proposed by Malaysia and joined by ASEAN, China, Hong Kong, Taiwan, Japan and South Korea for dialogue and consultation. Meanwhile, Australia and New Zealand created the Australian New Zealand Closer Economic Relationship Trade Agreement (ANZCERTA).[18]

12. In Latin America, first, dependency theory claims that Latin American economies were exploited by imperialism and transformed into capitalist economies immediately after World War II. Their integration into capitalism was achieved through center-periphery relations where the surplus generated by the periphery is drawn off toward the center. Thus, the development of the "core" requires the underdevelopment of "periphery."[19] Second, Latin American countries pursued industrialization through import substitution strategies, which faced limits from problems of resource allocation, cost-benefit in economies of scale, and supply of

capital and technology.[20] Third, the petrodollars flew into Latin American countries with low interest rates in the early 1970s. In 1982, the world economy faced global recession while the United States raised the interest rates to curb domestic inflation. The Mexican government announced the incapability of its debt service without rescheduling, which was managed by IMF intervention and the Baker Plan.[21] Fourth, after the debt crisis, Latin American economies recovered through market liberalization with forced austerity policies. They followed the East-Asian economic development model of export-led growth strategies.[22] In fact, the five states of Costa Rica, El Salvador, Guatemala, Honduras, and Nicaragua had already formed the Central American Common Market (CACM) for free trade in 1960.[23] In the same year, the Latin American Free Trade Association (LAFTA) was established, but its function was extremely limited. In 1969, Bolivia, Colombia, Chile, Ecuador, and Peru joined the Andean Common Market (ANCOM); and Venezuela followed in 1973, but Chile withdrew in 1976. The thirteen English-speaking countries in the Caribbean joined the Caribbean Community and Common Market (CARICOM) in 1973.[24] Most importantly, the eleven Latin American governments created the Latin American Integration Association (LAIA) in 1980 to promote linkages among their countries. A series of U.S. initiatives followed to lead many Latin American countries to negotiate framework agreements with the United States. The Southern Cone Common Market (MERCOSUR) was created in 1995 by Brazil, Argentina, Paraguay, and Uruguay, with Chile as a special partner. It was observed that Brazil-led Mercosur negotiated with U.S.-led NAFTA on FTAA. The Group of Rio, made up of nineteen Latin American countries, held its fifth annual summit in Santiago, Chile in 2001.[25]

13. On the other hand, (a) for the Arab states, the Organization of the Petroleum Exporting Countries (OPEC) is a permanent, intergovernmental Organization, created at the Baghdad Conference on September 10–14, 1960, by Iran, Iraq, Kuwait, Saudi Arabia and Venezuela. The five Founding Members were later joined by eight other Members: Qatar (1961); Indonesia (1962); Socialist Peoples Libyan Arab Jamahiriya (1962); United Arab Emirates (1967); Algeria (1969); Nigeria (1971); Ecuador (1973–1992) and Gabon (1975–1994).[26] The Gulf Cooperation Council (GCC) was joined in 1981 by the United Arab Emirates, Bahrain, Saudi Arabia, Oman, Qatar, and Kuwait. The Arab Maghreb Union (AMU) was established in 1989 by Algeria, Libya, Mauritania, Morocco, Tunisia, and Egypt (joined 1994). The Middle East and North Africa (MENA) project convened with Algeria, Egypt, Iraq, Jordan, Morocco, Tunisia, and both Yemen in 1994.[27] (b) For the African states, the African Economic Community (AEC) was agreed upon in Abuja, Nigeria in 1991 pursuing regional economic integration. The Economic Community of West African States (ECOWAS) was created by sixteen member states. The Preferential Trade Area for Eastern and Southern Africa (FTA) was merged into the Common Market for Eastern and Southern Africa (COMESA) by the twenty-two African member states in 1993. The Central African states created the Central African Economic Community (CEAO) and the Central African Economic and Customs Union (UDEAC), while the Southern Africa states created the Southern African Customs Union (SACU) and the Southern African

Development Cooperation (SADC) to promote trade between member states.[28] (c) For the eastern European states, on June 20, 1990, the Russian Federation (RF), Belarus, and Ukraine agreed to create a Commonwealth of Independent States (CIS),[29] which fifteen members joined as independent sovereign states. In March 1996, the RF signed a "treaty of the four" with Belarus, Kazakhstan, and Kyrghyzstan as a common market, and created two-state Union with Belarus in April 1997. The RF and Ukraine signed a treaty on economic cooperation in 1998 separately. The trade volume of the RF with Ukraine, Belarus, and Kazakhstan had been larger among CIS member states. "The Five" framework was established by RF, Azerbaijan, Georgia, Moldova, Ukraine, and from 1999, Uzbekistan. Meanwhile, the RF has been disturbed by the export of oil and gas from Kazakhstan and Azerbaijan to Western markets through bypassing RF territory.[30]

Theoretical Background of Regional Integration

14. The theories of regional integration are divided into two categories: international economics and international relations. Taking economics first, contemporary trade theories explain gains from trade through competitiveness. "If trade is liberalized, then (a) each country will tend to increase the output of that good in which it has *a comparative advantage* and will tend to decrease the output of that good in which it has a comparative disadvantage; (b) each country will export the good in which it has a comparative advantage and import the other; (c) world output will tend to become more efficient (so to expand the production possibility frontier of the world); (d) each country will gain from free trade relative to autarky; and (e) the gains enjoyed by a country will be greater the more favorable its terms of trade, that is, the greater the difference between relative prices before and after trade is liberalized."[31] "Economies of scale that are due to the division of labor, or that are accompanied by product differentiation, imply that trade between economies with modest comparative cost differences will be largely intra-industry, and that trade between economies with substantial comparative cost differences will be largely inter-industry."[32] Comparative advantage lies in factor-endowments: countries tend to have comparative advantage in those goods made by intensively using their relatively abundant factors of endowments. The Hecksher-Ohlin theory explains the relationships between comparative advantage and factor prices. A country has a comparative advantage in the good that is relatively intensive in the country's relatively abundant factor. Free international trade between two countries will cause factor prices in the countries to become more equal. If both countries continue to produce both goods with free trade, their factor prices will actually be equal. An increase in the relative price of the labor intensive good will increase the wage rate relative to both commodity prices and reduce the rent relative to both commodity prices. At constant prices, an increase in one factor endowment will increase by a greater portion the output of the good intensive in that factor and will reduce the output of the other good.[33]

15. Despite the benefits of an open trade regime, there have been some reasons to protect domestic industries. First, industries which are critical to national interests are protected such as in energy, transportation, communications, and defense industries including aircraft and missiles. Second, if a new industry (infant industry) has comparative advantage in a country but is well established in foreign countries, it is protected when it has difficulties in supplying capital and technology at the beginning stage. This is closely related to economies of scale due to the narrow domestic market. The idea of infant industry protection is in favor of import substitution strategy. Third, if a country has an intention to develop or to maintain a certain industry or industries due to pressures from domestic politics, protection measures are taken such as in the case of infant industry. Fourth, foreign direct investment (FDI) is a type of capital mobility between different economies by creating a multinational firm, but the host countries may try to impose various restrictions to hold favorable returns. Finally, the mobility of labor forces between countries are very much restricted even between EU or NAFTA member countries because of two reasons: to protect their own advanced technology and to avoid political pressures from unemployment and decline of wages. The instruments of protection are tariffs and nontariff barriers. Tariffs are preferred and generally imposed by two types: flat rate per unit of imports and ad valorem (a fixed proportion of import values). Nontariff barriers include import quotas, health and sanitary regulations, consumer protection registration, variable levies, and rules of origin. Price discrimination in foreign trade includes dumping, which is widely regarded as an unfair trade practice. The United States and EU have imposed heavy penalties on antidumping cases as a measure of protection. Regional economic integration tends to reduce disparities of economic development between member countries through the gradual process of moving from general trade relations to free trade areas, custom unions, common markets, and full economic unions.

16. The students of international relations explain regional integration by four theoretical categories: realism, liberalism, constructivism, and globalization. With a heritage drawn from Thucydides, Machiavelli, and Hobbes, *realism* has dominated international relations (IR) theory since World War II as an opposite concept to utopianism, legalism or idealism. Realists assume that international relations are associated with the threat of violence because the state of nature is a state of war in anarchy which means the absence of a central authority; states are the principal or dominant actors and the position of non-state actors is lesser important; the state is a unitary actor because political differences within the state are integrated into a single unit; the state is a rational actor by taking the proper decision-making process of the system; and national security of realists is usually in the top priority within the hierarchy of international issues.[34] Since states seek relative gains with the compliance of partners, there are two barriers considered in international cooperation: cheating from partners and relative achievement of gains. "According to realists, states worry that today's friend may be tomorrow's enemy in war, and fear that achievements of joint gains that advantage a friend in the present might produce a more dangerous potential foe in the future. As a result, states must give serious attention to the gains of

partners,"[35] to prevent others from achieving advances in their relative capabilities. Realists maintain a balance of power as equilibrium by a bipolar or multipolar system to avoid the triumph of a dominant power. Economic interdependence not only enhances prospects of peace but also raises risks of conflict. The existence of hegemonic power contributes to enforcing stability such as the role of the United States in the post-cold war period,[36] although the dominant power faces the growth of the rival power center, which is created voluntarily by efforts of political actors. Therefore, realists view that prospects for regional integration through international cooperation are pessimistic in real sense because there is obvious limit of full cooperation between powers. The U.S.-China relations in the post-cold war period, for example, well-explained realism: the Bush administration considers China as a potential competitor rather than a strategic partner.

17. *Liberalism* dominated much of political and economic thought in the eighteenth centuries, particularly in Great Britain and the United States. Adam Smith and David Ricardo were in favor of economic individualism under *laissez-faire* by maximizing the role of individual entrepreneurs and minimizing state intervention in the market. Jeremy Bentham viewed people as rational to choose the best for themselves without government interference. In contemporary liberalism, Andrew Moravcsik assumes that the main actors in international politics are individuals and private groups who are rational; states (or other political institutions) represent some subset of domestic society, on the basis of whose interests state officials define state preferences and act purposively in world politics; and the patterns of interdependent state preferences impose a binding constraint on state behavior.[37] Moravcsik views three variants of liberal theory: ideational, commercial, and republican liberalism. Ideational liberalism (social perspective) is based on social identities and values as a basic determinant of state preferences causing interstate conflict or cooperation. Social identities become compatible by legitimate borders, political institutions, and socioeconomic equality, where international cooperation is likely. Commercial liberalism (economic perspective) explains the individual and collective behavior of states based on the patterns of market incentives. If economic benefits are greater for powerful private actors, their incentive to press governments to facilitate transactions becomes greater. The expansion of the international economy made it more costly for states to go to war due to benefits from economic interdependence. Republican liberalism (political perspective) is based on representation and rent-seeking. When the mode of domestic political representation is biased in favor of particular groups, their monopoly power dominates government institutions for their interests, which creates economic inefficiency and conflict with unfavorable groups. Liberal democratic institutions can provide "democratic peace" through the self-adjustment process, which is supportive for international cooperation.[38] The emergence of neoliberalism in the 1980s came to consider international institutions as playing a major role.[39]

18. The debate between realism and liberalism is based on that state action is influenced by "structure" and "process" with institutions and that between neorealsim

and neoliberalism is based on a shared commitment to rationalism. However, Alexander Wendt states "Rationalism offers a fundamentally behavioral conception of process and institutions: they change behavior but not identities and interests."[40] Since this regime could not change identities and interests through process, Wendt introduced a social theory explaining "identities and interests" named *constructivism* as a new IR theory.[41] He views that people act toward objects on the basis of the meanings that the objects have for them; actors acquire identities by participating in orientations and practices of members engaged in social interactions over time; and identities are the basis of interests. Amitav Archarya applies constructivist theory for constructing regional security communities, which are groups of states that have renounced the use of force as a means of resolving intra-regional conflicts. Since state interests emerge from a process of interaction and socialization, he suggests three elements in making security communities: institutions, norms and identity. First, the regional institution (formal or informal) facilitates the development of trust, a regional culture, belief in a common destiny, and social learning. Multilateralism could involve the less formal norms of international society through consultation, dialogue and socialization. Second, norms (legal or social) are standards of behavior such as rights and obligations, which contribute to international order by forbidding actions which are subversive of collective goals. For example, legal norms are "respect for justice and the rule of law" and social norms are a "principle of consensus." Third, Identity is role-specific understandings and expectations about self, and identification are one of the instruments of regional integration. It is necessary to develop a collective sense of identity: who we are and how we differ from others, while external recognition is helpful to build collective identities of regional security communities.[42] Non-governmental organizations have been working in line with constructivism as a second track diplomacy, particularly in conflicting relations.

19. In the post-cold war period, an obvious trend of *globalization* has appeared as a set of economic and political structures and processes.[43] Globalization assumes that states and other entities interact in the international system; capitalism is the essence of historical development; a particular dominant mechanism may contribute to disparities of economic development; and economic factors are absolutely critical in explaining the evolution of the capitalist system.[44] The major causes of globalization are as follows:[45] first, the collapse of communism terminated the ideological confrontation between nation states. Restrictions arising from ideological competition of the cold war have been largely relaxed as the new system pursues common prosperity in a peaceful environment. Second, the revolutionary advancement of computer technology expedites information to pass through national borders via internet with high speed data processing systems, wireless telephones, satellite television, fax machines, printers and copiers, and other digital instruments for communications.[46] Third, the generalization of air transportation, owing to the rise of household income and reduced fare from mass usage, saves time and space for face-to-face human contact, which also stimulates family travel around the world.[47] Fourth, the trade barriers have been significantly reduced through bilateral, multilateral and regional arrangements,

which increase cross-border transactions of goods and services, demanding greater manpower. Also the Internet shopping malls promote immediate transactions, which overcome the problems of space and time. Fifth, the financial markets depend on electronic transactions at computer terminals, so that capital mobility becomes a matter of seconds around the world. Employment information is circulated through the Internet around the world, so that qualified workers can find jobs much easier and faster than before, although physical and administrative barriers still exist in the labor market. Sixth and finally, some cross-national studies evidenced the convergence of productivity from easier factor movement including faster transfer of new technology.[48] The above environment has expedited globalization and economic integration.

Figure 2. Capitalistic Efficiency versus Democratic Equality

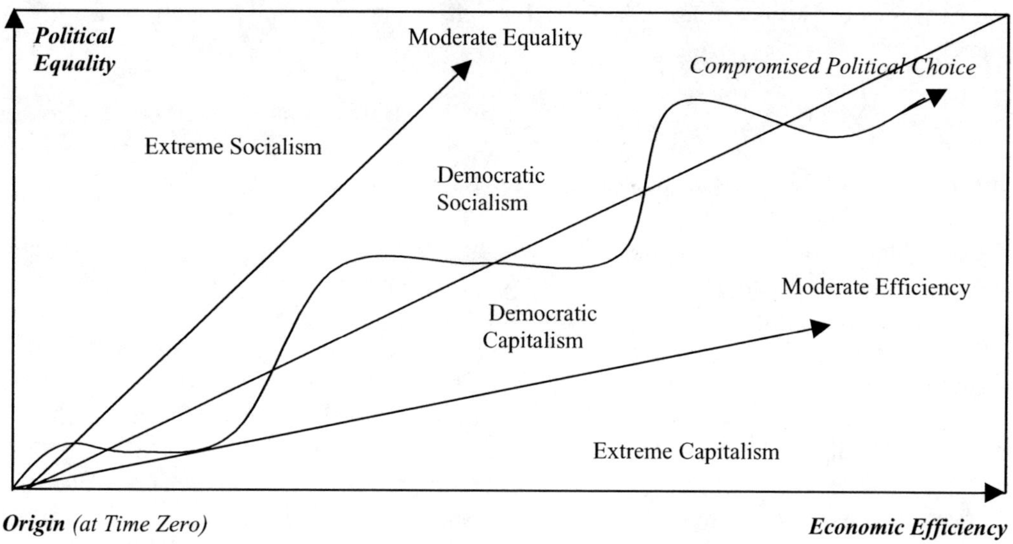

20. The impact of globalization on politics, economy, national security, and socio-culture, is wide and deep by overcoming time and space.[49] First, international pressures from global or regional superpowers are so influential that nation-states lose their independence in the decision-making process of government policies.[50] Regional economic integration pushes nation-states to move toward political integration of the region as intended in European Union.[51] Second, a nation's economy benefits from market liberalization by taking gains from trade, but income disparities between rich and poor nations remain widened because infant industries cannot be protected from foreign invaders.[52] The import substitution strategies in economic development are possibly interrupted by foreign competitors in the WTO system. Third, trade and investment by multinational corporations without national borders raise economic commitment with other nationals so that business interests cause complications in international relations. A strong economic bond with rival countries prevents or reduces possible military conflicts between nation-states, although imbalances of trade and investment cause more disputes on the tactical level.[53] Fourth, an increasing

number of non-governmental organizations is becoming influential in foreign relations, while the independence of nation-states is continuously declining. The international norms and rules help private agents to build up cohesiveness of their organizations. Fifth, globalization expedites convergence and homogenization, rather than the clash, of different cultures and civilization in the long run because economic integration helps political integration, which expedites cultural changes.[54] In globalization, economic interdependence is so strong that different cultures are converged into harmonious ways of life in each region without a "clash" if the third world countries achieve a level of reasonable income through modernization. Finally, it is understandable that some solutions on the strategic level cannot resolve all of problems on the tactical level in the region or world. The fundamental goal of regional integration lies in pursuing economic efficiency and political equality of nation-states with acceptable compromise through political choice, although it is difficult for both objectives to find a middle point.

21. A critical dilemma arising from political and economic integration lies in endless conflict between capitalistic efficiency and democratic equality in both macro and micro levels.[55] The fall of communism gave us a lesson that a socialist system could not maintain its political-military structure because of economic inefficiency. Then, is the capitalistic democracy the end of history?[56] How about the democratic socialist system, which is now popular in some European states? China has pursued a socialist market economy as a transition form from a socialist system to a capitalist system that may be the best way that China can choose. Meanwhile, Russia and Eastern European countries are struggling in the process of transforming towards a democratic capitalist system, working to build up efficient economies under a democratic political system. On the state level, it is a political choice of the people whether a state goes with democratic capitalism or democratic socialism where the former emphasizes economic efficiency while the latter focuses on political equality. If a state faces economic difficulties under a socialist government, it is possible to switch its system toward capitalism through the self-adjusting function of democracy, and the opposite would possibly happen. Therefore, people's choice of the political-economic system remains between moderate efficiency and moderate equality, which is a cyclical behavior of the people depending on economic situations rather than dialectic or ideological challenges for a new system,[57] as shown in Figure 2. On the regional level, income disparities between states will create further problems in the age of globalization. Inequality of average incomes between member states would be an debatable issue in the process of regional integration, but we can not equalize initial conditions of each nation. If nation states join an economic union (economic federalism), all economic policies are commonly adopted by member states, which means that individual firms in the region have equal opportunities in all economic activities. Then, efficiency of firms will be improved within the region through uninterrupted movement of factor inputs, which will partially reduce income disparities between member states. However, if a state chooses separate fiscal policies from regional guidelines, the way of income distribution of that state remains unchanged.

Economic Integration of the Asia-Pacific Region: APEC

22. Despite little geopolitical coherence between member economies, APEC was created by twelve founding members in 1989, and its membership expanded to twenty-one spreading to four continents of Asia, Australia, North America, and South America. The success of APEC owes to followings: Asian economic growth and increasing economic interdependence between their economies, rising protectionism against Asian manufacturing exports to Japan and other OECD countries, the change of paradigm from confrontation to cooperation by removing barriers created under the cold war, and a new trend of regional and global integration experienced in EU and NAFTA.[58] APEC has a broad geographical structure of its members in terms of ASEAN, EAEC, ANZCERTA, NAFTA and FTAA. ASEAN is the first subset of APEC consisting of ten member states pursuing economic integration by reducing trade barriers and improving its relations with other economies. EAEC is the second subset of APEC consisting of ASEAN plus five Northeast economies despite limited function of dialogue and consultation. ANZCERTA is the third subset of APEC with Australia and New Zealand having increasing trade relations with ASEAN and EAEC. Both Chile and Peru establish the fourth subset of APEC linking South America because Chile is a member state of Mercosur linking Brazil and Argentina, while Peru is that of the ANCOM linking Venezuela, Bolivia, Colombia, and Ecuador. NAFTA, as a region, is the fifth subset of APEC, which is a global connection of Asia with North America. In addition, APEC can reach South America through NAFTA by 2005 when FTAA is effective. We are very optimistic that APEC can provide a global link through its five subsets. In 1996 EU and ASEAN plus Three (including Japan, China and Korea) joined the Asian-Europe Meeting (ASEM) with the European Union,[59] which is another approach of Asian economies to link themselves to other region aggressively and independently without commitment of other non-Asian members of APEC such as America and Australia. Thus, APEC maintains a structure of sub-regional, regional, and global dimension of primary connections associated with secondary linkages.

23. Since its inauguration, APEC held its third annual meeting in Seoul, South Korea in 1991 at the ministerial level, and the Seoul APEC Declaration set its objectives, scope of activities, and mode of operations. The APEC Leaders Meeting held on Blake Island, Seattle, in 1993, envisioned a community of Asia-Pacific economies based on the sprit of openness and partnership to pursue continuous economic growth; to reduce trade and investment barriers; to share the benefits of economic growth; to improve education and training, to advance in telecommunications and transportation; and to protect the environment. In 1994, in Bogor, Indonesia, APEC Leaders presented the Bogor Declaration of Common Resolve: the vision of open trading with the industrial economies achieving the goal of free and open trade and investment no later than the year 2010 and developing economies no later than the year 2020. In 1995, in Osaka, Japan, APEC Leaders adopted the Osaka Action Plan, establishing the three pillars of APEC activities: trade and investment liberalization, business facilitation, and economic and technical cooperation. In 1996 in Manila,

APEC Leaders adopted the Manila Action Plan, launching the implementation phase of free and open trade and investment agenda to achieve the objectives outlined in Bogor. In 1998 in Kuala Lumpur, APEC Leaders adopted the Kuala Lumpur Action Program on Skills Development to contribute towards sustainable growth and equitable development, to reduce economic disparities, and to improve the social well-being of the people, through upgrading and improvement of skills. In 2000 in Bandar, Brunei Darussalam, APEC Leaders addressed the challenges of the new economy: managing globalization, providing the action agenda for the new economy, creating new opportunities, and strengthening the multilateral trading system. APEC 2001 held in Shanghai, China under the theme of "Meeting New Challenges in the New Century: Achieving Common Prosperity through Participation and Cooperation," focused on three sub-themes of "sharing the benefits of globalization and the new economy, advancing trade and investment, and promoting sustainable economic growth."[60] APEC is moving slowly as a open regional forum as originally intended.

24. APEC relations can be examined in terms of its sub-regional, regional, and global elements. For the United States, first, the fall of communism changed the paradigm of international relations from military confrontation toward economic cooperation, and domestic priorities moves from defense to non-defense, emphasizing social welfare for the U.S. citizens. Second, the center of global economic power has been shifting to the Asia-Pacific region so that U.S. commitment with the Asia-Pacific region would be continuously necessary. Third, the conversion of resources from military to domestic needs limits defense budgets, and some types of security communities like ARF would be preferable rather than expensive bilateral or multilateral alliances if the burdens are not shared.[61] The United States joined APEC to void exclusion from Asia Pacific affairs and to prevent its combining of economic and security affairs. Despite its early passive intentions, the United States has been able to access Asian markets favorably through bilateral or multilateral negotiations based on her superpower position. As the Asian economies rise, the United States faces two-front threat from Europe and Asia. "The EU has launched the euro, a new association agreement with Mexico, and negotiations with Mercosur; East Asia is pursuing the Asian Monetary Fund (AMF) and the East Asian free trade area (EAFTA). The result is a clear and steady erosion of both the U.S. position on the global economic scene and the multilateral rules and institutions that it has traditionally championed."[62] By activating FTAA by 2005, the United States will integrate economies of North and South Americas, and may create a Transatlantic Free Trade Area (TAFTA) with EU as a counter measure.[63] However, it encourages East Asian economies to create EAFTA and AMF to protect Asian interests. ASEM is now at the stage of information exchange, but can be transformed into a free trade area to encounter possible losses. Washington expects ARF to be a security community like NATO,[64] but regional diversity and lack of common security issues makes it difficult to build up its identity with common interests.

25. In the 1960s and 1970s, Japan desired to counterbalance European integration, to contain American protectionism, and to provide collective leadership to maintain the global order of trade and investment through bilateral and multilateral negotiations. Since the mid-1980s Japan began to pay attention to Asia because of crisis of the global trading system (GATT), unilateral pressures from Washington, and private sector interests in Asia. The Ministry of International Trade and Industry (MITI) recognized in 1988 that Japan's role was to promote the horizontal division of labor in Asia and to reduce Asia's dependence upon the U.S. market.[65] Japan joined APEC as a founding member with the three principles of liberalization, facilitation, and economic cooperation. Japan considers APEC as a consultative body based on voluntarism and focuses on confidence-building through open regionalism and consistency with GATT/WTO. Japan views that APEC favors community-building with gradualism, while EU pursues institution-building. As two Japanese observers have written, "What originally motivated the drive to set up a European institutional structure was the need to present a united front against the Soviet-dominated Eastern bloc; today partisans of European regionalism are concerned about competing economically with the United States, Japan, and the industrializing economies of East Asia."[66] The United States and Japan have parallel geopolitical interests in economics and security, so harmonization based on the rule of the game is essential, although both are competitive in trade and investment in the regional markets. While negative critics were controversial from Japanese commercialism in 1980s,[67] it has been suggested that Japan should play an appropriate role in collective security of the region in line with the United States, because it is not realistic for one side alone to maintain regional security and stability continuously. The proper role of Japan in maintaining regional security is helpful for its market expansion to ASEAN countries.[68] Positive development of Japan-China relations is also essential for APEC. Two economies are mutually beneficial in trade and investment if China gains capital and technology and Japan gains export markets. Finally, current recession in Japan without fundamental reforms may cause capital flight and emigration from Japan,[69] which could invite further recession, and that is not desirable for economic recovery of the region and the world.

26. China joined APEC with Taiwan and Hong Kong in 1991 because of its economic interests linked to the region; not to be excluded in the process of regional integration; strategic concerns about challenges from and competition with ASEAN; and to keep a stronger voice in regional affairs as an emerging power. China desires APEC to keep the "Asian way" as follows: first, China wants APEC to remain an open, flexible, and realistic economic cooperation forum rather than a closed and institutionalized group; consultations and voluntary commitments rather than binding agreements; and not mandatory directives or hard negotiations. Second, China wants the actions of APEC to take fully into account the divergent developmental conditions of members with freedom to arrange action plans in accordance with its own timetable. Third, China likes the progress of APEC based on the principles of equality, equity and mutual benefits from trade and investment. Finally, economic cooperation is strengthened along with liberalization and facilitation of trade and investment.[70] China

expressed five more principles in 1994: mutual respect and consultative consensus; gradual progress and stable growth; opening with nondiscrimination; comprehensive cooperation and mutual benefit; and reducing the development gap for common prosperity.[71] Due to rapid economic growth, China has become a major player in the Asia Pacific region, but faces challenges: economic transformation toward the socialist market economy and liberalization pressures from the global market. Weixing Hu describes China's costs of economic integration in four ways: trade interdependence is vulnerable to political pressures from the West; disparities of economic development between provinces require political attention; rising local economies force Beijing to change power relationships with local governments; and China's industries stay in a core-periphery structure based on vertical division of labor.[72] China pursues economic growth along with territorial unification, but both objectives are contradictory. It is a smart choice for China to maximize benefits from economic integration subject to minimizing risks of national security. China engages in multilateral security dialogues with ASEAN through ARF. It will join WTO by 2001 as the 143rd member-state, and will host the Summer Olympic games in Beijing in 2008.[73]

27. The ASEAN leaders realized that intra-ASEAN trade and investment are imperative for their economic growth, and formed the ASEAN Free Trade Area (AFTA) in 1992 by agreeing to trade liberalization within ten years. ASEAN joined extra-regional cooperation organizations, including EAEC and APEC for economy and ARF for security as insurance policies against future uncertainty. ASEAN conducts almost three-fourth of its trade with APEC countries, and its investment share is even higher. APEC could produce competitive forces to dilute ASEAN, but might complement ASEAN's economic integration by reducing transaction costs. Since the ASEAN leaders worry about the negative side, it is desired that the principles of APEC preserve ASEAN's identity and cohesion; are based on equality, equity, and mutual benefit, taking into account the difference of development stages; strengthen the open, multilateral economic and trading systems in the world; provide a consultative forum on economic issues without mandatory directives; strengthen the capacity of participants by facilitation and consultation; and proceed gradually and pragmatically especially in its institutionalization.[74] ASEAN is able to participate more actively in the APEC process, particularly in their commitments in the action plans, after being more prepared to deal with upcoming issues. Developing a monitoring mechanism is desirable for APEC to check its progress of action plans. As Michael G. Plummer indicated, ASEAN is the core of APEC, which cannot exist without the former and APEC moves forward only if ASEAN member states are not against it. While "pan-regionalism" reflects the ASEAN approach to economic development with regionalism, APEC has influenced the direction of ASEAN economic cooperation in general and AFTA in particular in return. Recently, ASEAN and related states have involved in studies on "ASEAN plus three" FTA and a Japan-ASEAN FTA, implying that Japan and China become competitive in ASEAN markets. Thus, Plummer writes, "APEC will continue to be nested in ASEAN in that the subregional organization is playing a central role in

molding the direction of APEC to be consistent with the goals of ASEAN economic cooperation."[75]

28. NAFTA integrates the three economies of North America to counter Europe and Asia. The strength of APEC will be tested by its capability ruling interactions among subregional trade arrangements (SRTAs). To nest NAFTA in APEC, it is desirable to investigate underlying differences of the political economies between Asia Pacific and North America, as suggested by Maxwell A. Cameron. Formal trade agreements between North America and Asia-Pacific within APEC will cause problems, because Asian countries have little incentive to undertake reforms while NAFTA has no power to enforce the reforms. Asian economies, particularly the four tigers and next tiers demonstrated sustainable growth with more savings and investment than economies of NAFTA. However, despite high growth, most Asian economies have maintained low levels of income inequality compared to others such as in Latin America. The patterns of trade and investment of NAFTA showed high degrees of interdependence. Mexico and Canada export three quarters of their goods and services to North America, and sixty percent of their FDI comes from the United States, while none of Asian countries depends absolutely on North America except the Philippines. NAFTA, led by the United States, has imposed strong principles of *laissez-faire*, but no single Asian economy can play an overwhelming role in trade and investment arrangements in APEC. Compared with NAFTA, regionalism in Asia-Pacific is based on forms of persuasion rather than structural mandates associated with hegemony.[76]The degree of economic development in APEC varies from the OECD level to the lowest developing economies. Diversities and disparities of economic development between subregions of APEC require a relaxed version of trade and investment arrangements. The concept of open subregionalism is preferable in nesting of NAFTA in APEC, because it applies the open regionalism with competitive liberalization to accelerate free trade among SRTAs. However, regionalism threatens the export-led growth strategies of the Asian economies, which favor the multilateralism of EU and NAFTA.

Table 1. Gross National Products of Selected Economic Groups

Group	*GNP (US$ Billion)*	*Population (Million)*	*GNP Per capita US$*	*Percent Of World GNP*
APEC	16,213	2,495	6,498	56.17
AFTA	575	507	1,113	1.99
Japan-Korea-China	5,547	1,418	3,912	19.22
ANZCERTA	436	23	18,974	1.51
NAFTA	8,914	397	22,454	30.89
APEC-Others	741	150	4,940	2.56
South America FTA	1,458	334	4,365	5.05
EU-15	8,280	375	21,420	28.69
World	28,862	5,897	4,894	100.00

Source: Robert Scollay and John P. Gilbert, *New Regional Trading Arrangements in the Asia Pacific?* (Policy Analyses #63), Washington, DC: Institute for International Economics, May 2001, pp. 50-51. Data Source: World Bank, World Development Report 1999/2000.

Table 2. Trade Shares of Northeast Asian Economies (Percent)
(Left Column is Imports and Right Column is Exports for 1996-1998)

Country	*Japan*		*South Korea*		*China*		*Hong Kong*		*Taiwan*	
Japan	x		19.61	10.79	20.52	17.85	13.32	5.97	27.01	9.58
South Korea	4.41	5.81	x		10.06	4.71	4.71	1.39	4.70	1.73
China	12.31	5.22	6.47	9.28	x		38.41	34.57	3.44	12.56
Hong Kong	0.68	6.15	0.67	8.07	5.10	22.30	x		4.58	11.57
Taiwan	3.89	6.49	1.76	3.45	11.70	1.94	7.68	2.47	x	
Northeast Asia	*21.28*	*28.51*	*28.51*	*31.58*	*47.38*	*46.52*	*64.12*	*44.40*	*39.72*	*35.43*
Southeast Asia	*14.74*	*15.59*	*8.51*	*14.01*	*8.51*	*6.58*	*10.33*	*6.38*	*13.61*	*12.11*
East Asia	36.02	39.25	37.01	45.60	55.89	53.10	74.45	50.78	53.33	47.54
ANZCERTA	5.00	2.27	4.86	1.82	2.50	1.32	1.26	1.52	3.24	1.55
NAFTA	*26.37*	*31.19*	*23.72*	*18.79*	*13.50*	*20.17*	*8.44*	*23.89*	*20.46*	*27.97*
World	100.00		100.00		100.00		100.00		100.00	

Source: Scollay & Gilbert, *New Regional Trading Arrangements in the Asia Pacific?*, pp.31-2.

29. The recent development of *subregional trade arrangements* in the Asia Pacific region such as a Korea-Japan-China FTA has been a concern of the megablocs (EU and NAFTA) in terms of its function as either building blocs or stumbling blocs. The judgment criteria lie in two categories: first, SRTAs or RTAs should enhance economic welfare of their members as well as that of the world, while avoiding negative effects on the welfare of nonmembers. Second, they should create incentives for "the negotiation of further arrangements satisfying the first criterion as well as for further progress toward global free trade via multilateral liberalization."[77] A question arises from whether subregionalization within the Asia-Pacific region is constructive toward the free trade goals of APEC. Subregionalization is an intermediate step and an indirect route for a single state to reach regional integration, by expediting trade liberalization through efficient negotiations with neighboring countries owing to similar identities or common interests. However, two negative opinions are expressed on this development: first, it is argued that large trade blocs (including an Asian FTA initiated by a Japan-Korea-China FTA) may face strong incentives to pursue the enhancement of their own welfare at the expense of the other two blocs, which will lead to destructive trade wars.[78] Second, if the SRTAs are overlapped, the fragmentation of the regional economy may cause a particular product of exports or imports to be held to different rules depending on its origin or destination due to different arrangements of each SRTA.[79] In fact, open regionalism is based on two principles in trade: to apply regional rules for member states, and multilateral rules for non-member states. Open subregionalism applies the same rules of regionalism applied for its regional system. As long as principles and rules of SRTAs or RTAs are consistent with multilateral rules of WTO /GATT, they would not interrupt but reenforce the global trade regime in the long run. It is good for small economies because they can avoid unilateral pressures from super economies through collective actions of organized member states. However, if gradual emergence of an East Asian trade bloc strengthens its collective power aggressively against EU and NAFTA, the world economy moves toward trilateral competition, and the structure and function of APEC needs to be revised.[80]

30. Table 1 shows that GNP of APEC members was 56.17% of the world economy in 1998, consisting of 30.89% from NAFTA, 19.22% from Japan-Korea-China, 1.99% from ASEAN-10, 1.51% from CER, and 2.56% from others in APEC, while EU was 28.69%. Table 2 shows intratrade relations of Northeast-5 and extratrade relations of Northeast-5 with ASEAN, CER and NAFTA during the period of 1996-1998. It is observed that economic interdependency is high between the Northeast Asian countries; Japan and South Korea have been trading high volumes with ASEAN; trade volumes of China, Hong Kong and Taiwan with ASEAN remain at a similar level of South Korea, but will rise continuously owing to geopolitical benefits; trade surpluses of Japan and China with the United States were $61.8 billion and $70.2 billion in 1999, that may cause trade disputes; and Northeast-5 and NAFTA are the main interest blocs of APEC.

Regional Economic Integration and the Korean Peninsula

31. The Korean peninsula has been a crossroads facing conflict between major powers even in the post-cold war period.[81] The Koreas' future depends largely on improvement of relations between the United States and China. For South Korea, the United States provided its national security through a bilateral alliance in the cold war period, which made South Korea possible to construct a cornerstone for economic development and democratization. The United States supplied capital and technology with attractive export markets absorbing its labor-intensive goods in the early stage of economic development and capital- and technology-intensive goods in the later period. A half-century security alliance made them major trading partners with each other exceeding sixty billion dollars of annual trade. Many leading intellectuals in government, business, and society in South Korea have been trained in colleges and universities, research institutes, and government programs in the United States. The effect of national security relations spilled over into economic and social development, so that South Korea has been largely westernized towards American values and systems. Meanwhile, China is rising as a regional and global power replacing in the role of the Soviet Union in the Northeast Asia, although it is still in a developing economic stage. China has been using North Korea as a strategic buffer against the United States by supplying weapons and necessities, including food and energy. Since China is most influential in North Korea, positive development of Seoul-Beijing relations is essential to ensure peace and stability in the Korea peninsula. China has attractive markets of trade and investment for South Korea due to inexpensive labor forces, 1.3 billion potential consumers, lower transportation costs, and cultural affinity with a long history. China is appropriate for South Korea to diversify its trade and investment with vertical and horizontal division of labor. Since Korea is too small to threaten China, Seoul's approach to Beijing has been relatively acceptable to its leaders and people. Thus, the United States and China are equally important for South Korea to maintain its economic development and national security without external intervention.

32. Being in the opposition camp of communism against the South, North Korea has been in near to collapse as the fall of the Soviet Union and Eastern European countries. Politically, the disappearance of global communism made the North Korean socialist party lose cohesiveness and loyalty. As South Korea was successful in northern politics by normalizing diplomatic relations with China and Russia, North Korea became isolated without improving its relations with the United States and Japan as counterbalances. Economically, its trade with former Soviet Union and its satellites fell almost to zero in the early 1990s as trade with Russia and China began to require cash transactions. As a result, North Korea experienced serious shortage of food and energy which was exacerbated by poor harvests in the mid-1990s. Fearing outflow of refugees from the North Korean border and strategic imbalance in the Korean peninsula, China subsidized grain and fuel continuously. Strategically, Pyongyang used its nuclear weapons for negotiations with the United States. The Clinton administration signed the Agreed Framework with North Korea by supplying 500,000 tons of heavy oil annually until two white water reactors are delivered to freeze its plutonium production. Finally, when its brinkmanship diplomacy was ineffective, Pyongyang approached South Korea in an attempt to improve its relations with the United States. After the North-South summit in June 2000, Kim Jung Il invited U.S. Secretary of State Madeline Albright to Pyongyang and sent his second man Cho Myong-Rok to Washington. But the new Bush administration has maintained a strong stance against North Korea by requiring transparency with verification and withdrawal of conventional weapons from the front line. Kim Jung Il visited Moscow in August 2001. Chinese President Jiang Zemin visited Pyongyang the following month, promising more aid and encouraging conciliatory policies toward the South.[82] A consensus suggests that the only medicine for survival of North Korea is to open its door and to liberalize its domestic politics. North Korea needs the United States as much as China.[83]

33. The Koreas should engage with regional powers for economic integration, either with or without unification. To link the Korean peninsula to regional integration, it is desirable to analyze interrelations of regional powers based on the four theories discussed previously, to which trade theories are equally applied. The first theory is based on realism. Realists believe that the Korean peninsula is in strategic confrontation between the United States and China (ignoring Japan and Russia). It is assumed that China's GDP reaches that of the United States within a couple of decades when it catches up major advanced military technology; China will build up military power continuously that stimulates an arms race against the United States and Japan; and China will claim territorial sovereignty on Taiwan and the Spratly Islands. Realists call for Washington to take military containment strategies against China, increasing its defense budget, strengthening bilateral alliances with Korea, Japan, and Taiwan, and increasing arms sales to allied nations. In line with this, Washington restricts exports of strategic materials and transfer of sensitive technology to foreign countries, and U.S. trade with and investment in China are restricted to consumer goods to avoid helping military industries in China. As a result, the gains from trade decline so that the production possibility frontier of the world cannot be maximized. This is a welfare loss

to both sides without a winner. Pursuing both strategies of military containment along with economic engagement, Washington prepares proper contingency plans against China to minimize risks of external threats caused by maximizing U.S. economic efficiency. It is difficult to compromise contradictory objectives of both strategies if they are pursued together. In fact, the rise of trade and investment increases economic interdependence, which widens opportunity costs of war, so that states will avoid military intervention as a means of settling conflicts. Expanded economic interactions expedite socio-cultural understanding among trading partners, which promotes regional integration and stimulates military alliance.[84] The priority of economic security is higher than that of military security in some areas, such as the Gulf region. Realism is not favorable thinking to deal with regional economic integration in the post-cold war period because of many actors affecting regional integration other than states.

Table 3. Welfare Effects of Asian FTAs on Regions (Percent of Initial GDP)

Country Or Group	(a) Japan and South Korea	(b) Japan-South Korea-China	(c) East Asia ("b" plus AFTA)	(d) W. Pacific ("c" plus CER)
Japan	0.01	0.25	0.34	0.57
South Korea	- 0.28	0.80	0.81	1.20
China	- 0.05	2.09	1.96	1.94
Taiwan	- 0.05	- 0.84	- 1.10	- 1.08
Indonesia	- 0.01	- 0.15	0.69	0.71
United States	- 0.01	- 0.02	- 0.03	- 0.06
European Union	- 0.01	- 0.02	- 0.02	- 0.02
The World	- 0.01	0.09	0.11	0.16

Source: Scollay & Gilbert, *New Regional Trading Arrangements in the Asia Pacific?*, pp. 98-69. Western Pacific includes East Asia plus ANZCERTA (shortly CER including Australia and New Zealand).

Table 4. Welfare Effects of a Korea-U.S. FTA on Regions (Percent of Initial GDP)

	Full Liberalization		Excluding Agriculture	
	Medium Run	Long Run	Medium Run	Long Run
Japan	- 0.04	- 0.07	- 0.02	- 0.04
South Korea	*0.91*	*2.41*	*0.38*	*0.09*
ChinaHongKong	- 0.06	- 0.11	- 0.05	- 0.08
Taiwan	- 0.10	- 0.17	- 0.03	- 0.06
ASEAN	- 0.08	- 0.14	- 0.05	- 0.08
United States	*0.05*	*0.13*	*0.02*	*0.06*
Sum of World	0.01	0.03	0.00	0.01

Source: Inbom Choi and Jeffery J. Schott, *Free Trade between Korea and the United States?*, Washington, DC: Institute for International Economics, April 2001, p. 56.

34. The second theory, based on liberalism, suggests that basic determinants of state preferences are representation and rent-seeking in government, market incentives in business, and social identity and values in society. In linking the Korean peninsula to regional integration, those input factors are considered in making choices among available alternatives. The first approach is to form a free trade area in Northeast Asia, which is a set of possible alternatives for Korea to join regional integration. The

concept of the East Asia Free Trade Area (EAFTA) is in line with the EAEG or EAEC suggested by Malaysia.[85] This idea has been accepted favorably by Japan and China since the Asian financial crisis in 1997. Scollay and Gilbert examined the economic effects of alternative regional trade arrangements in the Asia-Pacific region as shown in Table 3.[86] By using Computable General Equilibrium (CGE) techniques, they generated the welfare effects of planned FTAs on each country and region. In their findings, first, a Japan-South Korea FTA generates negative welfare effects except in smaller gains for Japan. Second, a Japan-South Korea-China FTA generates significant positive welfare gains for three member states at the cost of ASEAN and other countries. Third, a Western Pacific FTA generates very significant welfare gains to all member states such as Japan 0.57%, South Korea 1.20%, China 1.94%, Indonesia 0.71%, Australia 1.05%, and New Zealand 4.32% of initial GDP. Fourth, the United States and European Union would be the worst, creating losers for all subregional FTAs in Asia. In sum, the simulation shows that the best choice for Asian countries is to form a Western Pacific FTA, including countries of Northeast Asia, ASEAN, and CER, which causes a significant loss of welfare for the United States (- 0.06%) and European Union (-0.02%). From the Koreas' point of view, the wisest choice would be to create a Japan-South Korea-China FTA first, and gradually expand its memberships to ASEAN countries, and to CER in this first approach.

35. The second approach under liberalism for Korea to join regional economies would be to create a FTA with the United States. It is desirable for South Korea and the United States to create a FTA because they have common interests in politics, economy and national security in the Northeast Asian region, which are fundamental determinants of state preferences. Inbom Choi and Jeffrey J. Schott examined welfare effects of creating a free trade area between South Korea and the United States by using CGE techniques.[87] The study simulated two alternative scenarios that all tariffs are removed between the United States and Korea on a preferential basis in the first, and only nonagricultural tariffs are removed in the second. Table 4 shows the net welfare effects of a Korea-United States FTA on regions in terms of proportion of initial GDP. Their study concluded the following: first, "the bilateral trade relationship is already robust but deplete with troublesome barriers." In 1999, Korea-U.S. trade in goods and services reached $65 billion which was 20% of total Korean trade and 3% of America's; and the U.S. share of total FDI in Korea was 32%, which was 0.71% of total U.S. FDI abroad. Removal of trade and investment barriers would increase volumes of trade and investment substantially. Second, both the United States and Korea gain from the formation of a preferential FTA. Under full liberalization, South Korea gains 2.41% of GDP and the United States gains 0.13% of GDP in the long run, although some other countries including Japan, China-Hong Kong, Taiwan, and ASEAN show significant loss of welfare. Exclusion of the agricultural sector in trade reduces welfare effects, while long-run effects are much better than medium-run ones. Third, "a bilateral free trade pact would further reinforce the strong ties that already bind the two countries together." However, one's gains from creating a new FTA at the costs of others may

invite counteractions pursuing other FTAs between loser countries and the United States to take their losses back.

36. The third theory, based on constructivism, believes that both social identities and common interests are constructed by participating in orientations and practices, not by rationalism of structure and process. Constructivists want to connect the Korean peninsula to the region by confidence-building not by institution-building at the first stage. These are two examples of linking economic assistance and national security. The first case is the US-DPRK Village Wind Power Pilot Project, which is "the first attempt by a US non-governmental organization to work side-by-side with North Koreans in cooperative development. Previously, nongovernmental organizations have been limited by both the American and the North Korean governments to delivering food aid to North Korea. The project installed seven wind turbine towers in a rural village on the west coast of North Korea. The towers provide clean, renewable energy to the village's medical clinic, kindergarten, and households. In addition to meeting urgent humanitarian needs, this pilot project enables North Korea to demonstrate that it is willing to conform to international standards for development assistance. It is thus seen as a stepping stone from which North Korea can enter the international development community."[88] The second case is the ARF in which North Korea joined in 2000 as a member state. The Chairman's statement of the 7th ARF in Bangkok, Thailand on July 27, 2000, indicates that "The Ministers welcomed the participation for the first time of the Democratic People's Republic of Korea (DPRK) at the 7th ARF Ministerial Meeting in Bangkok. With regard to the issue of membership, the Ministers reaffirmed the decision taken at the Fifth ARF and agreed that with the current 23 participants, the focus should now be on consolidating the process of dialogue and cooperation among the present participants of the ARF."[89] Constructivists believe that nongovernmental activities with peoples of North Korea contribute to their confidence-building with the United States and western countries, while participation of North Korean officials in ARF increases dialogues through formal and informal contacts which also contribute to their confidence-building with South Korea, the United States, and other ARF member states.

37. The fourth theory, based on globalization, is related to North Korea's hesitation towards openness. First, opening domestic markets to foreigners means that North Korea enters into a free trade system of the world without protectionist measures for its domestic industries. The competition is so severe from the world market that the North Korean firms must supply better quality of products with lower prices for the similar items in order to survive. This requires proper education and training domestically and internationally to modernize the process of production, marketing, and management. Education enhances potential capabilities, awakens self-consciousness, and improves natural judgment on different systems. They will recognize the superiority of democratic capitalism when they turn their eyes on its totalitarian regime and its people suffering because of its failed system. Second, the rise of trade and investment requires more people to work for domestic and foreign trading firms, and

rapidly increases the number of North Korean nationals working in foreign countries. At the early stage, the North Korean government can monitor a small number of people staying overseas, but it would be too expensive to keep a large number of watchers in foreign soil as trade volumes rise. If the cost of censorship is too high, North Korean exports lose competitiveness so that the government cannot control information flowing from outside into North Korea. Third, the rise of household income forms a middle class, who will expect rights to participate in the mainstream of domestic politics. The business communities historically enjoy more political power than the government sector because the former pays more taxes than the latter. Thus, economic growth creates a middle class demanding more political influence. Fourth, as discussed in paragraph 20, foreign trade is based on reciprocity. As foreign trade and investment rise, foreign firms in North Korea will demand the same treatment as North Korean firms receive in their countries. North Korea should follow general norms and rules of the world community as a member to avoid unnecessary losses from retaliation or economic sanctions. North Korea cannot remains isolated, so it must prepare for openness and political liberalization for its survival. Globalization demands costs for dictators, but brings benefits to the people through democratization caused by economic development.[90]

The Prospects of Inter-Korean Economic Cooperation

38. The previous section discussed relationships between regional integration and the Korean peninsula based on four theories. This section will discuss how regional integration is related to inter-Korean economic cooperation. If South Korea gets positive gains from regional integration, the spillover effect will help South Korea to assist North Korea. If North Korea is not ready to receive economic assistance from South Korea, regional integration would not be meaningful to the North, as would inter-Korean economic cooperation. Economic assistance programs require two basic conditions: one is that the giver should have sustainable capabilities to supply goods and services with capital and technology, and the other is that the taker should get ready to maximize utilization of external assistance for its continuous economic growth. However, some believe that North Korea is currently not ready to receive external assistance as a qualified taker. North Korea has pursued economic development without a transformation of its failed economic system as evidenced in the fall of communism a decade ago (see paragraph 9). It is a precondition for North Korea to adjust its political system towards the globalized world in order to make economic assistance workable. The open economy can expand the production possibility frontier through gains from trade, but the autarkic economy cannot make it. If North Korea remains isolated, its economy declines continuously, which threatens the survival of the regime. If North Korea opens its door to the world without political liberalization, the regime will also collapse by the waves of freedom. Both openness and isolation will cause the regime to collapse, which is a dilemma of Kim Jung Il who wants to keep his inherited power forever. The only option for him to survive lies in pursuing the combined strategies of economic openness with political liberalization, although the

two strategies are difficult to compromise. For example, DPRK opened a free trade zone in Rajin-Sunbong in the early 1990s to exploit capitalistic profits, but failed to attract foreign capital because of lack of infrastructure and legal provisions. But the real reason behind the scene was that the political system of North Korea remained unchanged.

39. The problems of the North Korean economy lie fundamentally in the socialist system itself. First, the centrally planned economy distorts allocation of resources creating idle capacities in one industry while creating bottlenecks in the other. As a result, national production capabilities shrink year after year. Its actual military expenditures are estimated to exceed 30% of the total national budget,[91] which reduces investment in the private sector such as infrastructure, including power generation, transportation, and communications. The lack of infrastructure raises the costs of production and distribution, and reduces economic efficiency as a whole. Second, North Korea has been classified as a terrorist state by the United States, so that it is impossible to get loans from the international organizations such as IMF and the World Bank. Since the defaulted outstanding debt of North Korea is believed to be $12 billion, most foreign commercial banks refuse to give loans to North Korea, even with high risk-premiums. Science and technology of North Korea fall far short of South Korea's except in weapons and missiles. Totalitarian brainwashing pushes creativity away from individual interests. The government monopolizes information without sharing it with necessary people. Scientists and intellectuals are censored by the state, which reduces their creativity. Lack of foreign equipment and overseas education hinders technology transfer. Third, North Korean exports attract few customers because of low quality products without varieties and lack of marketing networks. It is assumed that one-fourth of labor forces are used for monitoring people in North Korea, and at least two hours a day are subjected brainwashing forced by the labor party. Because the people are mentally and physically tired in daily life, it is hard to believe that efficiency can survive in North Korea. Finally, North Korea has no self-adjusting function. The workers are waiting for orders or directions from top to bottom. They are working passively in order to avoid direct responsibilities in a worst case of scenario. Thus, it is obvious that external assistance to North Korea cannot be used for its economic takeoff to escape from the vicious circle.[92]

40. The current administration of South Korea has been consistently supportive to help North Korea although Pyongyang is not properly ready. However, South Korea itself has problems in inter-Korean economic cooperation because of its limited capabilities. Politically, the South Korean voters are gradually dissatisfied with the Sunshine Policy giving unconditional aid to the North without reciprocity.[93] Since external assistance to North Korea provides no verification in distribution, it is believed that donated food, clothing, and medicine go not to the needed people but to the core elite groups of the labor party or government. It is not acceptable that humanitarian aid is used to strengthen energy of loyal party members to suppress their own people. No confidence in North Korea exists in South Korea as U.S. President George W. Bush

himself once expressed.[94] Economically, potential economic capabilities of South Korea are too small to push the North Korean economy to take off from the deserted land. The people of South Korea do not want to give their hardly earned money to the North without hope of revival. They believe that the current political and economic situations of North Korea are not ready to mobilize external assistance to revive its economy, so that their assistance to North Korea is bottomless and a waste of resources earned from their hard work. It is agreed that economic assistance to the North without a change of its political system is not a fundamental medicine to cure its ailing economy, but rather a temporary measure of relief. Strategically, if the North Korean economy is fully recovered by economic assistance from the South, Pyongyang may build up its military power to attack the South, which is the worst fear that the people of South Korea worry about. It was reported that North Korea purchased helicopters and MIG fighters through Kazakhstan and made deals to purchase weapons from Russia despite its claimed economic hardship.[95] Therefore, the conservatives of South Korea stand strongly against further economic assistance to the North and support the tough policy of the Bush Administration against North Korea,[96] demanding transparency with verification as well as withdrawal of conventional weapons far from the front. Those conditions will limit South Korea's economic cooperation with the North.

41. We have observed that North Korea is not ready yet to capitalize external economic assistance to transform its political and economic system, and that the Sunshine Policy of South Korea faces a strong counter-force from the inside because of the concerns described above. From these two factors, we must start to consider inter-Korean economic cooperation. The objectives of this cooperation are self-sufficiency in necessities for the North in the short term, transformation of the North Korean economy toward a market system in the medium term, and integration of the two economies in the long term. In the short run, North Korea needs food, clothing, and medicine to fight hunger and disease. Concerning humanitarian aid, South Korea has supplied grain, agricultural products, fertilizer, clothing, and medicine directly or coordinated with the United Nations as temporary relief measures. In the medium run, North Korea should coordinate its resource allocation with South Korea in the process of transformation to reduce adjustment costs in a unified Korea. Seoul can support the economic transformation of North Korea in factor mobilization, resource allocation, overseas marketing, and capitalist know-how such as introduction of property rights, application of a price system, and privatization of state-owned enterprises. Sufficient supply of capital and technology is essential for North Korea to take off from the deserted land, but it is impossible for North Korea to access foreign capital markets as long as U.S. sanctions remain unchanged. The first thing to be done for North Korea to access international capital market is to resolve military problems with the United States and South Korea, including development and proliferation of missiles, as well as withdrawal of conventional weapons from the front. This is fundamental for peace and stability in the Korean peninsula, which should be resolved subject to transparency and verification as soon as possible. It is important for North Korea to show its true intention to respect peace and stability on the peninsula not by words, but by actions.

The threat of breaking the Agreed Framework with brinkmanship by North Korea may cause a serious problem with the United States, which could not be an option if North Korea does not want to be another Iraq.[97] Inter-Korean arms reduction would be the second step of strategic conciliation.

42. In the first step, if North Korea is released from U.S. economic sanctions after its resolving military issues with the United States and removing its name from the list of terrorists,[98] North Korea could access IMF and the World Bank by joining as a member with the submission of economic statistics reports. Second, it could borrow money from commercial banks in foreign countries by normalizing diplomatic relations, through international capital markets, and inter-bank loans. Third, Seoul could contribute a substantial sum of money as a "peace dividend" by diverting its defense budget to the non-defense sector after signing a peace treaty with disarmament between the two Koreas. Fourth, North Korea expects $10 billion worth of World War Two compensation from Japan once their diplomatic relations are normalized. Fifth, Pyongyang could obtain foreign exchange by attracting FDI for industries having comparative advantage, and creating a trade surplus from exports as well as from foreign travelers. Fifth, once the North Korean economy is revived, domestic savings and other surpluses will be an important source for investment. Labor exports would bring in foreign exchanges, by such manual labor as wood-cutting in Siberia or cleaning at foreign facilities. Sixth, self-sufficiency in grain production could reduce foreign exchange demand for its imports as humanitarian aid helped previously. The second step is for the two Koreas to coordinate in resource allocation. It is desirable to reduce adjustment costs in the unified Korea by balancing the industrial structure in the peninsula. The priority of North Korean investment is in agriculture for self-sufficiency of food production, labor-intensive industries for comparative advantage, and infrastructure arranged by needed basis but more than sufficient in advanced time. The third step of cooperation lies in efficient operations with productivity growth through joint-ventures for technology transfer, marketing networks, and training in management skills. The fourth step is to transform the socialist system by allowing personal property rights, adjusting to the price mechanism, and privatizing state owned industries.[99] However, the "most important revolution" would be the "revolution in minds, in our heads, in us ourselves"[100] as Mikhail Gorbachev declared in November 1990.

43. South Korea should also improve its capabilities by enhancing competition in politics, economy and society; while North Korea improves its economic readiness for a unified Korea. In *politics and government*, unfair competition in the electoral process of South Korea reduces the efficiency of the political system. Each political party forms a nomination committee to select the candidates running for electoral districts of the National Assembly. Since the chairman of each party organizes the nomination committee, it is similar to the political party chairman selecting the candidates running for members of the National Assembly. In other words, the chairman of the political party steals the first-election rights of party members in each

electoral district, which is against even basic principles of democracy. Thus, South Korean politics are controlled by a dictatorship of chairman of each political party. It may be easy for political factions to fortify their preoccupied power within the party, but monopoly in politics disturbs the normal function of the democratic system and reduces its efficiency. In the United States, the primary election requires that candidates of all levels compete with each other as party members within each electoral district. No candidate can be chosen by someone other than party members of each electoral district. South Korea should give primary election rights back to the people.[101] In addition, the campaign funding law should be uniformly enforced by the government because the unlawful collection of campaign funds jeopardizes fair competition in campaign advertising. If soft money is not controlled, it could be a source of corruption in the future. Meanwhile, Political appointees and career officers in the administration should clearly recognize their professional roles. Some career officers such as foreign services and uniform officers believe that they deserve the highest position within the ministry, which makes them opportunists and weakens professionalism in the government. Finally, the government must have a system of checks-and-balances in its organization. The efficiency of administration depends on individual capability, which is enhanced by harmonized working environment without factional prejudice and hidden discrimination by unfairness.

44. In *economy and business*, economic problems in South Korea are caused by lack of market competition with an abundance of government intervention. The traditional welfare theorem states that a government cannot do any better than the market, and market efficiency is achieved by the Pareto optimal allocation of resources, which defines that no one could be better off by reallocating resources without making someone else worse off.[102] While public goods are contributing to market failures, the government attaches both imperfect competition and external effects to overcome those failures.[103] The contradiction remains in the policy reality everywhere although the state pursues the harmonized measures in various ways. The goals of government intervention in the market lie in either maintaining capitalistic efficiency or promoting socialistic equality (paragraph 21). The ultimate goal is to secure continuous growth without losing equality. Another problem of the role of government is government failures that raise operational costs without achieving the goals. Anne O. Krueger pointed out two elements of government failures: failures of commission and failures of omission. The former comes from inappropriate state intervention, while the latter comes from negligence of state intervention.[104] It is observed that market failures and government failures exist together in South Korea. Since the nature of power shows increasing returns to scale, incumbent political power is used to acquire economic power, and economic power is used to acquire political power, which generates monopolies in politics and economy through the political-economic complex in the system.[105] The financial crisis in 1997 provided lessons, but nevertheless corruption exists and more reforms are still needed.[106] Despite obvious evidences of a tax evasion case of major newspaper owners in South Korea, for example, the opposition party was strongly against the charge of tax evasion. Both monopoly and corruption reduce

economic efficiency, which negatively affects growth of GNP and personal income in average. If nothing is done for above problems, the damage would be widened.

45. In *society and education*, it has been recently reported that an increasing number of South Korean students is coming to the United States for early education even for elementary school. This is a kind of "exit" because "voice" is not working through the political process. When each individual is healthy and capable, the society would be dynamic and productive. Education must be to develop potential capabilities of a person, by acquiring knowledge for wise judgment, harmonizing emotion for bravery, and strengthening body for energy. Those elements are necessary for individual to join society as a healthy member. However, foreigners may say that education in South Korea looks like a battle to attack Mount-Admission because admission to a certain university seems to guarantee their future. Severe competition for college admissions makes high school boys stay in the classroom day and night for additional lessons, so that they do not have time to enjoy exercises with friends and to engage in emotional training. As a result, the final product of education is less fruitful but more egoistic than that of balanced education in advanced countries. In addition, unbalanced investment in education causes problems in society. South Korea produces many degree holders of graduate schools each year, while many positions of manual workers are rising but not filled, a wasting resources. Over-investment in education creates bottlenecks in one sector and idle capacities in the other in labor supply. It would be unhealthy for society and unproductive for the economy if highly educated people have no jobs,[107] but ironically, this is a problem of resource allocation created by market forces in South Korea. Meanwhile, the rigidity of the labor market is a serious problem in South Korea because wages are much higher than market prices due to oligopoly of labor unions. High wages force domestic industries to move abroad, which reduces domestic employment. The bottom line is that the firms can survive in the world markets only by making profits. If firms could not survive, there would be no winners because nobody has job.[108] Finally, a healthy society is happy and productive and expands the nation's capabilities. It is urgent for South Korea to stop "Exit."

Summary and Conclusion

46. This study has analyzed relations between regional integration and the Korean peninsula with inter-Korean economic cooperation. In economics, contemporary trade theories explain gains from trade by taking comparative advantage, expanding the production possibility frontier and generating welfare gains to trading partners. In international relations, disappearance of enemies in the post-cold war period discourages realists, but encourages liberalists and constructivists, while a new trend of regional integration expedites globalization. The impact of regionalization as well as globalization is wide and deep. Politically, international pressures from global or regional superpowers are so influential that nation-states lose their independence in their decision-making. Economically, income disparities between core and periphery remain widened because infant industries cannot be protected. Strategically, a strong economic bond with rival countries reduces possible military conflict between nation-

states, although trade imbalance causes more disputes on the tactical level. In society, non-governmental organizations become influential, while power of nation-states declines. In culture, globalization expedites convergence and homogenization, rather than the clash, of different cultures or civilization in the long run, because economic integration helps political integration, which expedites cultural changes.

47. Although regional integration appears to be growing trend, it is not a universal solution. For example, APEC was created by twelve founding member states in 1989 and its membership was expanded to twenty-one across four continents. APEC is based on the sprit of openness and partnership to pursue continuous economic growth, to reduce trade and investment barriers, to share benefits of economic development, to improve education and training, to advance in telecommunications and transportation, and to protect the environment. A problem of APEC lies in disparities of economic development between subregions including Northeast Asia, Southeast Asia, the Western Pacific, North America, and South America. Each supports subregionalism, applying regionalism for member states and multilateralism for non-member states. It is agreed that subregionalization is an intermediate step and indirect route for a small state to reach regional integration. A recent trend of subregionalization such as a Korea-Japan-China FTA has been a concern of Europe and America because a new Asian FTA will benefit member states at the cost of EU and NAFTA, and invites increasing competition between three megablocs. Figure 3 shows the relationship between regionalization and economic development. Assuming the position "+" to be an origin, Quadrant I represents the best (EU and NAFTA) indicating positive signs in both horizontal and vertical factors, while quadrant III represents the worst (Middle East and Central Asia) indicating negative signs in both. Quadrant II is developed but less regionalized, and Quadrant IV is less developed but regionalized. Those imply that openness of trade and investment has positively contributed to economic growth, and advanced economies have experienced regional integration earlier than others.

Figure 3. Regionalizaiton and Economic Development

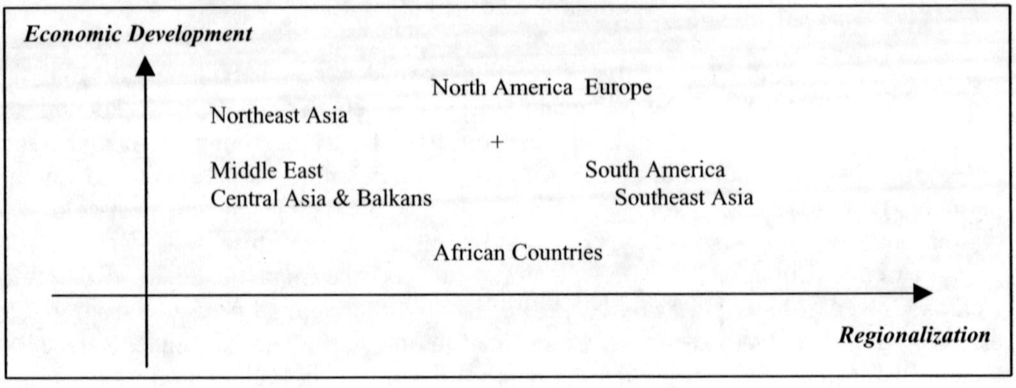

48. Regional integration is helpful for inter-Korean economic cooperation if South Korea benefits from it and its spillover effects are transferred to North Korea, which is currently isolated from regional integration. The benefits will go directly to North Korea if Pyongyang opens its door to the world. In fact, economic assistant programs need two requirements: the giver should have sustainable capabilities to supply goods and services, while the taker should get ready to capitalize external assistance for its economic development. On the one hand, the theory of globalism explains that foreign trade and investment invite democratization, so that North Korea cannot maintain its totalitarian system if it pursues economic development. Market openness invites freedom waves into its society, which threatens its regime. Meanwhile, continuous isolation pushes its economy down to the bottom, which also threatens its survival. Therefore, North Korea has a limited policy option: economic transformation along with political reform. In reality, the leadership of North Korea is gradually moving toward openness, but faces barriers due to its military intention threatening South Korea. As long as Pyongyang develops weapons of mass destruction and deploys its conventional weapons near Seoul, North-South confrontation remains unchanged in reality. As long as transparency and verification are not provided, the sunshine policy is not sustainable because of possible cheating and comparative gains by the North. The U.S. military strategists would not allow North Korea to play the game for cheating and more gains from blind engagement in order to maintain regional peace and stability. If North Korea wants economic gains, it should pay the price by cooperating with South Korea and its allies in political-military affairs honestly. On the other hand, South Korea has very limited economic capabilities to support the North. In other words, inter-Korean economic cooperation is limited because North Korea is not ready to utilize external assistance and South Korea has limited capabilities to rescue the North, which must be resolved by mutual efforts.

49. *Policy Recommendations to North Korea*: (a) In international relations, North Korea should normalize its diplomatic relations with the United States and Japan as soon as possible. To delay to gain more is, in fact, to lose more in terms of time cost in economic development. (b) In domestic politics, North Korea should liberalize its political system because it is impossible to control information by the state in the age of globalization. People will know anyway that the lagged political system would not work. (c) To improve its economy, North Korea should open the market by introducing the price system just like China in 1978. Do not hesitate to transform its socialist system, which was buried a decade ago. (d) Strategically, the world would not allow either North Korea or South Korea to attack the other side. The heavy burden of military spending reduces productive investment, and invites economic decline. It would be smart to sign a peace treaty with South Korea, guaranteed by both the United States and China. (e) The world powers are busy to resolve their own problems. Do not expect foreign countries to solve the Korean problems. South Korea is the only state to volunteer to help North Korea. Keep in mind that there is no place for North Korea to go but to collapse if it is not ready to capitalize economic assistance from the South. (f) The world is smart enough to recognize the negotiation tactics of North

Korea, which was part of the doctrine used for communist expansion during the cold war period. If North Korea hesitates to take these actions, the survival of its regime would be hopeless. The ball is in Pyongyang's court and nobody feels in any hurry to resolve North Korean problems, except the leaders of North Korea itself.

50. *Policy Recommendation to South Korea*: The Sunshine Policy was successful in attracting Kim Jung Il to appear on the scene, although he had to do the same for his own good. It is obvious that South Korea has very limited capabilities to assist North Korea, so that massive economic assistance from the South would not be sustainable. Therefore, South Korea should focus on the expansion of the nation's capabilities in politics, economy, and society. (a) South Korea should introduce natural freshness into politics by inviting fair competition and removing the dictatorship of political party chairmen. It is possible to create a system of primary elections for candidates running for the National Assembly by prohibiting a system of party-ruled nominations. The campaign funding laws should be fairly enforced by the government. (b) In the economy, major problems of South Korea are caused by a lack of market competition with an abundance of government intervention, resulting in both market failures and government failures. The government should do the right things, and don't do the wrong things, and expedite reforms continuously. (c) South Korea should stop "Exit" by building the system of "Voice" as soon as possible. It should resolve the problems of college admissions, either by renaming all schools by serial numbers or removing the names of problem-making schools, and or introducing a ceiling system in employment. Surplus of high intellectuals and shortage of manual workers create social problems, which also should be resolved. (d) The leaders of South Korea should not use inter-Korean relations for their political advantage. Instead, national policy should be chosen by the consensus of the people. A huge amount of tax money should not be used without approval of the National Assembly representing the people. (e) Some people of South Korea blame both government and business, and they believe that they are not responsible for nation's problems. "If we know that we are wrong, we can fix it." But if we do not know that we are wrong (because we are not responsible), we cannot fix it. Socrates taught us "Know yourself!" The citizens of South Korea should recognize that they are the people who are responsible for nation's problems.

Endnotes

[1] Michael Schulz, Frederik Soderbaum and Joakim Ojendal, "A Framework for Understanding Regionalization," in the same authors, ed., *Regionalization in a Globaling World: A Comparative Perspective on Forms, Actors and Processes*, New York: ZED Books, 2001, p. 3.
[2] "Bagehot Ideas, at last," *The Economist*, June 30th, 2001, p. 54. Politicians are now having the arguments that should have been aired during the election. "He was outraged by Tony Blair's refusal in a television interview to say that a Labour government should help the poor by increasing taxes on the rich."
[3] Schulz, Soderbaum and Ojendal, ed., *Regionalization in a Globaling World*, 264-5.
[4] Editorial, "Chadenfreude Economics," *The Wall Street Journal*, July 10, 2001, p. A18.
[5] "China and Korea: Fraternal Meetings," *The Economists*, September 8th, 2001, p. 45.
[6] Robert Gilpin, "APEC in a New International Order," in Donald C. Hellmann and Kenneth B. Pyle, ed., *From APEC to Xanadu: Creating a Viable Community in the Post-Cold War Pacific*, Armonk, New York: M.E. Sharpe, 1997, p. 15.
[7] Harold James, *International Monetary Cooperation Since Bretton Woods*, Washington, DC: International Monetary Fund, 1996, pp. 22-57, Chapter 2. "Prosperity Has No Fixed Limits." Because the International Trade Organization (ITO) was never ratified by the U.S. Congress, GATT became a weaker substitute.
[8] Rondo Cameron, *A Concise Economic History of the World: From Paleolithic Times to the Present*, 3rd ed., New York: Oxford University Press, 1997, pp. 371-5. Jackson J. Spielvogel, *Western Civilization: Comprehensive Volume*, New York: West Publishing Company, 1997, pp. 995-1001.
[9] Anders Aslund, *How Russia Became a Market Economy*, Washington, DC: The Brookings Institution, 1999, pp. 109-115. Alternative Currency and Payments Arrangements.
[10] Rudiger Dornbusch, Wilhelm Nolling, and Richard Layard, ed., *Postwar Economic Reconstruction and Lessons for the East Today*, Cambridge, Massachusetts: MIT Press, 1993. Edward F. Denison and William K. Chung, *How Japan's Economy Grew So Fast: The Sources of Postwar Expansion*, Washington, D.C.: The Brookings Institution, 1976.
[11] Willem Molle, *The Economics of European Integration: Theory, Practice, Policy*, 3rd ed., Brookfield, Vermont: Ashgate Publishing Company, 1997, pp. 27-51.
[12] Holand Hunter, "Soviet Economic Problems and Alternative Policy Responses" in Morris Bornstein, ed., *The Soviet Economy: Continuity and Change*, Boulder, Colorado: Westview Press, 1981, pp. 345-62. R. W. Davies, "Economic Planning in the USSR" in the same book, pp. 7-38.
[13] Jan S. Prybyla, "On Systemic Transition: Will China Go Capitalist?" in Carl Linden and Jan S. Prybyla, ed., *Russia and China on the Eve of a New Millennium*, New Brunswick, New Jersey: Transaction Publishers, 1997, pp. 209-49. Charles Wolf Jr., "China's Capitalists Join the Party," *The New York Times on the Web*, August 13, 2001. Erik Eckholm, "Chinese Censors Shut Down Marxist Journal Critical of Jiang," *The New York Times on the Web*, Aug 16, 2001. For a negative view, see Gordon G. Chang, *The Coming Collapse of China*, New York: Random House, 2001.
[14] Norris C. Clement and et al., *North American Economic Integration: Theory and Practice*, Northampton, Massachusetts: Edward Elgar, 1999, pp. 55-122. Ralph H. Folsom, *NAFTA in a Nutshell*, St. Paul, Minnesota: West Group, 1999, pp. 247-8.
[15] Amitav Acharya, *Constructing a Security Community in Southeast Asia: ASEAN and the Problem of Regional Order*, New York: Routeledge, 2001, pp. 1-14.

[16] See http://www.aseansec.org/newasean/archive.html for "Chairman's Statement: The First ASEAN Regional Forum," Bangkok, 25 July 1994. EU, Russia and China joined as founding members.

[17] See http://www.apecsec.org.sg/member/dateofjoin.html for the date of joining of member states; and Hellmann and Pyle, ed., *From APEC to Xanadu,* pp. 203-38.

[18] Cedric Dupont, "European Integration and APEC: The Search for Institutional Blueprints," in Vinod K. Aggarwal and Charles E. Morrison, ed., *Asia-Pacific Crossroads: Regime Creation and Future of APEC*, New York: St. Martin's Press, 1998, pp. 364-7.

[19] Gerald M. Meier, *Leading Issues in Economic Development*, 5th ed., New York: Oxford University Press, 1989, p. 105-10, II.C.1. Dependency Theories of Underdevelopment.

[20] *Ibid*., pp. 297-304, VI.A.4. Import Substitution and pp. 305-10, VI.A.5. Export Promotion. For further, see Raul Prebisch, "Five States in My Thinking on Development," in Gerald M. Meier and Dudley Seers, *Pioneers in Development*, New York: Oxford University Press, 1984, pp. 175-91. Prebisch (1901-1986) lectures that the terms of trade of primary exports from the periphery are deteriorated in comparison with those of manufacturing imports from the center. So the periphery countries abandon the market-oriented development strategies and adopt import substitution industrialization strategies.

[21] William R. Cline, *International Debt Reexamined*, Washington., DC: Institute for Intlernation-al Economics, 1995.

[22] Ching-yuan Lin, "East Asia and Latin America as Contrasting Models," *Economic Development and Cultural Change* Volume 36 Number 3 Supplement (April 1988): s153-s197.

[23] "Central America: Small, Vulnerable – and Disunited," *The Economist*, August 11, 2001, pp. 28-9.

[24] Don D. Marshall, *Caribbean Political Economy at the Crossroads: NAFTA and Regional Development- alism*, New York: St. Martin's Press, Inc., 1998, pp. 43-99.

[25] Reuters, "Latin American Leaders Appeal to Bush on Argentina," *The New York Times on the Web*, August 18, 2001; and Associate Press, "Argentine Debt Crisis Takes Stage as Latin American Leaders Gather," *Interactive Wall Street Journal*, August 17, 2001.

[26] See http://www.opec.org/ with clicking "About APEC" and "History" by order.

[27] Said El-Naggar, ed., *Economic Development of the Arab Countries*, Washington, DC: IMF, 1993; and Said El-Naggar, ed., The Uruguay Round and the Arab Countries, Washington, DC: IMF, 1996.

[28] Zubair Iqbal and Mohsin S. Khan, ed., *Trade Reform and Regional Integration in Africa*, Washington, DC: IMF, 1998, pp. 327-506; I. G. Gatel, ed., *Policies for African Development*, Wash., DC: IMF, 1992.

[29] IMF, *Russian Federation (Economic Review)*, Washington, DC: IMF, 1992; and IMF, *Common Issues and InterRepublic Relations in the Former U.S.S.R.* (*Economic Review)*, Washington., DC: IMF, 1992.

[30] Stephen White, *Russia's New Politics: The Management of a Postcommunist Society*, New York: Cambridge University Press, 2000, pp. 244-7 and 250. For Caspian energy, "Jan H. Kalicki, "Caspian Energy at the Crossroads," *Foreign Affairs*, Vol. 80, No. 5 (Sept./Oct. 2001), pp. 120-34. For transition, see Georg Winckler, ed., *Central and Eastern Europe Road to Growth*, Washington, DC: IMF, 1992; and Thane Gustafson, *Capitalism Russian-Style*, New York: Cambridge University Press, 1999.

[31] Wilfred J. Ethier, *Modern International Economics*, New York: W. W. Norton & Company, 1983, p. 47.

[32] *Ibid*., p. 48.

[33] Paul R. Krugman and Maurice Obstfeld, *International Economics: Theory and Practice*, 3rd ed., New York: HarperCollins College Publishers, 1994, pp. 64-86.
[34] Paul R. Viotti and Mark V. Kauppi, *International Relations Theory: Realism, Pluralism, Globalism, and Beyond*, Boston, Massachusetts: Allyn and Bacon, 1999, pp. 54-198. For major works of realists, see Edward Hallett Carr, *The Twenty Years' Crisis 1919-1939*, New York: Harpers & Row, 1964; Hans J. Morgenthau, *Politics among Nations: The Struggle for Power and Peace*, brief ed., New York: McGraw-Hill, Inc., 1993; Raymond Aron, *International Relations: A Theory of Peace and War*, Garden City, New Jersey: Doubleday, 1973; Kenneth N. Waltz, *Man, the State, and War: A Theoretical Analysis*, New York: Columbia University Press, 1959; Waltz, *Theory of International Politics*, New York: Random House, 1979; Robert Gilpin, *U.S. Power and the Multinational Corporation: The Political Economy of Foreign Direct Investment*, New York: Basic Book, 1975; Gilpin, *War and Change in World Politics*, New York: Cambridge University Press, 1981. For neorealism, see Richard Ashley, "The Poverty of Neorealism," in Robert O. Keohane, ed., *Neorealism and Its Critics*, New York: Columbia U. Press, 1986, pp. 255-300.
[35] Joseph M. Grieco, "Anarchy and the Limits of Cooperation: A Realist Critique of the Newest Liberal Institutionalism" in Charles Lipson and Benjamin J. Cohen, ed., *Theory and Structure in International Political Economy: An International Organization Reader*, Cambridge, MA: The MIT Press, 1999, p. 11.
[36] Robert O. Keohane, *After Hegemony: Cooperation and Discord in the World Political Economy*, Princeton, New Jersey: Princeton University Press, 1984.
[37] Andrew Moravcsik, "Taking Preferences Seriously: A Liberal Theory of International Politics," in Lipson and Cohen, ed., *Theory and Structure in International Political Economy:* pp. 36-44.
[38] *Ibid.*, pp. 44-53, Variants of Liberal Theory.
[39] Joseph S. Nye, "Neorealism and Neoliberalism," *World Politics*, 40 (January 1988): 235-51; and Jack Knight, "Explaining the Rise of Neoliberalism: The Mechanisms of Institutional Change," in John L. Campbell and Ove K. Pederson, ed., *The Rise of Neoliberalism and Institutional Analysis*, Princeton, New Jersey: Princeton University Press, 2001, pp. 27-50.
[40] Alexander Wendt, "Anarchy Is What States Make of It: The Social Construction of Power Politics," in Lipson and Cohen, ed., *Theory and Structure in International Pol. Economy*, p. 76.
[41] *Ibid.*, p. 77. See Robert O. Keohane, "International Institutions: Two Approaches," *International Studies Quarterly* 32 (December 1988), pp. 379-96; and Nicholas Onuf, *World of Our Making*, Columbia, South Carolina: University of South Carolina Press, 1989.
[42] Amitav Acharya, *Constructing a Security Community in Southeast Asia: ASEAN and the Problem of Regional Order*, New York: Routledge, 2001, pp. 14-46.
[43] Samuel S. Kim, "Korea and Globalization (Segyehwa): A Framework for Analysis," in Samuel S. Kim, ed., *Korea's Globalization*, New York: Cambridge University Press, 2000, p. 18. "I define globalization as a set of process of stretching and intensifying worldwide interconnectedness in all aspects of human relations and transactions – economic, social, cultural, environmental, political, diplomatic, and security –such that events, decisions, and activities in one part of the world have immediate consequences for individuals, groups, and states in other parts of the world."
[44] Viotti and Kauppi, *International Relations Theory,* pp. 341-2. Philip G. Cerny, "Globalization and the Changing Logic of Collective Action," *International Organization*, 49 (4) (Autumn 1995), pp. 595-625.
[45] Robert W. Cox, "A Perspective on Globalization," in James H. Mittelman, ed., *Golbalization: Critical Reflections,* Boulder, Colorado: Lynne Rienner Publishers, Inc., 1996, pp. 21-32; Bill

Emmott, "The 20th Century," *The Economist*, September 11-17, 1999, p. 41; Karl Polanyi, *The Great Transformation: The Political and Economic Origins of Our Time*, Boston: Beacon Press, 1957.

[46] "The Internet's New Borders," *The Economist*, August 11, 2001, pp. 1-2. "Special Report: Geography and the Net -- Putting It in Its Place," in the same issue, pp. 18-20.

[47] Operating costs per mile for the world's airlines fell by 60 percent between 1960 and 1990 (for 30 years), while maritime transport costs fell by more than two-third between 1920 and 1990 (for 70 years).

[48] Dale W. Jorgenson, *Productivity (Vol. 2): International Comparisons of Economic Growth*, Cambridge, Massachusetts: The MIT Press, 1995; and Kevin H. O'Rourke and Jeffrey G. Williamson, *Globalization and History: The Evolution of a Nineteenth Century Atlantic Economy*, Cambridge, Mass.: MIT Press, 1999. The former views convergence of productivity, and the latter does that of factor prices.

[49] Nurit Kliot and David Newman, ed., *Geopolitics at the End of the Twentieth Century" The Changing World Political Map*, Portland, Oregon: Frank Cass, 2000; and Wheegook Kim, "From Confrontation to Cooperation: A New paradigm for Inter-Korean Relations," *The Korean Journal of Defense Analysis*, Vol. XI, No. 2 (Winter 1999), pp. 42-3.

[50] Martin Wolf, "Will the Nation-State Survive Globalization?," *Foreign Affairs*, Vol. 80, No. 1 (January/February 2001), pp. 178-90.

[51] Susan Strange, *The Retreat of the State: The Diffusion of Power in the World Economy*, trans., Victoria Elliott, New York: Cambridge University Press, 1996; and Jean-Marie Guehenno, *The End of the Nation-State*, Minneapolis, Minnesota: University of Minnesota Press, 1993; and Bruce R. Scott, "The Great Divide in the Global Village," *Foreign Affairs*, Vol. 80, No. 1 (January/February 2001), pp. 160-77.

[52] Judith Miller, "Globalization Widens Rich-Poor Gap, U..N. Report Says," *The New York Times on the Web*, July 13, 1999; Barbara Stallings, ed., Global Change, *Regional Response: The New International Context of Development*, New York: Cambridge University Press, 1995, pp. 1-30.

[53] Joseph S. Nye, "Hard Power, Soft Power," *Boston Globe*, August 6, 1999.

[54] Kenichi Omae, *The End of the Nation State: The Rise of Regional Economies*, New York: Free Press, 1995, p. 21. Samuel P. Huntington, *The Clash of Civilization: Remarking of the World Order*, New York: A Touchstone Book, 1996.

[55] Merilee S. Grindle, "In Quest of the Political: The Political Economy of Development Policymaking," in Gerald M. Meier and Joseph E. Stiglitz, *Frontiers of Development Economics: The Future in Pers*pective, New York: Oxford University Press, 2001, 345-80.

[56] Francis Fukuyama, *The End of History and The Last Man*, New York: Avon Books, 1992. For another view, see Fareed Zakaria, "The Rise of Illiberal Democracy," *Foreign Affairs*, Vol. 76, No. 6. (November /December 1997), pp. 22-43.

[57] Ralf Dahrendorf, "The Third Way and Liberty: An Authoritarian Streak in Europe's New Center," *Foreign Affairs*, Vol. 78, No. 5 (September/October 1999), p. 15.

[58] Charles E. Morrison, "APEC: The Evolution of an Institution," in Aggarwal and Morrison, *Asia-Pacific Crossroads: Regime Creation and Future of APEC*, pp. 1-22.

[59] Robert C. Hine, "Bring Two Continents: EU-ASEAN Trade and Investment," in Roger Strange, Jim Slater and Corrado Molteni, ed., *The European Union and ASEAN: Trade and Investment Issues*, New York: St. Martin's Press, LLC, 2000, pp. 14-5.

[60] Hellmann and Pyle, ed., *From APEC to Xanadu: Creating a Viable Community in the Post-Cold War Pacific*, pp. 203-238; and http://www.apecsec.org.sg/apec_organization/brochure2001.html. John J. Tkacik, Dana R. Dillon, Balbina Hwang, and Sara J Fitzgerald, "Prparing for the

APEC Summit: Mobilizing Asina Allies for War," *Backgrounder: Executive Summary* No. 1487, The Heritage Foundation, October 4, 2001. Regarding a new development of Sino-American relations after terrorist attack, see Phillpe C. Saunders, "Can 9-11 Provide a Fresh Start for Sino-U.S. Relations?" *Special-Policy-Fourm #33*, Nautilus Institute, November 1, 2001 at http://www.nautilus.org/fora/Special-Policy-Forum/33_Saunders.html.

[61] Disappearance of immediate enemies or gradual emergence of nationalism in the post cold war period reduces the significance of military alliance with the United States such as in Japan and South Korea.

[62] C. Fred Bergsten, "America's Two-Front Economic Conflict," *Foreign Affairs* Vol. 80, No. 2 (March /April 2001), 00. 16-27.

[63] Review & Outlook, "A Trans-Atlantic Single Market?," *Interactive Wall Street Journal*, July 27, 2001. "The British chancellor of the exchequer, Gordon Brown, wants to pave the way for what in the fullness of time could be a trans-Atlantic single market. He called yesterday for a first step of abolishing all industrial tariffs between the European Union and the United States. Mr. Brown's initiative deserves support."

[64] Dennis C. Blair and John T. Hanley Jr., "From Wheels to Webs: Reconstructing Asia-Pacific Security Arrangements," *The Washington Quarterly*, Vol. 24, No. 1 (Winter 2001), pp. 7-17; and Emanuel Alder and Michael N. Barnett, *Security Communities (Cambridge Studies in International Relations 62)*, New York: Cambridge University Press, December 1998.

[65] Yoshinobu Yamamoto and Tsutomu Kikuchi, "Japan's Approach to APEC and Regime Creation in the Asia-Pacific," in Aggarwal and Morrison, *Asia-Pacific Crossroads*, pp. 193.

[66] Akio Watanabe and Tsutomu Kikuchi, "Japan's Perspective on PAEC: Community or Associations?" in Hellmann and Pyle, ed., *From APEC to Xanadu*, p. 136.

[67] *Ibid*., p. 207. Negative criticism came from Japanese commercialism in the 1980s. (a) The United States helped Japan to rebuild its political and economic system of democratic capitalism. (b) Japan could use resources entirely to build its economy under the U.S. security umbrella while others spent high defense budget. (c) Japan made huge profits by supplying goods and services to Korean War and Vietnam War. (d) Japan had golden opportunities to export labor-intensive products to the United States in the 1960s and 1970s until late comers were restricted in the 1980s. (e) Japan commercialized U.S.-supplied technology to penetrate the U.S. market; (f) Japan maintained huge trade deficit with the United States and others, but protected Japanese markets. (g) Japanese overseas investment was not for infrastructure but for consumer goods, which was not helpful for economic growth of the host countries.

[68] Kenneth B. Pyle, "The Context of APEC: U.S.- Japan Relations," in Hellmann and Pyle, ed., *From APEC to Xanadu*, pp. 98-125.

[69] Leonard J. Schoppa, "Japan, the Reluctant Reformer," *Foreign Affairs*, Vol. 80, No. 5 (September/ October 2001), pp. 76-90. "Japan's citizens have learned to find private solutions to their country's many ills, just as Japanese corporations have moved more and more of their operations overseas. But this trend has only driven Japan into deeper economic straits." The people choose "exit" strategies if the government does not hear "voice" as policy input. See Albert O. Hirschman, *Exit, Voice and Loyalty: Responses to Decline in Firms, Organizations, and States*, Cambridge, MA: Harvard University Press, 1970; S. Schiavo-Campo and P. S. A. Sundaram, *To Serve and To Preserve: Improving Public Administration in Competitive World*, Manila, Philippines: Asian Development Bank, 2001, pp. 497-532; James Brooke, "Accelerating Decline in Japan Evokes Rust Belt Comparisons," *The New York Times on the Web*, August 31, 2001. "The reality is that the de-industrialization is happening very rapidly in Japan."

[70] Zhang Yunling, "China and APEC: Interests, Opportunities, and Challenges," in Hellmann and Pyle, ed., *From APEC to Xanadu*, pp. 195-202.

[71] Zhang Yunling, "China and APEC," in Aggarwal and Morrison, *Asia-Pacific Crossroads*, pp. 222-3.
[72] Weixing Hu, "Economic and Security Cooperation in Northeast Asia: A Chinese Perspective," in Tsuneo Akaha, *Politics and Economics in Northeast Asia: National and Regionalism in Connection*, New York: St. Martin's Press, pp. 109-133.
[73] Leslie Chang, "Olympics Chief Softens Position on Monitoring Rights in China," *The Wall Street Journal*, August 28, 2001, A8. "The International Olympic Committee's new president, Jacques Rogge, appeared to step back from previous suggestions that the IOC would monitor human rights in China in the lead-up to the 2008 Summer Games in Beijing…The IOC is not a political body."
[74] Hadi Soesastro, "APEC: An ASEAN Perspective," in Hellmann and Pyle, ed., *From APEC to Xanadu*, pp. 174-94; and Yoshino Fumio, "ASEAN in APEC," Sekiguchi Sueo and Noda Makito, *Road to ASEAN-10: Japanese Perspective on Economic Integration*, New York: JCIE, 1999, pp. 37-59.
[75] Michael G. Plummer, "ASEAN and Institutional Nesting in the Asia-Pacific: Leading from behind in APEC," in Aggarwal and Morrison, *Asia-Pacific Crossroads*, pp. 279-314.
[76] Maxwell A. Cameron, "Nesting NAFTA in APAC: The Political Economy of Open Subregionalism," in Aggarwal and Morrison, *Asia-Pacific Crossroads*, pp. 257-78.
[77] Robert Scollay and John P. Gilbert, *New Regional Trading Arrangements in the Asia Pacific?* (Policy Analyses #63), Washington, DC: Institute for International Economics, May 2001, p. 15.
[78] A. O. Krueger, "Are Preferential Trading Arrangements Trade-Liberalizing or Protectionist?," *Journal of Economic Perspectives*, Vol. 13, No. 4 (Winter 1999), 105-24.
[79] A. Panagariya, "The Regionalism Debate: An Overview," *World Economy*, Vol. 22 (1999), 447-511.
[80] Fred Bergsten, "Towards a Tripartite World," *The Economist* on the Web, July 13, 2000; and "The Uneasy Triangle," *The Economist* on the Web, March 15, 2001.
[81] Robert A. Scalapino, "The Changing Order in Northeast Asia and Prospects for U.S.-Japan-China-Korea Relations," in Lee-Jay Cho, Myung-Kwang Park and Choong-nam Kim, ed., *Korea and the Asia-Pacific Region*, Hawaii: East-West Center, 2001, pp. 35-64.
[82] Doug Struck, "North Korea, China Rekindle Old Flame: With U.S.-N. Korean Talks Frozen, China Bolsters Ties with Kim," *The Washington Post Internet*, September 5, 2001.
[83] William T. Pendley, "Restructuring U.S.-Korea Relations and the U.S. East Asia Strategy for the Twenty -First Century," in Lee-Jay Cho, Myung-Kwang Park and Choong-nam Kim, ed., *Korea and the Asia-Pacific Region*, Hawaii: East-West Center, 2001, pp. 65-103.
[84] Chung-in Moon and Dae-Won Ko, "Korea's Perspective on Economic and Security Cooperation in Northeast Asia," in Tsuneo Akaha, ed., *Politics and Economics in Northeast Asia: Nationalism and Regionalism in Contention*, New York: St. Martin's Press, 1999, pp. 177-205.
[85] Yong-Kul Won, "East Asian Economic Integration: A Korean Perspective," *The Journal of East Asian Affairs*, Vol. XV, No. 1 (Spring/Summer 2001), pp. 72-96; Joshua Kurlantzick, "Is East Asia Integrating?," *The Washington Quarterly*, Vol. 24, Nol 4 (Autumn 2001), pp. 19-28.
[86] Robert Scollay and John P. Gilbert, *New Regional Trading Arrangements in the Asia Pacific?* (Policy Analyses #63), Washington, DC: Institute for International Economics, May 2001.
[87] Inbom Choi and Jeffrey J. Schott, *Free Trade between Korea and the United States?* (Policy Analyses #62), Washington, DC: Institute for International Economics, April 2001.
[88] http://www.nautilus.org/dprkrenew/index.html, http://www.nautilus.org/admin/staff/peter.html, and http://www.nautilus.org/dprkrenew/wpowerarticle.html.
[89] http://www.aseansec.org/menu.asp?action=3&content=2.

[90] Wheegook Kim, "Democracy and Economic Development in South Korea and its Application," *International Journal of Korean Studies*, Vol. II, No. 1 (Fall/Winter 1998), pp. 69-99. Samuel S. Kim, ed., *Korea's Globalization*, New York: Cambridge University Press, 2000.
[91] The Ministry of National Defense, *Defense White Paper 2000*, Seoul: Korea: Ministry of National Defense, 2000, pp. 48 and 271.
[92] For the likelihood of reform, see Marcus Noland, *Avoiding the Apocalypse: The Future of the Two Koreas*, Washington, DC: Institute for International Economics, June 2000, pp. 281-4. "There is little sign that the North Korean regime is contemplating such output boosting reforms."
[93] James Brooke, "Relations with North Korea May Suffer after Seoul Cabinet Walkout," *The New York Times on the Web*, September 4, 2001. "The sunshine policy is failing because the government just pushes money into North Korea," … ""It seems that North Korea just gets what it wants. While South Korea keeps giving this money, in the end we are getting nothing. We feel really dumb and stupid."
[94]Kongdan Oh and Ralph C. Hassig, "Guessing Right and Guessing Wrong about Engagement," *The Journal of East Asian Affairs*, Vol. XV, No. 1. (Spring/Summer 2001), p. 30. "I do have some skepticism about the leader of North Korea, but that's not going to preclude us from trying to achieve…"
[95] "DPRK Arms Control," *NAPSNet Daily Report*, September 10, 2001, Berkeley, California: Nautilus Institute at http://www.nautilus.org/. "the DPRK has imported US$344.3 million worth of various weapons from the PRC, Japan, Russia and Poland since 1991...the DPRK has exported US$914million worth of weapons including missiles and missile parts, missile launching pads, machine guns…and ammunition."
[96] Chong-Wook Chung, "Has North Korea Really Changed?," *Korea Focus*, Vol. 9, No. 2 (March-April 2001), pp. 53-64. "As long as North Korea remains a garrison state, and unless it abandons its military-led political system, it will be impossible for Pyongyang to undertake genuine reform and opening."
[97] Leon V. Sigal, "Reversing US Missteps toward North Korea," *The Boston Globe*, June 23, 2001, p. A 15. "Pyongyang is now warning that it will walk away from the talks if Washington persists. This would spark resentment in Seoul and, in return, anger in Washington."
[98] Wheegook Kim, "From Confrontation to Cooperation: A New paradigm for Inter-Korean Relations," *The Korean Journal of Defense Analysis*, Vol. XI, No. 2 (Winter 1999), pp. 65-72.
[99] Soogil Young, Chang-Jae Lee and Hyoungsoo Zang, "Preparing for the Economic Integration of Two Koreas: Policy Challenges to South Korea, in Marcus Noland, ed., *Economic Integration of the Korean Peninsula*, Washington, DC: Institute for International Economics, January 1998, pp. 251-71.
[100] Stephen White, *Russia's New Politics: The Management of a Postcommunist Society,* p. 28.
[101] George Sorensen, *Democracy and Democratization: Processes and Prospects in a Changing World*, 2nd ed., Boulder, Colorado: Westview Press, 1998, pp. 24-63; and Robert Michels, *Political Parties: A Sociological Study of the Oligarchical Tendencies of Modern Democracy*, translated by Eden and Cedar Paul, New Brunswick, New Jersey: Transaction Publishers, 1999.
[102] Amartya Sen, Nicholas Stern, and Joseph Stiglitz, "Roundtable Discussion, Development Strategies: The Roles of the State and the Private Sector," in World Bank, *Annual Conference on Development Economics 1990* (Proceedings), New York: Oxford University Press, pp. 421-35. P. R. G. Layard and A. A. Walters, *Microeconomic Theory*, New York: McGraw-Hill, 1978, pp. 22-2. State intervention is justified to recover the efficiency in case of market failure due to external effects, public goods, and imperfect competition caused by uncertainty and inadequate information, increasing returns to scale, and entry barriers.

[103] The World Bank, *World Development Report 1997: The State in A Changing World*, New York: Oxford University Press, 1998, p. 27. Public goods are generally provided by governments for infrastructure, defense, law and order, education, public health, antipoverty programs, disaster relief, and so on. They are measures for equality and national security and are necessary to maintain a healthy nation state.

[104] Anne O. Krueger, "Government Failures in Development," *The Journal of Economic Perspectives* 4 (3) (Summer 1990), p. 9-23.

[105] Adam Przeworski and et al., *Sustainable Democracy*, New York: Cambridge University Press, 1995, p. 40, quoted from Frederic C. Lane, *Profits from Power: Protection Rent and Violence Controlling Enterprises*, Albany: State University of New York Press, 1979.

[106] See http://www.keia.org/2korea's%20Economy-full.pdf, Part II. Korea's Structural Reform.

[107] Walter W. McMahon, *Education and Development: Measuring the Social Benefits*, New York: Oxford University Press, 1999, pp. 155-178; George Psacharopoulos and Maureen Woodhal, *Education for Development: An Analysis of Investment Choices*, Washington, DC: The World Bank, 1985, pp. 29-71; Indermit S. Gill and Cho-Sun Ihm, "Republic of Korea," in Indermit S. Gill, Fred Fluitman and Amit Dar, *Vocational Education and Training Reform: Matching Skills to Markets and Budgets*, New York: Oxford University Press, March 2000, pp. 261-93.

[108] Yong Cheol Kim and Chung-in Moon, "Globalization and Workers in South Korea," in Samuel S. Kim, ed., *Korea's Globalization*, New York: Cambridge University Press, 2000, pp. 54-75.

Chapter III
From Confrontation to Cooperation: A New Paradigm of Inter-Korean Relations[*]

Introduction

The fall of the Berlin wall in 1989 introduced a decade of gradual adjustment of the world power structure towards a new order for the coming century. It was the beginning of changes in international relations, from military confrontation to economic cooperation in the post–Cold War period, applying the theory of pluralism rather than that of realism. The increase of trade and investment with lowered international barriers has expedited globalization and accelerated the convergence of different cultures, as technological advancements have brought borderless flows of information. These developments represent the victory of capitalist efficiency over central planning in pursuit of socialist equality. Most of the failed socialist states have transformed their systems in the direction of liberal democracy and a market economy. North Korea, however, remains isolated and hardly changed. Its government's controlling grip has only tightened, and its scarce resources are being used to develop missiles and weapons of mass destruction while the regime continuously requests foreign aid to deal with hundreds of thousands deaths annually from hunger and disease.

Pyongyang's fundamental dilemma in policy choice lies in the conflict between two different goals: political stability and economic development. If North Korea opens the door to trade and investment, waves of freedom will threaten the regime's survival. If North Korea (DPRK) remains closed, on the other hand, the people will continue to suffer from accumulated economic difficulties, also threatening the regime. The wise strategic choice lies in gradual and simultaneous development of politics and the economy, a path China has successfully pursued since 1978. However, Pyongyang has been too cautious to choose that type of balanced policy, so that by delaying openness it has paid more time costs in growth than it has gained from negotiations. Pyongyang seems to understand the mistakes it has made through its survival strategies in the past, and if the missile talks with the United States do bring a breakthrough in building a new peace mechanism on the Korean peninsula, a turning point may be at hand for the North Korean leadership to pursue gradual transformation towards a market economy.

Since South Korea (ROK) has been North Korea's counterpart in military confrontation, it is also partially responsible for the failure to dismantle the Cold War structure on the peninsula. It is true that hard-line conservatives in South Korea dominated the policy-making process in the government until Kim Dae-jung (DJ) took over as president, in February 1998. Despite many difficulties, his engagement policy has been successful in dealing with North Korea and coordinating with the regional

---

[*] Published by *The Korea Journal of Defense Analysis* XI (2) (Winter 1999): 35-77. Reprinted by the permission of the publisher.

powers since that course is in the best interests of all related parties. Meanwhile, the DPRK has utilized the weaknesses of the engagement policy to maximize its benefits in negotiating with Washington and Seoul, as shown in the cases of its missile launch, submarine infiltration, and the North-South naval clash in the Yellow Sea in June 1999. However, inter-Korean economic cooperation will improve step by step as soon as the DPRK begins to change towards openness and agrees to be a normal member of the world community. It is helpful that, as DJ consistently pursues conciliation and cooperation with the North, the South Korean economy is rapidly recovering from the Asian financial crisis.

The fifty years of military confrontation on the Korean peninsula are a by-product of World War Two, Cold War confrontation, and the status quo strategy of the four regional powers in the post–Cold War period.[1] More directly, North Korea cannot survive if China does not supply grain and fuel. But why does China support North Korea? It is obvious that China does not want to face US forces at its Korean border. Pyongyang has blamed the US forces in South Korea for the continued division of the peninsula, but many South Koreans believe it is China that is the major obstacle to Korean unification. As the world environment is prepared for peace and prosperity through globalization, the East Asian regional powers, particularly the United States and China, have been pursuing an engagement policy and potential partnership in the twenty-first century. It must be hoped that the two Koreas will follow their example.

This study sets four goals, to be pursued in four main sections. In the first section the impact of global and regional developments on the Korean peninsula is assessed in terms of globalization of nation-states, which is accelerating the convergence of different cultures and forcing the two Koreas to pursue peaceful coexistence. Second, North Korea's survival strategies are evaluated through a systems analysis of cases such as the naval clash between the North and South in 1999. Third, the engagement policy of the DJ administration in South Korea is examined in terms of strengths to be enhanced and weaknesses to be overcome. Finally, a new paradigm of inter-Korean relations is investigated based on the report of US-DPRK coordinator William J. Perry, which will stimulate discussions on impending diplomatic issues which Pyongyang has pursued over the long period of negotiations with Washington and Seoul. The study's findings will contribute to policymaking options for the two Koreas and the regional powers as they seek peace and prosperity. As long as North Korea plays the game by the rules as a member of the world community, the two Koreas will peacefully approach reconciliation, to their own benefit.

The systems approach will be applied to examine a proposed new paradigm of inter-Korean relations, shifting from Cold War military confrontation to post–Cold War economic cooperation. The *system* is the Korean peninsula, with two sovereign governments, North and South. Each government has *subsystems* of politics, national security, economy, and sociocultural elements. The global and regional environment is the *suprasystem* affecting the system and its subsystems. It is assumed that rational actors make decisions in the system. The first step of the systems approach considers three types of *interactions* among suprasystem, system, and subsystems: interactions between suprasystem and system, between the two systems of North and South Korea, and between subsystems within the system. This refers to the interactions between the global environment and North Korea, between the two Koreas, and between politics and the economy in both North and South Korea. The second step of the systems approach considers *feedback operations* for output adjustment to the system goals by repeatedly inserting revised policy input, that is derived from unsatisfactory policy output, into the system.

Globalization and Regional Convergence

The collapse of communism in 1991, ending the Cold War, was the bloodless victory, in politics, of democracy and in the economy, capitalism. Since liberal democracy is "the end point of mankind's ideological evolution and the final form of human government,"[2] the world has become more peaceful and stable, without ideological competition except in a few cases. The tradeoff between democratic equality and capitalist efficiency, however, creates a miniature cold war problem: how to sustain economic growth in global markets with fair income distribution in cohesive societies pursuing individual happiness. Some European leaders have invented a theory, the Third Way, to combine efficiency and equality in the system. The third way is not a third theory but one of many ways that might be chosen between efficiency (dollars) and equality (rights) such that the tradeoff point is vague and unclear.[3] "The third way presupposes a more Hegelian view of the world,"[4] but it is a cyclical phenomenon rather than a dialectic one. American affirmative actions law, for example, has in the pursuit of social equality protected minority interests, but the law may be abolished in the future in order to improve economic efficiency.

Revolutionary globalization has arisen from the unlimited transfer of knowledge and technology through borderless information flow based on advanced science and technology. Nation-states, even authoritarian regimes, can no longer monopolize information because of the availability of internet communications, wireless digital telephone connections, satellite television, fax machines, digital video disks, printers and copiers, and various other technological elements. If a government were to try to control individual communications, the costs would be too high for its economy to bear.[5] For example, the number of Chinese internet users hit four million in June 1999 and are to have reached five to eight million by the end of the year. Considering that forty percent of all users are in the 21-to-25 age group, the number will continue to increase.[6] If China wanted to control internet communications to stop the flow of political criticism, its government would have to hire experts numbering at least five percent of internet users. Even then, what about those who use satellite TV, wireless telephones, and fax machines? Information control raises overhead costs, reducing competitiveness. Therefore, no-control is the best policy for all governments, so that the world can enjoy the free flow of information without barriers.[7]

The world financial market is no exception in globalization.[8] The rise of world trade has expanded nations' production possibility frontiers through utilization of comparative advantage. The abandonment of the gold standard and liberalization of exchange rates not only expedited the flow of goods and services but raised the level of foreign direct investments and capital mobility. As trade barriers have broken down, national economies have become more and more integrated with each other. High-speed data processing systems provide immediate transactions at computer terminals around the world and produce fast delivery with low cost of necessary information. Problems have arisen, however, in emerging markets due to capital outflows, falling currencies, failing banks, and loss of confidence, as experienced in the Asian financial crisis in the second half of 1997.[9] The recovery and adjustment process has been painful, and the survival of national currencies in the global market is in question.[10] If the Euro becomes successful along with other regional currencies,[11] there could be eventual convergence to a single world currency system without foreign exchange problems.[12]

The convergence of productivity has been evidenced in cross-national studies, showing technological globalization as a part of economic integration. The concepts of convergence include homogenization, catch-up, gross convergence, explained convergence, residual convergence, asymptotically perfect convergence, and bounded convergence.[13] Economic growth is based on both factor mobilization and productivity growth. The major engine of productivity growth has been advancing knowledge and technical progress. Information technology has expedited the transfer of knowledge and technology among nation-states. Financial globalization has stimulated the rise of multinational firms, which has forced the host countries to catch up on advanced technologies, learning by doing, purchasing innovation licenses, and hiring expensive foreign engineers to obtain technological know-how. The developing countries have invested in general education and professional training in research and development, in addition to physical capital accumulation. They purchase weapons and equipment from foreign countries on the condition of technology transfer. These developments are due to the shorter product life cycle, which contributes to productivity convergence and technological globalization.

The global market has continuously reduced tariffs and other barriers at national borders. Both Europe and North America–Mexico have created regional economic blocs, the EEC and NAFTA, respectively,[14] and additional regional blocs will appear in Latin America, Asia, and Africa. The World Trade Organization has been balancing the protectionist trends of all members to settle trade disputes multilaterally.[15] If the world were to converge into a single market from the various regional markets, there would be no border transaction costs. Thus, there would be no difference between foreign and domestic trade since there would be no barriers or controls by any government in the global market. The invisible hand enhances efficiency in allocating world resources without bottlenecks and idle capacities, so world production is maximized to its full potential. The current degree of market liberalization has not yet gone this far. It is still true, however, that barriers and controls posed by any government will produce a certain amount of costs due to inefficient resource allocation in the global sense, so it is better for a nation-state to follow the global trend of borderless free trade.[16]

Thus, globalization comes from the disappearance of ideological competition, the revolution of information technology, uninterrupted free factor mobility, productivity convergence, and trade liberalization. It overcomes time and space in transportation and communications, continuously forcing the world to be integrated and introducing historical changes such as the following:[17] Politically, international pressures from global and regional superpowers are so influential that nation-states lose their independence in policy decision-making.[18] Economically, a nation's economy benefits from market liberalization by taking its comparative advantages, but the income gap between rich and poor nations is widening because infant industries cannot be protected from foreign invaders.[19] Strategically, borderless trade and investment expands economic commitment to other nations so that business interests cause complications in international relations. This economic bond prevents or reduces possible conflicts between nation-states. From the socio-cultural point of view,[20] in the long run globalization expedites the convergence, rather than the clash, of different cultures and civilizations, since as the world becomes integrated the boundaries of politics and culture are weaker than those of the economies.[21]

The Korean peninsula has been at the geopolitical center of Northeast Asia, and since the dawn of the twentieth century the fate of Koreans has been largely decided by regional powers. Thc current inter-Korean military confrontation is an extension of the Cold War, with China and Russia on the north facing the United States and Japan on the south, though Japan and Russia remain in minor roles.[22] With the fall of the socialist countries, China's rise allowed North Korea to survive. Because the regional powers did not adjust to the new world order in the last decade, inter-Korean relations failed to progress. As long as Sino-American relations develop positively in the coming century, Seoul's engagement policy will contribute to peace and prosperity for the two Koreas. The ripple effect of two-power relations on the Korean peninsula has been evidenced in the past. For example, China bullied Taiwan by launching missiles over Taipei in March 1996, and North Korea bullied Seoul by dispatching submarines and ships and launching a missile over the East Sea (Sea of Japan). Bipolar relations in the region have been closely reflected on the Korean peninsula.

Is China really a threat to the United States economically, strategically, or politically? Economically, China's annual growth rate was 6.04 percent on average during the period 1978–1995. Its GNP was 3.5 percent of world GNP (the United States' GNP was 25.6 percent), and its per capita income ranked eighty-first in 1997.[23] Based on an average annual growth rate of 4.5 percent in the period 1995–2015, China's per capita income will reach $6,398 (against the United States' $30,268, 4.78 times that of China) at the end of the period.[24] It should be observed that the Chinese economy can be expected to face difficulties in the future, as follows:[25] (a) Transition economy: China faces problems of loss-making state enterprises,[26] proliferating non-performing banks, and the weak fiscal position of its central government.[27] (b) Insufficient factor mobility: The foreign direct investment in China was $45 billion at its peak in 1997 (80 percent from overseas Chinese), but out-flight of capital was $35 billion in the same year. Its trade volume in 1997 was 3 percent of total world trade (similar to that of South Korea). (c) Slow productivity growth: the transfer of advanced technology from overseas to China is limited, and China-produced high-tech equipment may remain in the second generation of technology. (d) Economic inefficiency: the single-party political system allows corruption in the political-economic complex due to the lack of checks and balances,[28] distorting resource allocation and reducing efficiency. (e) Shortage of grain and energy: Increases in population and personal income push grain demand tremendously in China, while the structural shift of its industries from labor- to capital-intensive requires rapidly expanded energy supplies. This causes a shortage of grain and energy in China,[29] creating bottlenecks that will critically constrain the Chinese economy in the future. Thus, China remains a developing country transforming its socialist system towards a market economy,[30] and has many problems to overcome.[31]

The theory of China as a strategic threat arose following the collapse of the Soviet Union, based mainly on die-hard concepts of the Cold War and disturbances of the international status quo generated by China's increasing assertiveness and its growing national potential. This theory needs to be reevaluated, as follows:[32] (a) Military capabilities: China's defense spending is only 4.5 percent of global defense spending (the United States makes up 33.9 percent), and its naval and air force capabilities remain far below the current technology.[33] (b) Territorial assertiveness: China has claimed sovereign rights over Taiwan and islands in South China Sea, including the Senkaku Islands (disputed with Japan), the Paracel Islands (disputed with Vietnam), the Spratly Islands (disputed with the Philippines and other neighbors). Nevertheless, some believe that "the South China Sea will remain an 'American lake' well into next century."[34] (c) Nuclear weapons: Chinese missiles can threaten US naval forces, but they are so primitive that their accuracy and ability to hit North America is in doubt, and the United States is developing a missile defense system.[35] (d) Arms transfer: China's arms transfers to Pakistan and Iran may precipitate a nuclear arms race, but the main goal of this transfer lies in China's opposing and balancing Western interests. China is cooperative in the arms control regime. (e) Regional hegemony: China wants to maintain the balance of power in the region for its own national security, not for the purpose of hegemony. It engages with Russia and endeavors to contain Japan against American hegemony in Asia.[36] In fact, Gerald Segal argues, "China does not matter because it is a potential strategic partner for the West."[37]

Politically, China has a fundamental problem of democratization, which has been closely linked to the human rights question in the United Nations.[38] The issues are as follows: (a) Single-party politics: The Chinese Communist Party monopolizes domestic politics with its outdated socialist ideology, which is shifting to nationalism.[39]

The slow pace of democratization causes problems, but China has chosen a course in which politics lags behind the economy in order to avoid national disintegration. It is recognized that China's overall human rights situation has improved. (b) The middle class: If Chinese average annual personal income passes $5,000, Beijing fears that the new middle class will demand more political power, and that the regime will be unable to control the "freedom waves." The central government must choose either a federal system or disintegration forced on it by regional powers or ethnic groups.[40] (c) The issue of Taiwan: China repeatedly insists that Taiwan is a part of its territory, and the United States does not support Taiwan's independence movement or its bid for United Nations membership.[41] (d) The Korean peninsula: China uses North Korea as a buffer zone in order to secure its own border with Korea, while it cultivates its economic relations with South Korea in order to achieve a balance with the Japanese economy for the future. (e) Peacekeeping role: China has been active in UN peacekeeping activities. China was milder than Russia on the issue of Kosovo and agreed to the dispatch of UN forces to East Timor.[42]

The global and regional environments affect the system through interactions.[43] Information technology has expedited globalization by reducing time and space, and has accelerated the convergence of different elements on the levels of the suprasystem, the system, and the subsystems, both vertically and horizontally. The information age has introduced unlimited competition, from the level of individuals to various levels of organization, to the level of the world system, maximizing global efficiency by minimizing local costs. The United States' hegemonic power and foreign policy leadership may maintain the efficiency of the world system in the age of globalization. Washington leads multipolar regional powers in what is now a uni-multipolar world,[44] acting constructively to resolve regional conflicts such as the case of East Timor. However, the regional powers have been resisting the hegemonic power, believing that it has limited resources and will be unable to endure forever.[45] China is not an adversary of the United States, but instead is a potential strategic partner in maintaining the region's stability and prosperity.[46] US constructive engagement with China is mutually beneficial since the two countries need each other. As long as Washington and Beijing are engaged for peace and prosperity, inter-Korean relations will stand on the same plane, moving towards conciliation and cooperation.

Evaluation of North Korean Survival Strategies

The collapse of the socialist countries and their ideology in 1991 brought North Korea serious problems in politics, economy, national security, and social system. The regime recognized the serious consequences if its Juche ideology faded away through gradual loss of public support in the post–Cold War period, despite years of harsh brainwashing of the population and continually more strident control of information. When Seoul approached Moscow and Beijing for diplomatic normalization, North Korea felt isolated and needed to seek some measures to maintain the regime's political independence from external pressures. South Korea, allied with the United States, was building up its armed forces, while North Korea was losing its military bonds with Russia and China.[47] Pyongyang tried to take protective measures against possible external threats. While the economy of South Korea was prospering, the DPRK economy was declining continuously in the 1990s. The lack of foreign exchange in North Korea made it impossible to purchase weapons and equipment from foreign countries and difficult to supply appropriate food and energy for its soldiers, which reduced the level of military training, lowered soldiers' morale, and weakened combat readiness.

The DPRK's intention to develop nuclear weapons was one attempt to escape from the difficulties of domestic instability, diplomatic isolation, economic hardship, and military inferiority to the South. North Korea agreed to freeze nuclear development and signed the Agreed Framework with the United States in Geneva, Switzerland, in October 1994, gaining two light water reactors and 500,000 gallons of heavy oil a year until final delivery of the reactors. On 17 August 1998, the *New York Times* reported that the DPRK was building underground facilities near Yongbyon, and Washington suspected the site was for processing plutonium.[48] Two weeks later, the DPRK launched a Daepodong I missile towards Japan over the East Sea.[49] After hard negotiations, North Korea allowed a US inspection team to visit the site[50] and the team found no evidence of enriching plutonium. The United States recognized that the Agreed Framework did not regulate nuclear missile delivery systems but only nuclear warheads, and the matter became subject to party-politics criticism.[51] The US Congress reviewed American policies toward the DPRK, while North Korea insisted that it had launched an artificial satellite for peaceful use, not an armed missile.

The new possibility that a North Korean ICBM might reach Alaska or Hawaii was a surprising threat to South Korean, Japanese and US national security. Though the Japan was very sensitive to the first firing of the Daepodong I,[52] South Korea responded mildly, for the following reasons: First, the DPRK's missile threat to the South was strategically no different from that posed by the previously deployed Rodong missiles with their range of 500 miles that covers the entire territory of South Korea. Second, ROK President Roh Tae Woo had declared South Korea nuclear free, surrendering its sovereignty in this matter to the United Nations, so that South Korea believed that the problem now belonged to Washington, not to Seoul. Third, the DJ administration wanted to maintain smooth relations with the DPRK based on its engagement policy and did not criticize North Korea when it insisted it had launched a satellite instead of a missile. In a way, the DPRK's missile launch brought forward the reality that time is no longer on the side of the United States or South Korea but instead favors North Korea.[53] As a result, Washington began to deal with the DPRK on issues of missile development and nonproliferation.[54]

Meanwhile, DPRK vessels have been entering the south of the Northern Limit Line (NLL) every year but have always retreated when approached by South Korean gunboats. This year for the first time they refused to retreat and this year was the first time the ROK vessels touched the North Korean vessels. The ROK vessels had been taking progressively stronger measures during the entire two weeks beginning with repeated warnings. ROK naval vessels bumped and nudged the DPRK vessels back in the direction of NLL, but finally the North Korean ships opened fire on 15 June. Self-defensive counterfire from the ROK Navy resulted in the sinking of seven DPRK ships, with dozens of deaths. Pyongyang's intentions in this naval action were as follows:[55] (a) The territorial dispute was expected to bring benefits to the DPRK in negotiating with Washington because of lack of legal validity of the NLL. (b) Armed violations by the North might damage the South's "sunshine policy," as harsh outbursts were expected from ROK opposition politicians. (c) The armed clash might widen the gap in parallel policy coordination between Washington and Seoul, through anticipated differing responses. (d) The recognition of North Korea's military aggressiveness in combat, and hopefully their success, would be helpful in enhancing the morale of the DPRK military. (e) The two-faced tactics of the DPRK — attacking a secondary target while talking peace to obtain the main objectives — would be helpful and produce no harm in dealing with the United States and South Korea. The ROK's unexpected victory in the clash demonstrated the naval superiority of the South against the North. Inter-Korean relations went cold, the high-level talks were halted, and scheduled tours to the Kumgang Mountains were cancelled.

What is the reality of the North Korean system? Let us review its subsystems first, including politics, economy, military, and society. The DPRK's domestic politics appear calm and stable, but there are many hidden elements that threaten the regime with the possibility of sudden explosions — such as a failed military coup in 1995. The fall of communism cast a pessimistic light on the ideology of Juche, and despite their superficial expressions of loyalty to the regime, necessary for their own survival, the ruling elite and intellectuals have become discouraged, as reported by defector Hwang Jang-yop.[56] Political stability depends on public support of the regime, coming largely from material satisfaction. Starvation and hunger-related diseases caused the death of two to three million North Koreans from 1994 to 1998, rendering the central government incapable of controlling the local population, as shown in increasing numbers of escapees to China seeking food. Growing corruption, black market activities, and other anti-system behavior has increased public anger.[57] External food aid bolsters the fragile private food system in the North, but potential demand for food contributes to the need for opening the system, since a new round of famine-related deaths will seriously shake the regime if food aid is not continued. The North Korean regime has ruthlessly oppressed the political opposition by condemning political enemies to inhumane prison camps. Though the regime continues to control the people with socialist brainwashing, the effectiveness of such tactics will decline since the regime cannot indefinitely avoid the freedom waves of the information age.

In foreign relations, the DPRK has ignored the generalized norms and rules of the international community, so it is not easy for it to obtain broader cooperation with foreign countries. North Korea has been involved in selling drugs, counterfeiting, and terrorist activities such as the blowing up of a Korean airliner and the bomb attack on a ROK presidential delegation in Burma. During the Cold War period, terrorism was considered a part of the military confrontation, but the world community has been angered to see terrorism carried out by a state government after the Cold War. So long as the DPRK is isolated from the world economy, terrorism does not seriously affect its autarkic economy. Once it opens the door to foreign trade and investment, however, the risk of doing business with North Korea will raise the cost of insurance and thus production, reducing its competition in the world market. If a North Korean firm, for example, wants to borrow money from a US bank in order to build a domestic plant, the bank will charge the highest interest because it has the highest risk in the world. The existence of military threat and political risk removes all attraction from investment in the country. Its diplomatic isolation raises economic costs in various ways in trade and investment. The lack of communication with other countries interrupts the flow of information and reduces the speed of transfer of science and technology. As a result, it is obvious that the country will remain in ignorance and poverty and lag far behind the standard of the current global civilization.

The North Korean economy has declined continuously since 1989,[58] though increased food aid has provided some relief recently.[59] The DPRK has tried to justify its economic failures in four ways: US economic sanctions on DPRK, expanded military spending forced by the presence of US forces in South Korea, collapse of the Soviet Union and its satellites countries, and its poor economic planning and performance. Though North Korea tries to find external excuses, the fundamental reasons for its poor economic performance exist within its own system, even if observers might concede partial agreement with its claims.[60] (a) The centrally planned economy creates bottlenecks and idle capacities in resource allocation, reducing economic efficiency. (b) The compensation returned by party loyalty rather than individual achievement and the nonexistence of property rights reduce workers' motivation, and with it, productivity. (c) The self-sanctioned autarkic economy refuses foreign trade and investment, restricting the production possibility frontier. (d) The over-expanded military, with its separate budget, absorbs too much of the country's resources for the economy to sustain and reduces investment in the private sector. (e) Information control, political censorship of intellectuals, and brainwashing of the population reduce individual motivation and creativity, preventing invention and innovation and delaying transfer of science and technology. (f) The costs of maintaining the socialist totalitarian system are too high: eliminating the political opposition, organizing public movements, homogenizing the population's way of thinking, and pursuing other self-serving political operations (g) Corruption prevails in non-democratic countries, and its impact on the economy becomes serious when trade and investment are expanded. This damages efficiency and equality in the long run. (h) The socialist totalitarian system has lost dynamic and static self-adjustment functions, and exacts unnecessary costs due to the lack of coordination vertically and horizontally.[61]

The supply side of economic growth resides in two elements: factor mobilization and productivity growth.[62] Factor mobilization has been difficult in North Korea due to the lack of capital inflow caused by diplomatic isolation and an unattractive economic environment, waste of resources caused by misallocation, military expansion, and reckless political operations. Productivity growth is also in trouble in North Korea due to the lack of domestic invention and innovation, foreign technology transfer, and motivation for people to work hard, as discussed above. The demand side of economic growth comprises domestic consumption and foreign exports linked to international marketing capability. The DPRK distributes consumer goods by rationing according to previously decided central planning. Its exports declined rapidly after the collapse of communism, and US economic sanctions interrupted DPRK foreign trade. The problem was caused by the Stalinist system, not by external pressures. The impact of the US economic sanctions on DPRK exports must be small until the late 1980s considering that its exports to European countries consisted largely of raw materials until their collapse. Since the fall of Soviet Union in 1991, US sanctions have prevented American firms—which represent a large chunk of world purchasing power—from buying North Korean goods directly; this applies equally to raw materials as well as manufactured products. However, the DPRK system remains unchanged, the lift of U.S. sanctions would not be enough to create a big push for its economic take-off.

The DPRK military spent over 25 percent of the country's GNP in recent years, while the ROK military spent less than 3.5 percent of GNP.[63] Despite that high ratio, the absolute amount of North Korean military spending was 2.5 times lower than South Korea's in the mid-1990s because its economy is so much smaller.[64] Military expansion has been one of major reasons for the DPRK economic collapse; the over-expansion of the DPRK military from 1970 to 1990 drained investment in the private sector, which reduced industrial productivity,[65] The DPRK was unable to import advanced weapons and equipment from foreign countries, or to replace spare parts for its existing weapon systems, as evidenced by its importing used MiG-21s from Kazakhstan.[66] South Korean intelligence believes that around 30 percent of DPRK conventional weapons and equipment are functioning, but the remaining 70 percent are over thirty years old — too old to use in combat. The victory of the ROK Navy over the DPRK in the Yellow Sea illustrates the current condition of DPRK weapons and equipment.[67]

North Korea may choose from among the following survival strategies: (a) Pursue economic growth by normalizing foreign relations with Washington, Tokyo, and others. (b) Pursue economic cooperation with the South through NGO transactions first, and through state-to-state relations later. (c) Utilize US policy differences with South Korea in order to isolate Seoul from Washington. (d) To obtain maximum benefit in negotiations, use three types of nuclear threat: nuclear warheads, delivery systems, and missile technology sales. (e) Ask for war compensation, humanitarian aid, direct investment, and technology transfer from Japan after normalization of relations. (f) Approach international organizations for aid and loans after removal of US economic sanctions and after it has changed its terrorist reputation and become a member of the IMF and the World Bank by submitting proper economic statistics.[68] (g) Seek capital and technology from foreign countries around the world by improving diplomatic relations. (h) Try to control information flow into its system to protect the regime from the waves of liberal democracy and capitalism, and strengthen the armed forces, as the core of the regime, against internal and external threats.[69]

Can North Korea's survival strategies achieve the system's goals, political stability and economic prosperity? Real problems exist in setting and achieving these goals. (a) The DPRK faces serious conflict between its two strategic goals because the Juche system reduces economic efficiency while economic growth challenges the socialist system. (b) North Korean diplomatic normalization with Washington, Tokyo, and others does not guarantee economic growth equipped with factor mobilization and productivity improvement. (c) Inter-Korean economic cooperation is key to ending the vicious circle, but it would require a peace treaty and disarmament on the peninsula, a time-consuming process requiring patience. (d) Reciprocity is a state of equality between two parties. The DPRK is not accustomed to respecting such recognized values in foreign relations, which disturbs others and delays compromise.[70] (e) The time cost in economic growth is more expensive than the gains from brinkmanship-style negotiations. The cost of politics has been much higher than that of economics in North Korea since the DPRK leadership has been unable to recognize the time costs in economic development. Those barriers must be removed for North Korea to achieve its strategic goals.

ROK Engagement Policy toward the DPRK

In his inaugural speech in February 1998, President Kim Dae-jung declared the three principles of his engagement policy (which he likes to call the "sunshine policy") toward North Korea: no absorption intended, no military provocation tolerated, and peaceful coexistence pursued. It is a long-term strategy for Korean unification based on superiority of the South Korean system and expressing his determination to create and maintain peace and prosperity with confidence and endurance by helping the North to transform its system towards democracy and a market economy. To achieve these goals, the DJ leadership applies following principles: the separation of business from politics; reciprocity; unconditional efforts to solve the North Korean food shortage; intention to resume the discontinued inter-Korean dialogue; and endeavors to solve the separated-families problem.[71] The sunshine policy also encourages other nations to engage North Korea, which would be helpful in ending the vicious circle in economic development, but it has faced mild resistance from conservatives in and outside of South Korea.

The majority of South Korean people were confused by the engagement policy in the beginning.[72] Right-wing conservatives, including retirees from the armed forces and families of people who had escaped from the North, criticized the policy when the DPRK submarines appeared in the East Sea in 1998. The conservative media worried about the future of the policy when a spy ship appeared near the southern seashore. Opposition politicians argued the lack of reciprocity with the North when the DPRK refused to allow South Korean labels on rice and fertilizer bags delivered as food aid to the North from the South. There was criticism when the DPRK spent the funds obtained from Hyundai's tour operations to purchase forty MiG-21 fighters from Kazakhstan. Despite the critics, however, Seoul gained a diplomatic initiative through its aggressive approach to the North by providing flexibility (in dealing with DPRK) to Washington and Tokyo. Seoul had been concerned that the United States was achieving rapprochement with the North faster than the South was and feared diplomatic distance from Washington. The new policy welcomes other nations to approach the North positively for economic cooperation since it is helpful for the DPRK to open its society to the world community.[73]

Relatively calm about the engagement policy at first, North Korea came to believe that the policy would result in absorption of the socialist system in the long run because it would produce freedom waves from increasing contacts and material transactions.[74] As long as the transactions did not threaten the political order, the speed of economic cooperation would be expedited and the volume of transactions increased. Pyongyang tried to maximize economic gains from the generosity of the South by asking Seoul for more aid, trade, and investment. However, policy limitations exist in the South because of North Korea's failure to observe reciprocity and concern that a trade surplus from the South might finance further DPRK military buildup. A policy limit also exists in the North due to the fear of "freedom waves," which forces the authorities to tighten control measures. Another problem is that the DPRK heavily uses inter-Korean relations in domestic politics for tactical gains through propaganda, which causes inter-Korean relations to be inconsistent and unreliable. The naval clash between the two Koreas in June 1999 caused the discontinuation of high-level talks and the Kumgang Mountains tour, though both were soon rescheduled.[75]

The United States welcomed South Korea's engagement policy because it fits into the same framework as the US engagement policy toward China and the DPRK. When Seoul initially approached Pyongyang more eagerly than did Washington, the United States began to believe that Seoul was pursuing an aggressive and independent diplomacy toward the DPRK. Close policy coordination was required with the United States and other powers.[76] When Seoul tried to improve relations with Russia and Japan, Kim Dae-jung suggested six-party talks, though the efforts were not successful.[77] Meanwhile, the policy began to face difficulties due the differences between ROK domestic politics and US military strategies in Asia. Washington was more concerned about the DPRK's nuclear capability and its proliferation of weapons, while Seoul worried about economic recovery from the Asian financial crisis if inter-Korean relations were to go wrong. Washington wants Seoul to join the Theater Missile Defense (TMD) regime, while Seoul hesitates to do so because it does not address what constitutes the real threat from the North, and the TMD commitment worsens ROK-China relations.

China has supported the engagement policy[78] because it pursues peace and stability on the Korean peninsula, which is needed to avoid disruption of its transition economy. If the two-Koreas relationship worsens, Sino-American relations would be expected to follow the trend, which would hurt China's economy in various ways. China does not want Korean affairs to damage its foreign relations, China's primary goal. Also, China has a strategic interest in Korea. If North Korea remains hostile, Washington might prepare critical military measures to dismantle the DPRK nuclear capability, or it may strengthen containment with economic sanctions, pushing the DPRK into collapse despite Chinese support. If China does not support South Korea, it may lose its strategic leverage in a unified Korea dominated by Seoul. From the strategic point of view, China's role in Korea may be compared to the US role regarding Taiwan. China subsidizes the DPRK's survival by providing grain and energy, while the United States sells fighters and weapons to Taiwan. North Korea tries to push US forces out of the South, while Taiwan pursues its independence and tries to push China's influence off the island. China uses the DPRK as a buffer against the United States, while America uses Taiwan as an unsinkable aircraft carrier in case strategic containment of China is needed in the future.

The engagement policy is the best choice among Seoul's three alternatives - containment, disengagement, and engagement - though this policy has weaknesses in dealing with the North. (a) The policy does not have strong enough leverage to force the DPRK to pay the costs of ignoring norms and breaking rules of positive input. Despite much flexibility in the policy, the voters of South Korea and the United States are sensitive to the North Korean failures in reciprocity.[79] (b) Since the policy has broad room for differences in the interests of South Korea and the United States in dealing with North Korea, close policy coordination between them is important for goal achievement. (c) Regional power relations affect the engagement policy greatly; and inter-Korean relations are closely linked to Sino-American relations, so that their engagement is essential in dealing with North Korea. Accordingly, the policy actors should have confidence in negotiating and endurance in working toward desired outcomes, and the policy itself should be consistent in its procedures and flexible in responding to external shocks.[80] While the engagement policies of the United States and South Korea towards North Korea remain stalemated, policymakers in each government have begun to consider comprehensive ways of breaking through the impasse and making progress.

Meanwhile, South Korea has experienced several serious incidents with North Korea. A North Korean submarine carrying commandos appeared near the Eastern Sea in summer 1998, which aroused domestic critics of ROK politics. In August 1998 US intelligence found that the DPRK was building an underground nuclear facility in Kumchangri, which was considered a violation of the Agreed Framework. On 31 August 1998, North Korea launched a three-stage Daepodong I missile and announced that it would also launch the Daepodong II missile as soon as it was ready. The impact of those incidents on Korean affairs was tremendous. The US Congress forced the

Clinton administration to deliver its promised crude oil to North Korea after a complete inspection of the suspected nuclear site, but the Japanese Diet threatened to withhold the funds supporting KEDO operations if North Korea launched the second missile. Since the Agreed Framework freezes only North Korea's processing of enriched uranium, under the agreement the United States cannot regulate delivery systems or control the proliferation of missile sales and technology transfer to potential US adversaries. The United States believes that the DPRK nuclear issue should be resolved in order to keep US strategic interests in the future.

The bipartisan leadership of the US Congress perceived that the US foreign policy towards North Korea had failed and that the DPRK should be punished for its military provocations.[81] It was believed that US economic sanctions would not be effective as long as China supplied food and energy to the DPRK. Meanwhile, the nuclear tests of India and Pakistan in May 1999 led to the idea that the spread of nuclear weapons was only a matter of time, and that eventually those countries would have nuclear-warhead ballistic missiles. Since the fundamental goal of Kim Dae-jung's engagement policy was to avoid a second Korean war, a "crash scenario with hard landing" was not acceptable to the Korean people, and Washington could not pursue such a "hard landing" without Korea's agreement. The policy consensus in Washington and Seoul suggested a comprehensive engagement with North Korea,[82] and the Clinton administration appointed William J. Perry as a presidential adviser coordinating Korean affairs. It is expected that a package deal with Pyongyang can bring a breakthrough, making all parties happy by saving lives, time, and money. The time is ripe for the DPRK to make some changes.[83]

William J. Perry began his mission based on his professionalism and experiences in pursuing constructive engagement with China.[84] He met with theorists and practitioners broadly, visiting foreign governments—including North Korea in May 1999—for consultation. On 12 December 1999, soon after the Kumchangri inspection, based on Perry's efforts US special envoy Charles Kartman and Deputy Minister Kim Gye-gwan of North Korea announced in the so-called Berlin Agreement that their countries had pledged "to preserve a positive atmosphere conducive to improved bilateral relations and to peace and security in Northeast Asia and the Asia-Pacific region."[85] Three days later Perry reported to the US Congress his proposed US policy towards the DPRK. Foreign Minister Paek Nam-sun of North Korea reconfirmed the Berlin Agreement on 24 September 1999 in a speech at the United Nations General Assembly, saying that North Korea would "refrain from testing any long-range missiles for the duration of negotiations aimed at improving the relations."[86] The Berlin Agreement was based on understandings and expectations, and the Clinton administration made it clear that sanctions could be reapplied if necessary. The South Korean leadership recognized that these results represented a victory of the DJ administration's sunshine policy.[87]

William J. Perry's report included a three-step approach and five policy recommend-ations. The three steps were (1) restraint of DPRK missile launches and partial lifting of US sanctions together with parallel measures on the part of South Korea and Japan with respect to this engagement (short-term); (2) abandonment of DPRK missile development and sales, and technology transfer (mid-term); and (3) termination of the Cold War on the Korean peninsula (long-term). The five policies were to (1) choose a comprehensive and integrated approach towards North Korea; (2) strengthen the US policy enforcement system, including nomination of a senior-level envoy; (3) maintain the system by coordinating policies and cooperating with South Korea and Japan; (4) pursue bipartisan policies towards North Korea in the US Congress; and (5) prepare contingency plans for any emergency resulting from North Korean challenges.[88] The proposal is based on reciprocity, exchanging the DPRK's missile development and proliferation for meeting its critical needs for diplomatic normalization, economic cooperation, and security guarantees—though it recommends harsh punishment if North Korea does not comply with the proposed package deal.

President Clinton partially lifted US sanctions against North Korea on 17 September 1999, which would permit "the transfer of commercial and personal funds between the two countries and allow commercial air and sea transportation for passengers and cargo." According to the Associated Press, "Clinton's order would not affect counter-terrorism or nonproliferation controls on North Korea, which prohibit exports of military and sensitive dual-use items and most types of US assistance. Restrictions imposed by law, such as missile sanctions, will remain in place."[89] North Korea urged Washington to lift the remaining sanctions so as to make it a comprehensive and substantial measure.[90] In fact, the Berlin Agreement is a symbolic positive gesture expressing the DPRK's intention to engage with the United States. However, stopping missile launches temporarily does not mean that North Korea will halt its entire process of missile development. The DPRK is developing a missile delivery system and transferring missile technology with sales to US adversaries. Since the partial lifting of US sanctions against the DPRK was a part of the Agreed Framework, so far the game is even.[91]

The fundamental solution for the DPRK's problems lies in true abandonment of missile development and proliferation, pledged in written documents[92] and with oversight by US authorities. If this is done, Washington should lift all sanctions correspondingly by proving that North Korea is no longer sponsors terrorist activity. If North Korea does not have a real intention to abandon missile development and sales, negotiations will only strengthen its survival capabilities by allowing its economy to recover with inflows of capital and technology.[93] Real negotiations should begin now to resolve DPRK problems in a civilized way, where the options remain unchanged: engagement, non-interference (muddling through), and containment. However, there is a big difference from previous deals: time is not now on the North Korean side but on the American side. An *expanded containment policy* against North Korea would terminate the regime by reinforced containment, direct military measures, or both.

Under this scenario, South Korea would join the Theater Missile Defense, develop offensive missiles with a range of five hundred miles, and purchase advanced weapons and equipment from the United States, while the US forces would increase offensive capabilities in the region by adding troops. This would be the end of DJ's sunshine policy, and the two Koreas would have to pay the price.

Inter-Korean Economic Cooperation

Three Stages of North Korean Transformation:
An Optimistic Scenario for Thirty Years (2000–2030)

Stage & Subsystem (Period Taken)	*Initiation Stage* (Present to 2010)	*Progress Stage* (2011-2020)	*Mature Stage* (2021-2030)
Foreign Relations			
US–China	Confidence Building	Increased Engagement	Strategic Partners
US–DPRK	Confidence Building	Increased Engagement	N-S Equal Distance
ROK–DPRK	Confidence Building	Increased Engagement	Federal System
ROK–China	Increased Engagement	N-S Equal Distance	Strategic Partners
Domestic Politics			
Ideology	Socialism	Nationalism	Liberal Democracy
Political Parties	Single Party	1 ½ Parties	Two Parties
Human Rights	Slightly Relaxed	Moderately Relaxed	Largely Relaxed
Information Control	Largely Controlled	Moderately Relaxed	Largely Relaxed
Economy			
Market Openness	Partially Open (25%)	Half Open (50%)	Mostly Open (75%)
Trade/Investment	Labor -Intensive	Capital -Intensive	Tech -Intensive
Property Rights	Partially Open (25%)	Half Open (50%)	Mostly Open (75%)
Price System	Partially Open (25%)	Half Open (50%)	Mostly Open (75%)
Privatization	Partially Open (25%)	Half Open (50%)	Mostly Open (75%)
National Security			
Military Spending	Pre. Level (25% GNP)	Reduced	Largely Reduced
Force Level	Present Level	Reduced	Largely Reduced
Peace Regime	Confidence Building	Peace Treaty	N-S Alliance
Disarmament	Confidence Building	Disarmament	N-S Alliance
Military Exchange	Strategic Level	Tactical Level	N-S Alliance

Note: The degree of performance is assumed as of the end of each period.

The Berlin Agreement made the US comprehensive engagement policy with North Korea effective by suspending DPRK missile launches and announcing a partial lifting of US sanctions. Japan followed suit by restoring its relationship with the DPRK, disrupted by the missile launch,[94] while Seoul is improving investments and cultural exchanges with Pyongyang.[95] Thus, the first step of Perry's plan has been successful. The next step lies in abandonment of DPRK missile development and proliferation in order to terminate the Cold War structure on the Korean peninsula, which is the main focus of coming negotiations between Washington and Pyongyang. North Korea wants to approach Washington directly to raise the stakes by bypassing Seoul, despite its pursuit of NGO activities between the two Koreas (*Tongmi Bongnam*). South Korea does not necessarily need to beg for high-level talks since the DJ administration will be happy if North Korea is moving toward transformation by engaging with any other nations. North Korea will come to Seoul as soon as its leadership recognizes the need for South Korean help in attracting foreign investors—a different situation from what obtained under previous South Korean administrations.[96]

Assuming that North Korea maintains good faith with the United States in regard to the Berlin Agreement, we can consider an optimistic scenario transforming the DPRK system and subsystems by three stages of development: initiation, progress, and maturity, as shown in table V-1. The scenario is a rough prediction of changes for subsystems including foreign relations, domestic politics, economic transformation, and national security during each ten-year period. In the *initiation stage* (present-2010), the foreign relations between the United States and China, the United States and the DPRK, and the ROK and the DPRK would pursue bilateral confidence building, while those between China and the ROK would mature more than the three other relationships owing to their bilateral efforts and to US-China engagement. In politics, the socialist ideology and the communist party remain unchanged despite the death of communism. Human rights are slightly improved, while information control is largely continued. In the economy, the market is partially open to foreigners in specialized zones, while trade and investment favor labor-intensive industries due to comparative advantages in abundant labor but not in scarce capital and technology. Once the economy begins to open, property rights will be gradually introduced, along with initiation of a price mechanism, which will make the market more efficient, and a small number of state-owned enterprises will be privatized. For national security, North Korea will keeps its current level of military spending and forces, at around 25 percent of GNP in this period, and will try to build confidence with Seoul by exchanging high-ranking officers to work at the strategic level, which will be expanded gradually.

If the first stage is successful, North Korea will enter the *progress stage* (2011–2020) by expanding its first-stage efforts. If the second stage is successful, North Korea will enter the *mature stage* (2021–2030), which will make the system totally different, since one generation (thirty years) is more than enough for changes of all subsystems. At that time, the current leadership will fade away, and the third generation will take power. These are the people who have hated the old political rules and love Western democracy. The United States and China will become strategic partners, and the two Koreas will form a federation and work toward unification if they are not already unified. Accordingly, Washington and Beijing will meet with the Federal Korea, with equal distance from the North and the South except in diplomacy, finance, and national security affairs. The armed forces of the two will be unified or allied, and their civilianized societies will not have to worry about military coups. Domestic politics will pursue democracy, and the economy will rely on competition within the market system. Thus, North Korea after thirty years will become similar to the present South Korea in all subsystems.

The above scenario is a vision of two-Korea relations on the plane of history, for which the Korean people have to work together. North Korea tries to use the foreign powers for its economic recovery, bypassing Seoul because the superiority of South Korea threatens the North Korean regime's survival. However, this is a temporary posture. Information control is impossible in the age of globalization because of technological progress, and a regime's monopoly on information makes the society inefficient. It will fall far behind the standard of civilization in the rest of the world. Sooner or later, the North Korean people will know what is going on outside of their borders. The best way for the regime to escape from this dilemma lies in gradual and simultaneous—but not slow—development of politics and economy. Over a thirty-year period, economic takeoff does not pull the entire system, though it looks good in initially pushing the system forward. But the lag in the political sphere will interrupt economic growth in the future, and adjustment costs will be higher than expected. A good example can be found in South Korea, where the economy grew rapidly but was pulled back in later years, when underdeveloped politics disturbed resource allocation.

The objectives of economic cooperation between the two Koreas are to ensure self-sufficiency in necessities in the short term, support transformation of the economic subsystem in the medium term, and prepare for integration of the two economies in the long term. What can South Korea do to achieve these objectives? In the short run, North Korea needs food and medicine to escape from hunger and disease. For humanitarian aid, South Korea has supplied grain and agricultural products, fertilizer, clothing, and medicine directly or coordinated with the United Nations.[97] These are temporary relief measures required for the country's survival in its immediate difficulties. In the medium term, the economic transformation of North Korea should be coordinated with the South for economic integration to reduce adjustment costs in unified Korea. The North Korean economy should be transformed from a socialist to a capitalist system, just like the transition economies in China, Russia, and the eastern European countries. South Korea can support this transformation in factor mobilization, resource allocation, marketing in foreign countries, and transformation know-how, including introduction of property rights, application of the price system, and privatization of state-owned enterprises.

Factor mobilization is essential on the supply side of the economy in terms of capital and technology. North Korea could borrow money from the UN financial institutions by becoming a member, which would require a certain qualification process: removing its terrorist reputation and submitting economic data to the United Nations. It could also borrow money from commercial banks in foreign countries by normalizing diplomatic relations. The United States, Japan, and the OECD countries could provide financial assistance to North Korea if Pyongyang abandoned its missile program and proliferation, and became a reliable member of the international community. In addition to humanitarian aid, South Korea could contribute a substantial sum of money as a peace dividend by diverting its defense budget to the non-defense sector once the two Koreas signed a peace treaty with disarmament. North Korea could obtain foreign exchange by creating a trade surplus and attracting foreign direct investment for industries having comparative advantage. The foreign purchase of

DPRK land and other properties could be a part of foreign direct investment. North Korea expects $10 billion worth of World War Two compensation from Japan (though Japan is considering an amount less than $5 billion) once their diplomatic relations are normalized. Once the DPRK economy is revived, domestic savings and other surpluses will be important for investment. Labor exports would bring in foreign currency. DPRK workers could be sent overseas to perform such manual labor as wood-cutting in Siberia or cleaning foreign facilities, and their numbers could be gradually expanded.

The two Koreas might coordinate with each other in resource allocation. Considering that their economies will definitely be integrated sooner or later, the newly created industrial structure in the North should not duplicate what exists in the South. South Korea currently has idle capacities in automobile and shipbuilding industries; the DPRK should not invest further in these areas. This kind of planning will bring many savings by reducing adjustment costs in the unified Korea. In this sense, the economic growth model of Taiwan, focusing on light industries first, is better for North Korea as it would allow the economies in North and South to be mutually supportive. Agricultural investment has a priority in the North because (a) the DPRK has a comparative advantage in labor-intensive industries, (b) the production of grain reduces foreign exchange demand, and (c) self-sufficiency in grain production reduces future risk of famine, increasing popular political support.[98] South Korea can provide know-how about economic planning from its own experiences since 1962. The South would advise that investment in infrastructure should be balanced with other investments. Insufficient infrastructure, including energy, transportation, and communications, exacts heavy costs by delaying business activities, which reduces economic efficiency. The lack of harbor shipping systems and the unpaved highways and byways in the North will delay plant construction and import-export activities.

Productivity growth is essential for economic development, which comes from the progress of science and technology, resulting from the allocation of funds to human resources in terms of education and training as well as research and development.[99] Technology transfer, limited to the nonmilitary sector, from South to North would maximize mutual benefits. As long as there is no peace treaty between North and South Korea, it is obvious that sensitive technology cannot be transferred. South Korea can help the North by allowing the DPRK to use the South's international marketing network for its foreign sales. This would require the ROK firms to create joint-ventures with DPRK firms in various ways by supplying each other's comparative advantages. In the process of the economic transformation of North Korea, the first step is to allow personal property rights, which will stimulate workers' desires to accumulate wealth for their own sake. The second step is to train the people to adjust to the price system in the market, which will not be easy for people who have been brainwashed by their socialist leaders for many years. In the third step of privatization process, it is important to root out moral hazards, which have been problems in Russia, China, Vietnam, and North Korea. Corruption is the main source of inefficiency.[100] South Korea is in a good position to help North Korean transformation due to its previous experiences in economic planning, and there is no language barrier.

The types of economic cooperation are inter-Korean trade, direct investment, and financial and humanitarian aid. The market forces decide the economic activities in South Korea, though political consensus can guide public enterprises to invest in the North. The major part of North-South economic cooperation lies in financial assistance, which means a net transfer of assets from South to North free of charge. The transferred assets contribute to the economic growth of the North, reducing future unification costs. The cooperative mood on the Korean peninsula attracts foreign direct investment, which is helpful for both economies. Resource transfer reduces investment in the South, which affects the South Korean economy negatively. Transfer of funds helps to expand South Korean business in the North, which positively affects the ROK economy. If the economic engagement can reduce the military threat from the North, both economies can divert military spending to investment in the nonmilitary sector, stimulating both economies. The costs of financial aid are the amount of the net transfer and the reduced investment effects, while the benefits include unification cost reduction, disarmament effects, FDI and psychological gains, and business initiatives in the North.[101]

What is the problem with North-South economic cooperation, then? (a) The South fears that the North may use economic assistance to maintain its armed forces threatening the South, putting a severe limit on economic cooperation. The bottom line is that the North would have to remove its military threat to the South by signing a peace treaty and disarmament agreement, which should be guaranteed by the United States and China. (b) North Korea tries to maximize its economic interests without sacrifice of political monopoly, which is impossible. The economy will not revive without transformation of the current system, which includes political rigidity and a closed market. A gradual and simultaneous—but not slow—opening, with security measures, is the best way to solve the problem. The lifting of US economic sanctions might be helpful, but without system change within the DPRK the impact would be minimal. (c) Some technical problems disturb trade and investment: the continual trade imbalance between North and South, limited land transportation possibilities in the DMZ area, insufficient legal provision and restriction measures, and lack of inter-agency coordination. These problems should be solved as soon as possible. (d) The ROK economy is the main source of capital and technology for North Korea since South Korean firms have comparative advantages over foreign firms in various ways. Pyongyang tries to bypass Seoul in order to engage with the United States, which is not a workable approach. The North Korean leadership should remember that the smartest way is not one far from reality.

Summary and Conclusion

The Korean peninsula has been a geopolitical center of mixed interests for the world powers since the beginning of the twentieth century. The Japanese Empire invaded, reigned over, and exploited Korea for thirty-six years as a convenient colony that supplied cheap labor and raw materials for Japan's military expansion until its surrender in 1945. World War Two divided Korea into North and South at the thirty-eighth parallel. Five years later the Korean War exploded when North Korea invaded the South, and China intervened in the war to stop the US forces to control the entire peninsula. The Korean War ended, but the peninsula remained divided at the DMZ, encapsulating the military confrontation of the Cold War. As the two Koreas competed in an arms race, their economic differences widened. The collapse of communism threatened North Korea, but the rising economy of China has rescued it by supplying food and energy. Meanwhile, since 1991 South Korea has been improving bilateral relations with China and Russia, while North Korea has faced serious economic difficulties without any sign of change in the totalitarian socialist regime. Now is the time to shift relations from military confrontation to economic cooperation.

The study has sought a new paradigm of inter-Korean relations by analyzing globalization and regional convergence, survival strategies of North Korea, South Korean engagement policy and the aftermath of Perry's report, and issues of inter-Korean economic cooperation. In summary, first, the information age has introduced unlimited competition to the world system, maximizing global efficiency by minimizing local costs. The United States, as a hegemonic power, has maintained foreign policy leadership in preserving the world's efficiency in the age of globalization. Washington leads multipolar regional powers in the uni-multipolar world, while regional powers resist its hegemony believing that it has limited resources and will be unable to last forever. In this sense, US constructive engagement with China is mutually beneficial since both countries need each other. As long as Washington and Beijing are positively engaged as potential strategic partners, inter-Korean relations are on the same historical plane. When China becomes a friend of the United States, how can North Korea resist the winds of change?

Second, the Kim Dae-jung leadership of South Korea has consistently pursued an engagement policy with the North, as set forth in the three principles announced in his inauguration address. The policy-making process of his administration is well organized democratically, particularly in the National Security Committee (NSC), to which he has appointed qualified members with various voices from within and outside of the system. The NSC team knows the importance of policy tuning with allied and friendly countries. Also, the South Korean economy is rapidly recovering, and the statistics show positive trends despite some noise from conflicting interests during the adjustment process. The market is recovering its competitive posture, and exports have been expanded to previous levels. Foreign exchange reserves passed well over $70 billion by the end of 1999, owing to the rising trade surplus and foreign direct investment. A decade after the fall of Communism, South Korea has built its confidence in liberal democracy with a market economy. The feedback function of self-adjustment makes the system work properly, so that South Korea as a system is too healthy to be shaken by external threats, including those from North Korea.

Third, the economic difficulties of North Korea came from the system itself, not from outside. Most of the nation's available resources were allocated to the over-expanded armed forces, so that investment in the private sector declined, and the lack of capital accumulation reduced productivity growth and economic efficiency. The North Korean intention to develop nuclear weapons is a means of escaping from the current difficulties of political instability, diplomatic isolation, economic decline, and military inferiority to the South. However, the DPRK can never recover its economy without liberalizing the market. The "freedom waves" entering the country from openness might threaten the closed regime, but its isolated autarkic economy might also cause the regime to fall, without a sound. North Korea has no choice other than gradual and simultaneous—but not slow—development of politics and economy, the course that Deng's China has followed since 1978. Though time is essential in growth, North Korea has lost more in time costs than it has gained from long negotiations with the United States and South Korea. If the DPRK leadership fails in strategic engagement with Washington as provided by Perry's package, its economy will stagnate a decade longer, which will lead to the fall of the regime.

Fourth, South Korea's engagement policy is in line with the Perry package, which is on the negotiation table between Washington and Pyongyang. The U.S. intention is for the DPRK to abandon its missile program and nuclear proliferation entirely, in exchange for diplomatic normalization, receipt of economic assistance, and military security with or from the United States. The US government has released neither the Berlin Agreement nor Perry's report, but we can see that US-DPRK relations are moving forward positively, as evidenced by President Clinton's lifting of sanctions in September 1999. The remaining question is how much and how fast North Korea can harvest the fruits of this opportunity, if it can follow the direction of American foreign policy leadership. However, if North Korea has no true intention of giving up its missile program and proliferation, relations with the United States will return to the containment policy. In this case, time will not be on the DPRK's side but on the American side. The US would enforce harsh containment with tough military measures, including provisions for TMD, extension of the ROK's missile range to five hundred miles, increasing ROK purchases of offensive weapons, reinforcement of US war power in Korea, and preemptive strikes.

Fifth, if North Korea maintains good faith with the United States in dealing with its missile program and proliferation, US-DPRK relations will improve, similar to the current status of ROK-China relations, within the first decade. If the system moves quickly towards openness in this initiation stage, the ongoing forces will accelerate transformation in the second and third decades, the progress and mature stages. If there is no interruption, a thirty-year period of transformation will improve North Korea's situation and make it comparable to the current South Korea. In this regard, North-South economic cooperation is essential for factor mobilization, resource allocation, overseas marketing, and know-how for system transformation, such as allowing property rights, introducing a price mechanism, and privatizing state-owned enterprises.

In fact, South Korea is a key for North Korea to end the vicious circle of suffering from hunger and disease. The bottom line for North-South economic cooperation is for the two Koreas to sign a peace treaty including arms reduction and resulting removal of the Northern military threat. Political maneuvers by the DPRK intended to shake up the South are a waste of resources and delay its economic development.

The study concludes with four policy recommendations: first for the United States, second for China, third for North Korea, and last for South Korea.

Recommendations for Washington: It is important for the peace and stability of the world and the Northeast Asian region that North Korea abandons its missile development program and nuclear proliferation. President Clinton's announcement partially lifting US economic sanctions against North Korea is a positive sign of peaceful engagement with North Korea. However, (a) Washington should make sure that North Korea absolutely abandons developing and proliferating nuclear weapons, and makes that pledge in written documents and under US authorities' supervision. (b) If North Korea complies with the agreement, Washington should take actions providing diplomatic normalization, economic assistance with lifting of remaining sanctions, and national security by guaranteeing the North–South Korean peace treaty and disarmament agreement. (c) If North Korea has no true intention to give up its missile development program and nuclear proliferation, Washington should take steps to terminate the regime by providing for harsh containment with military measures, including TMD development and preemptive strikes. (d) In dealing with North Korea, the United States should closely consult with Seoul and Tokyo, since the deal is closely related to their national interests, South Korea and Japan have each bilaterally allied with the United States, and North Korea tries to create a gap and widen it to take advantage of the differences.

Recommendations for China: China is currently opposed to North Korean missile development and nuclear proliferation and supports the engagement policy of South Korea. Continuous economic difficulties in North Korea have made Pyongyang demand large amounts of food and energy from China, an endless flow into a bottomless container. The increasing influx of refugees from North Korea has brought social instability to China's border provinces, which is not desirable from China's viewpoint. Most of all, (a) Beijing's foreign policy towards the Korean peninsula needs to be fair to both sides and cooperative with Washington and Seoul in order to maintain regional peace and stability. (b) If North Korea does not give up its development of nuclear weapons and proliferation, China should declare that it will no longer supply additional food and energy to North Korea. (c) China should continuously advise North Korea to adopt the Chinese model of economic development by opening the markets first in several economic zones followed by political liberalization.

Recommendations for North Korea: (a) North Korea should exchange its nuclear development and proliferation for diplomatic normalization, economic assistance with total lifting of economic sanctions, and national security guarantees from the United States as soon as possible, without hesitation. (b) It should accept the engagement policy of South Korea through state-to-state relations according to international norms and rules of reciprocity, not by distorting its meaning for propaganda purposes. (c) North Korea's intention to bypass South Korea for direct engagement with Washington is undesirable and unproductive in North-South economic cooperation, and should be corrected. (d) The fundamental precondition for massive economic cooperation between the two Koreas is a peace treaty with a disarmament agreement, which should be guaranteed by the United States and China, plus Russia and Japan, if necessary. (e) The DPRK leadership should change its concept of national security from realism to pluralism, focusing on economic and social development rather than building military hardware and tightening domestic control over the elite political opposition. In a market economy, it is obvious that to control any system requires corresponding costs, reducing economic efficiency.

Recommendation for South Korea: (a) In pursuing the engagement policy with North Korea, South Korea should closely coordinate with regional powers, particularly with Washington and Beijing in order to maximize the policy efforts and to minimize unnecessary misunderstanding. (b) South Korea should not rush to help North Korea merely in order to use the issue for domestic politics, and should oblige North Korea to respect reciprocity in all international relations. (c) It is clearly in South Korean national interests for North Korea to normalize diplomatic relations with other nations including Washington and Tokyo. South Korea should not try to interrupt the DPRK's efforts but help them to expand their political and economic relations. (d) South Korea should sign a peace treaty and arms reduction agreement with the North in order to eliminate suspicions and limitations on North-South economic cooperation, which should be guaranteed by regional powers including the United States and China. (e) The Seoul government should continuously support NGO's economic cooperation with North Korea, which provides a foundation for state-to-state economic cooperation between Seoul and Pyongyang. (f) Since South Korea is economically not as strong as was West Germany in 1991, the Seoul government must continue to build up its national strength in order to help the North and to prepare a foundation for unification. The recovery of competition in the market is important, and the restructuring of banking industries and conglomerates without political influence should be expedited. (g) Politics should be competitive through elimination of factional monopolies in the political parties, and revising the election system to be fair and efficient, particularly in nominating candidates and raising campaign funds. (h) The entire country including government, business, and labor works together towards rebuilding social values by bringing violators of laws to justice without exception. It is import for the citizens groups to watch the fairness of law enforcement by the government authorities. In the absence of fair competition in politics and economy, the voices of citizens groups must be essential for reforms.

Endnotes

[1] Michael Oksenberg, "The Korean Peninsula and the Great Powers: Prospects for Cooperation Among the United States, China, Russia, and Japan," presented to the 53rd Annual Conference of the World Affairs Council under the theme, "Korea: One People, Two Worlds," held at the Asilomar Conference Center in Pacific Grove, California, 30 April – 2 May 1999, from *NAPSNet Special Report—WAC Conference*, Berkeley, California: Nautilus Institute, 28 May 1999. Oksenberg noted that the Korean peninsula combines the major global issues in one place.

[2] Francis Fukuyama, "By Way of an Introduction," in *The End of History and The Last Man* (New York: Avon Books, 1992), p. xi. For another view, see Fareed Zakaria, The Rise of Illiberal Democracy," *Foregn Affairs* 76, 6 (November/December 1997), pp.22-43

[3] Arthur M. Okun, *Equality and Efficiency: The Big Tradeoff* (Washington: Brookings Institution, 1975); John M. Leger, "How We Got Here," *Wall Street Journal Interactive Edition*, 27 September 1999.

[4] Ralf Dahrendorf, "The Third Way and Liberty: An Authoritarian Streak in Europe's New Center," *Foreign Affairs* 78, 5 (September/October 1999), p. 15.

[5] Robert O. Keohane and Joseph S. Nye, Jr., "Power and Interdependence in the Information Age," *Foreign Affairs* 77, 5 (September/October 1998), pp. 81–93.

[6] "PRC Internet Users Hit 4 Million," *Beijing Xinhua*, 14 July 1999, from *World News Connection*, 15 July 1999, FBIS-CHI-1999-0714. Si Liang, "China Strengthens the Protection of Network and Information Security," *Zongguo Tongxun She* (Hong Kong), 13 August 1999, from *World News Connection*, 30 August 1999, FBIS-CHI-1999-0829.

[7] For further discussion on this point, see Robert J. Saunders, Jeremy J. Warford, and Bjorn Wellerius, *Telecommunications and Economic Development*, 2d ed. (Baltimore: Johns Hopkins Univ. Press, 1994).

[8] R. Barry Johnston and V. Sundararajan, "Managing Financial Sector Liberalization: An Overview," in Johnston and Sundararajan, eds., *Sequencing Financial Sector Reforms: Country Experiences and Issues* (Washington, DC: International Monetary Fund, 1999), pp. 1–23. Bernard Wysocki, Jr., "Where We Stand," *Wall Street Journal Interactive Edition*, 27 September 1999. Wysocki says, "Capitalism may appear to have won the global ideological war. But plenty of battles remain."

[9] World Bank, *Global Economic Prospects and the Developing Countries: Beyond Financial Crisis* (Washington, DC: International Bank for Reconstruction and Development / World Bank, 1999), pp. 55–118; and World Bank, *World Development Report: Knowledge for Development* (Washington, DC: International Bank for Reconstruction and Development / World Bank, 1999), pp. 91–98.

[10] James Tobin, "Keynote Address: Financial Globalization: Can National Currencies Survive?" in *Annual World Bank Conference on Development Economics 1998* (Washington, DC: World Bank, 1999), pp. 63–76.

[11] For further information, see Paul R. Masson, Thomas H. Krueger, and Bart G. Turtelboom, eds., *EMU and the International Monetary System* (Washington, DC: International Monetary Fund, 1997).

[12] Stanley Fisher, "ABCED: Past Ten Years, Next Ten years," in *Annual World Bank Conference on Development Economics 1998*, p. 84. Kyujin Im, "Creation of the Asian Monetary Fund on the Shelf: Financial Cooperation between Korea, China, Japan Strengthened," *Maidas Donga Ilbo*, 11 September 1999.

[13] William J. Baumol, Richard R. Nelson, and Edward N. Wolff, eds., *Convergence of Productivity: Cross-National Studies and Historical Evidence* (New York: Oxford University

Press, 1994), pp. 7–11. For more on productivity, see Dale W. Jorgenson, *Productivity*, Vol. 2, *International Comparisons of Economic Growth* (Cambridge, MA: MIT Press, 1995).

[14] Further, see Willem Molle, *The Economics of European Integration: Theory, Practice, Policy*, 2d ed. (Brookfield, MA: Dartmouth Publishing Company, 1994); and James D. Robinson III and Kay R. Whitmore, *North American Free Trade Agreement: The Report of the Advisory Committee for Trade Policy and Negotiations (ACTPN)* (Washington, DC: US Government Printing Office, September 1992).

[15] For further discussion, see Ann O. Krueger, ed., *The WTO As an International Organization* (Chicago, IL: University of Chicago Press, 1998); and Marcus Noland, "Learning to Love the WTO," *Foreign Affairs* 78, 5 (September/October 1999), pp. 78–92. Regarding China's joining WTO, see Hua Ta-Chen, "Prospect of China's Accession of WTO and Cross-Strait Economic Relations and Trade," *Hong Kong Ta Kung Pao*, 21 September 1999, from *World News Connection*, 25 September 1999, FBIS-CHI-1999-0922.

[16] Lawrence H. Summers, "Reflections on Managing Global Integration," *Journal of Economic Perspectives* 13, 2 (Spring 1999), pp. 3–18. He considers three positions: economic integration, public economic management, and national sovereignty, and suggests three compromises: (a) to pursue integration in those areas where the conflicts are less obvious, (b) to finesse sovereign problems by highlighting the national benefits of internationally congenial behavior, and (c) to pursue integration at sub-global levels.

[17] Robert W. Cox, "A Perspective on Globalization," in James H. Mittelman, ed., *Globalization: Critical Reflections* (Boulder, CO: Lynne Rienner Publishers, 1996), pp. 21–30. Bill Emmott, "The 20th Century," *Economist*, 11–17 September 1999, p. 41. "Globalization—the shrinking of distance and the increasing interplay and interdependence—has been the theme of the whole century, and longer. It is far from complete."

[18] Susan Strange, *The Retreat of the State: The Diffusion of Power in the World Economy*, trans. Victoria Elliott (New York: Cambridge University Press, 1996); and Jean-Marie Guehenno, *The End of the Nation-State* (Minneapolis, MN: University of Minnesota Press, 1993).

[19] Judith Miller, "Globalization Widens Rich-Poor Gap, U.N. Report Says," *New York Times on the Web*, 13 July 1999; Barbara Stallings, ed., *Global Change, Regional Response: The New International Context of Development* (New York: Cambridge University Press, 1995), pp. 1–30; and Joon Ho Hong, "Seoul Will Hold a Forum: Discussions for Removal of Rich-Poor Gap," *Digital Chosun Ilbo*, 13 September 1999.

[20] Joseph S. Nye, "Hard Power, Soft Power," *Boston Globe*, 6 August 1999.

[21] See Samuel P. Huntington, *The Clash of Civilizations: Remaking of the World Order* (New York: A Touchstone Book, 1996); and Kenichi Omae, *The End of the Nation States: The Rise of Regional Economies* (New York: Free Press, 1995), p. 21. Omae writes, "There is not much evidence to support the notion that economic activity in today's borderless world follows either the political boundary lines of traditional nation-states or the cultural boundary lines of what Huntington calls 'civilization'."

[22] William J. Perry, in *NAPSNet Special Report—WAC Conference,* Part 1, 28 May 1999. He pointed out three factors contributing to Asian security: the US bilateral alliances with Japan, Australia, and the ROK; US forward troop deployment; and US engagement with China. Among the three, Sino-American strategic engagement is believed to be essential for regional peace and stability in the long run.

[23] Gerald Segal, "Does China Matter?" *Foreign Affairs* 78, 5 (September/October 1999), pp. 24–36. Applying purchasing power parity, the numbers for China improve, to 11.8 percent and sixty-fifth in rank, respectively.

[24] Angus Maddison, *Chinese Economic Performance in the Long Run* (Paris: OECD Development Center, 1998), p. 97; and "People's Daily Editorial: Urges PRC to Unite for Growth," *Beijing Xinhua* in English, 7 June 1999, from *World News Connection*, 8 June 1999, FBIS-CHI-1999-0607. The editorial notes, "As a big country with 56 ethnic groups, China faces many new problems and difficulties."

[25] Nicholas R. Lardy, "China and the Asian Contagion," *Foreign Affairs* 77, 4 (July/August 1998), pp. 78–88.

[26] Han Zhenjun, "Promoting State-Owned Enterprises Reform," *Beijing Liaowang*, 16 August 1999, in *World News Connection*, FBIS-CHI-1999-0915, 16 September 1999; Reuters, "China Communist Party to Mull State Sector Reforms," *New York Times on the Web*, September 19, 1999; "The Decision of the Central Committee of the Communist Party of China on Major Issues Concerning the Reform and Development of State-owned Enterprises," *Beijing Xinhua*, 22 September 1999, in *World News Connection*, 27 September 1999, FBIS-CHI-1999-0926. The twelve points of this article were adopted at the Fourth Plenum of the Fifteenth CPC Central Committee on 22 September 1999.

[27] Maddison, *Chinese Economic Performance in the Long Run*, p. 95.

[28] Similar corruption can be observed in Russia. See John F. Harris, "Clinton Warns Russian about Corruption," *Washington Post*, 13 September 1999, p. A16. See also Wang Weiguang, "Correctly Understand and Handle Conflicts of Interests among the People in the New Period," *Beijing Renmin Ribao*, 22 June 1999, from *World News Connection*, 25 June 1999, FBIS-CHI-1999-0624, regarding conflicts of interests among the people in the new period.

[29] Kent E. Calder, "Asia's Empty Gas Tank," *Foreign Affairs* 75, 2 (March/April 1996), pp. 55–69. The APEC's Advisory Committee for Energy predicted that China's oil imports would increase to 19 percent of Asia's oil imports by the year 2010 (Japan 37%, Korea 18%, Taiwan and Hong Kong 9%, ASEAN countries 27%, in the same year).

[30] Matt Forney, "China Learns Lessons on Adaptability: Ten Years after Tiananmen Students Gained Much of What They Sought," *Wall Street Journal*, 2 June 1999, p. A23.

[31] See "Special Reports: China, the People's Republic at 50," *Wall Street Journal Interactive Edition*, 13 September 1999. Related articles from this source include Leslie Chang, "Freer Markets Encourage Trade, New Bonds between Provinces"; Marcus Brauchli, "To Foreigners Who Sought a New Life, China's Market Reforms Are a Betrayal"; and Erik Guyot, "Foreign Companies Help Spark Corporate Reform across China."

[32] For pros and cons on this issue, see Richard Bernstein and Ross H. Munro, "China I: The Coming Conflict with America," *Foreign Affairs* 76, 2 (March/April 1997), pp. 18–32; Robert S. Ross, "China II: Beijing As a Conservative Power," *Foreign Affairs* 76, 2 (March/April 1997), pp. 33–44; and "Who's Afraid of China," *New York Times Magazine*, 1 August 1999.

[33] The figures are different from various researchers. Bernstein and Munro, "China I: The Coming Conflict with America," p. 25, insist that China's real annual defense budget amounts to a minimum of $87 billion more than Japan's, with some adjustments.

[34] Robert S. Ross, "China II: Beijing As a Conservative Power," p. 39.

[35] Bates Gill, "Power Plays While There's Less to the Chinese Threat than Meets the Eye," *Washington Post*, 20 June 1999, p. B01. "The United States will retain more than a 10-to-1 advantage in strategic warheads over China for many years to come."

[36] See Andrey Kirillov, "Russia, China Continue Talks on Military Cooperation," *Moscow ITAR-TASS*, 25 August 1999, from *World New Connection,* 26 August 1999, FBIS-CHI-1999-0825; and "Russia, China Sign Contract for Sale of SU-30MKK Jets," *Moscow Interfax*, 26 August 1999, from *World News Connection,* 26 August 1999, FBIS-CHI-1999-0826.

[37] Gerald Segal, "Does China Matter?" p. 32. For recent reports in the *Wall Street Journal Interactive Edition*, see "Special Reports: China, the People's Republic at 50" including Matt Forney, "PLA Makes a Big Move to Modernize, but Peace Is Needed to Finish the Job," and Karby Leggett, "Large Income Gap a New Woe for China's Army of Farmers."
[38] Chen Jian, *The China Challenge in the Twenty-First Century: Implications for US Foreign Policy* (Washington, DC: US Institute for Peace, 1998), pp. 20. For recent reports, see "Special Reports: China, the People's Republic at 50," in *Wall Street Journal Interactive Edition,* including He Qinglian, "Relation between China's Politics, Society Hurts Economic Reforms," and W. J. F. Jenner, "An Ever-Changing Past Gives Few Clues to China's Politics."
[39] John Pomfret, "China Special Report: Chinese Search for New Values," *Washington Post*, 26 September 1999, p. A1; and Pomfret, "In China, Celebration and Contradiction," *Washington Post*, 29 September 1999, p. A1. Time is the medicine for democratization. Economic development pulls political development and vice versa. It is obvious that the new generation of Chinese people will have an improved democratic system just as Western civilization has experienced political evolution.
[40] Chen Jian, *China Challenge*, p. 14. The author discusses Party failures, the Chinese search for faith, crime and corruption, private business, and what is "coolest" in China.
[41] WheeGook Kim, "The Impact of Sino-American Relations on Korean Unification," *Journal of East Asian Affairs* 11, 1 (Winter/Spring 1997), pp. 20–64; Chen Jian, *China Challenge*, pp. 19–20.
[42] Column Lynch, "UN Plans for E. Timor Authority," *Washington Post*, 16 September 1999, p. 17; "Indonesian Troops Leaving East Timor," *New York Times Internet*, 17 September 1999.
[43] For more on regional convergence in Asia, see Steven Radelet and Jeffrey Sachs, "Asia's Reemergence," *Foreign Affairs* 76, 6 (November/December 1997), pp. 44–59.
[44] Samuel P. Huntington, "The Lonely Superpower," *Foreign Affairs* 78, 2 (March/April 1999), p. 49.
[45] Tyler Marshal, "Anti-NATO Axis Could Pose Threat, Experts Say; Geopolitics: China-India-Russia Coalition after Kosovo," *Los Angeles Times*, 27 September 1999, p. A-1.
[46] Sheng Lijun, "China and the United States: Asymmetrical Strategic Partners," *Washington Quarterly* 22, 3 (Summer 1999), pp. 147–64.
[47] "North Korea–Russia Signs a New Diplomatic Agreement by Removing the Existing Article of Automatic Military Engagement," *JungAng Internet Service*, 14 September 1999.
[48] C. Kenneth Quinones, "North Korea's New Nuclear Site: Fact or Fiction," *International Journal of Korean Studies* 2, 1 (Fall/Winter 1998), pp. 45–51.
[49] Sheryl WuDunn, "North Korea Fires Missile over Japanese Territory," *New York Times on the Web*, 1 September 1999.
[50] Myung Chol Kim, "Farewell to 1994 Agreed Framework!," *NAPSNet Special Report*—PFO #23C, Berkeley, CA: Nautilus Institute, 24 November 1998. The author is an authorized representative of the DPRK in Tokyo, and this paper threatens the United States.
[51] Larry A. Niksch, "US Policy toward North Korea: The Agreed Framework's Fading Prospects and a Look at Alternative Policies," paper presented at the European Union Policy Seminar, "North Korean Scenarios 1998–2003 and EU Responses," sponsored by the Conflict Prevention Network of the European Union, 13 October 1998.
[52] WheeGook Kim, "DRPK's Satellite Launch and Its Aftermath," *Korea Defense Review*, October 1998, pp. 31–38. For Japan's sensitive response, see p. 33.
[53] For further discussion, see Morton I. Abramowitz, *Managing Change on the Korean Peninsula: Report of an Independent Task Force Sponsored by the Council on Foreign Relations* (New York: Council on Foreign Relations, 1998); and US Institute for Peace, *Mistrust and the*

Korean Peninsula: Dangers of Miscalculation, USIP Special Report (Washington, DC: US Institute for Peace, 1998).

[54] Il Woo Jee, "North Korea, Transfer Missile Technology to Iran and Syria," *Digital Chosun Ilbo*, 14 September 1999; "North Korea Can Deploy Nuclear Weapon within Four Months," *Hankyoreh Internet*, 20 August 1999; Hyo Sang Kang, "Chinese Ambassador to Washington, China Does NOT Want Nuclear Weapon Deployed by Either North or South," *Digital Chosun Ilbo*, 20 August 1999.

[55] Seung Dong Han, "Invading West Sea: Analyses for the West Sea Incident /Foreign Specialists," *Internet Hankyoreh*, 18 June 1999. This is an interview article with Selig Harrison, David Brown, Scott Snyder, Dakesada Hedesi, and Kimiya Dadaci. See also Korea Research Institute for Strategy, *The Policy Discussions Report: Evaluation of West Sea Incident and Policy Direction in the Future* (Seoul: Korea Research Institute for Strategy, 1999); and WheeGook Kim, "North–South Korean Naval Clash in West Sea and the Engagement Policy," *Korea Defense Review*, July 1999, pp. 21–26.

[56] Yong-sam Kim, "Excerpts from Hwang Chang-yop's November Letters," *Chosun Ilbo*, 14 February 1997, from *World News Connection*, 18 February 1997, FBIS-EAS-97-031; Eui Bong Hwang and Jong Shik Gong, "Sketch of Hwang Chang-yop Escape: The Messed Contradiction of North Korean System," *Maidas Donga Ilbo*, 13 February 1997; and Bang Hyung Nam, "Aftermath of Hwang Chang-yop's Escape: North-South-China Relations," *Maidas Donga Ilbo*, 13 February 1997.

[57] Andrew Natsios, *Special Report: The Politics of Famine in North Korea* (Washington, DC: US Institute for Peace, 1999).

[58] "Bank of Korea: DPRK Economy Shrinks for Ninth Straight Year," *Seoul Yonhap*, 26 August 1999, from *World News Connection*, 27 August 1999, FBIS-EAS-1999-0826.

[59] Doug Struck, "Famine in North Korea Is Easing, Official Says," *Washington Post*, 16 August 1999, p. A10; and Barbara Crossette, "North Korea Appears to Be Emerging from Years of Severe Famine," *New York Times on the Web*, 20 August 1999.

[60] Myong Chol Kim, "Kim Myong Chol on Paik's Article," *NAPSNet Policy Forum Online* 99–06, 16 June 1999. For a general approach, see Pyong Hoi Goo and Byong Jip Moon, eds., *The North Korean Economy: Theories and Practices* (Seoul: Korea Trade Association, 1996).

[61] WheeGook Kim, "Problems and Remedies of the North Korean Economy: A Strategic Approach," *Korean Journal of Defense Analysis* 8, 2 (Winter 1996), esp. "The Root of Problems," pp. 234–240.

[62] Paul Krugman, "The Myth of Asia's Miracle," *Foreign Affairs* 73, 6 (November/December 1994), pp. 62–78.

[63] Information Analysis Department, *North and South Korean Economic Indicators, Seoul: Ministry of National Defense* (Seoul: Ministry of Unification, various years).

[64] Ibid., various years.

[65] For military expansion and economic decline, see Paul Kennedy, *The Rise and Fall of the Great Powers: Economic Change and Military Conflict from 1500 to 2000* (New York: Vintage Books, 1989); and Robert W. DeGrasse Jr., *Military Expansion, Economic Decline: The Impact of Military Spending on US Economic Performance* (Armonk, NY: M. E. Sharpe, 1983). For defense economics, see Todd Sandler and Keith Hartley, *The Economics of Defense* (New York: Cambridge University Press, 1995); and Christian Schmidt, *The Economics of Military Expenditures: Military Expenditures, Economic Growth, and Fluctuations* (New York: St. Martin's Press, 1987).

[66] In Goo Kim and Yong Won Yoo, "North Korea Imported 40 MIG-21 from a CIS Nations," *Digital Chosun Ilbo*, 7 August 1999; Min Bae Kim, "MIG-21 Purchase Not Likely from

Revenue from Mt. Geumgang Tour," *Digital Chosun Ilbo*, 12 August 1999; and Judith Miller and Steve Levine, "To Appease US, Kazakhstan Acts on MIG Sales," *New York Times on the Web*, 12 September 1999.

[67] Ministry of National Defense, *Defense White Paper 1998* (Seoul: Government of Republic of Korea, 1998), pp. 57–69, esp. "North Korean Military Threat."

[68] Desaix Anderson in *NAPSNet Special Report—WAC Conference,* Part 1, 28 May 1999. He suggested immediate steps to be taken by the United States, Japan, and South Korea, including facilitating North Korea's joining the IMF.

[69] Nicholas Everstadt, "The Road from Berlin," *Digital Chosun Ilbo*, 13 September 1999. "The same September 1998 Supreme People's Assembly gathering that elevated Kim Jong-il to the DPRK's highest post also embraced a new official objective: to become a 'powerful and prosperous state' (*Kangsong Taeguk*)."

[70] John Locke, *Two Treatises on Government*, collectors ed. (Norwalk, CT: Easton Press, 1991), p. 127. "A state also of equality, wherein all the power and jurisdiction is reciprocal, no one having more than another, there being nothing more evident than that creatures of the same species and rank, promiscuously born to all the same advantages of Nature, and the use of the same faculties, should also be equal one amongst another, without subordination or subjection."

[71] Ministry of Unification, *Policy towards North Korea for Peace, Reconciliation and Cooperation* (Seoul: Korean Government, 1999), pp. 16–21.

[72] Young Dae Song, "A Year of Kim Jong-il Regime and the Policy towards North Korea," *Hankuk Ilbo*, 7 September 1999, p. 10. The article suggests three points: (a) conditional engagement with carrot and stick, (b) development of negotiation techniques with reciprocity, and (c) parallelism between US-DPRK and North-South relations.

[73] Won Sup Lee, "Lee Won Sup Column: Illusion and Reality of North–South Korean Talks First," *Hankyoreh Internet*, 28 September 1999.

[74] David Steinberg in *NAPSNet Special Report—WAC Conference,* Part 1, 28 May 1999. He noted that the sunshine policy is really a code name for absorption. See also "North Korea Reconfirms No Missile Test," *Hankyoreh Internet*, 26 September 1999. "The engagement or sunshine policy is an absorption strategy by transforming North Korea to the liberal democratic system, and even the South Korean authorities are mentioning in public that the sunshine policy is similar to that the US peace strategy caused to destroy former Soviet Union."

[75] There exist pains and gains from conflict between politics and economy. DPRK's contradictory behavior includes rejecting the sunshine policy but expanding Hyundai operations, resuming Beijing talks but confronting South Korea in the Yellow Sea, and seeking foreign investment but abducting a Korean-American businesswoman.

[76] US Institute for Peace, *Challenges of Building a Korean Peace Process: Political and Economic Transition on the Korean Peninsula* (Washington, DC: US Institute for Peace, 1998).

[77] Stephen E. Noerper, "Toward a New Stability: Challenges and Change on the Korean Peninsula," paper presented at the Thirteenth Asia-Pacific Roundtable, hosted by Institute of Strategic and International Studies, held in Kuala Lumpur, Malaysia, on 30 April – 2 May 1999, from *NAPSNet Special Report*, 3 June 1999. Russia will resume supplying the DPRK crude oil—possibly 400,000 to 500,000 tons in 1999. President Kim Dae-jung's four-day visit to Russia renewed support for six-party talks on security in Northeast Asia, to include Russia, since he hoped that a new DPRK-Russia relationship would help move North Korea from isolation and promote peace and security in Northeast Asia. Hitoshi Tanaka in *NAPSNet Special Report—WAC Conference,* Part 1, 28 May 1999, noted that the Japanese are concerned with DPRK spies, missile launches, ship incursions, abductions of Japanese nationals, and financial transfers from pachinko parlors in Japan. He added that Japan wants to see the realization of six-party talks.

[78] Beijing Reuters, "China Urges Rival Koreas to Improve Ties," CNN.com, 29 August 1999, Asia-Pacific News. "The North and the South are parties directly concerned with the peninsula issue, and the issue should be settled independently without interference from outside, through such political means as peaceful dialogue." The South Korean Defense Minister visited China on 23 August 1999 and said that South Korea sought a "cooperative partnership" with China, and requested Beijing "to support Seoul's effort to maintain stability on the Korean peninsula." Beijing Yonhap, "China Supports Korean Unification without Interference from Outside: Kim Yong Nam – Li Peng Talks," *JoongAng Ilbo* Internet Service, 4 June 1999.
[79] It is acceptable for South Korea to retaliate for the DPRK's military provocation because the principle of reciprocity should be applied as a part of the norms and rules of international relations.
[80] Ministry of Unification, "Policy towards North and the Position on Current Issues" (Seoul: Korean Government, 30 July 1999), p. 28.
[81] In off-the-record discussions at the Hudson Institute in November 1998, an invited speaker at a seminar, a senior staff member for an influential US representative, insisted that the only solution for the United States was a war against North Korea. A question from the floor was how the United States would enter the war without consensus with South Korea. For congressional activities, see Benjamin A. Gilman, "Introduction of H.R. 1835, North Korea Threat Reduction Act of 1999," in *Congressional Record*, 106th Congress, lst sess., 1999, Vol. 144.
[82] Richard L. Armitage, "A Comprehensive Approach to North Korea," Strategic Forum No. 159, (Washington, DC: US National Defense University, March 1999).
[83] Morton I. Abramowitz and James T. Laney, *US Policy toward North Korea: A Second Look* (New York: Council on Foreign Relations, July 1999). The council's first report was *Managing Change on the Korean Peninsula: Report of an Independent Task Force Sponsored by Council on Foreign Relations* (New York: Council on Foreign Relations, June 1998). Daryl M. Plunk, *Time for a New North Korea Policy*, executive summary No. 1304 (Washington, DC: Heritage Foundation, 2 July 1999). Plunk suggests four points: policy tuning with allies, aid to North Korea based on real concessions, creation of a peace corps for the North, and appointment of senior negotiators as special envoys.
[84] William Cohen, *The United States Security Strategy for the East Asia-Pacific Region* (Washington, DC: US Department of Defense, 1998), esp. "Comprehensive Engagement with China," p. 30.
[85] William Drozdiak, "N. Korean Pledge Eases Fears on Missile Test," *Washington Post*, 13 September 1999, p. A1.
[86] "Encouraging Pyongyang," *Asian Wall Street Journal* in *Wall Street Journal Interactive Edition*, 20 September 1999.
[87] Jooin Yom, "President Kim, DPRK-US Talks Is a Result of Win-Win Strategy," *Digital Chosun Ilbo*, 14 September 1999.
[88] Tae Kyu Oh, "Perry's Report: Three-Step Recommendation to Terminate the Cold War in the Korean Peninsula," *Hankyoreh Internet*, 14 September 1999; "The Summary of Perry's Report," *Hankyoreh Internet*, 15 September 1999.
[89] "Clinton Eases North Korea Sanctions," *New York Times on the Web*, 17 September 1999.
[90] Reuters, "N. Korea Urges US to Ease Sanctions Further," *New York Times on the Web*, 21 September 1999.
[91] The category of US economic sanctions against North Korea includes diplomatic relations, US 25-mile travel limit, trade embargo, exports, shipping, most favored nation, proliferation, terrorism, foreign assistance (human rights, communist states, security assistance, IFI lending).

See "North Korea Sanctions," by visiting http: //www.nautilus.org /library/security /references/ sanctions.html/.

[92] Jon Brook Wolfsthal, "Seizing an Opportunity in N. Korea," *NAPSNet Policy Forum Online* #9907C (Berkeley, CA: Nautilus Institute, 1999).

[93] Jung Hyun Kwon, "Urgent Interview with Kyong Won Kim and Young Sun Ha on US-DPRK Berlin Agreement," *Digital Chosun Ilbo*, 13 September 1999.

[94] "Japan-DPRK Relations," *NAPSNet Daily Report*, Berkeley, California, 22 September 1999. "China Daily ("Japan May Lift Sanctions on DPRK," Tokyo, 9/20/99, p. A11) reported that Japanese Prime Minister Keizo Obuchi said on September 19 that Japan may lift sanctions on the DPRK if the DPRK's freeze on missile test-firing becomes 'more certain.' We support it as a step forward for improving relations between the US and the DPRK."

[95] "Hyundai to Build $57 Million Gym in North Korea," *Wall Street Interactive Edition*, 20 September 1999; Byung Soo Park, "North-South Exchanges: DPRK Circus Will Visit Seoul in November," *Hankyoreh Internet*, 22 September 1999; In-ku Kim, "North Korea Asks South for Reforestation Aid," *Chosun Ilbo* (Seoul), 27 September 1999, from *NAPSNet Daily Report*, Berkeley, California, 28 September 1999.

[96] Ji-ho Kim, "Sunshine Policy May Encourage Pyongyang to Bypass Seoul, Experts Say," *Korea Herald* (Seoul), 28 September 1999, from *NAPSNet Daily Report*, on the same day. "Despite their official welcome of the rapid thaw in US-DPRK ties, there are concerns among some ROK unification officials and DPRK watchers that the DPRK may bypass the ROK in dealing with inter-Korean affairs. While ROK officials ask for more patience, many DPRK watchers doubt if such patience can bring about the desired results in the inter-Korean relationship. Some of them call on the ROK government to revise its reconciliatory policy toward the DPRK."

[97] Ministry of Unification, *Monthly Report: Inter-Korean Interchange & Cooperation and Humanitarian Projects*, Seoul, Korea: Korean Government, various issues. For further information, visit http:// www.unikorea.go.kr/.

[98] WheeGook Kim, "Problems and Remedies of the North Korean Economy: A Strategic Approach," *Korean Journal of Defense Analysis* 8, 2 (Winter 1996), p. 251.

[99] Regarding North Korean computer software technology, see Chan-Mo Park, "Current Status of Software Research and Development in North Korea," *International Journal of Korean Studies* 2, 1 (Spring/Summer 1999), pp. 144–59.

[100] Susan Rose-Ackerman, "Corruption and Development," in Boris Peskovic and Joseph E. Stiglitz, eds., *Annual World Bank Conference on Development Economics 1997* (Washington, DC: World Bank, 1997), pp. 37–57.

[101] WheeGook Kim, "Problems and Remedies," p. 254.

Chapter IV
Democracy and Economic Development in South Korea: An Application of Experiences to Transform North Korea*

Introduction

The South Korean economy was highly praised by foreign economists as a successful model of development and proudly joined OECD in late 1996 as the world's eleventh largest economy with over $10,000 of per capita income. Since then, a series of business bankruptcies and financial crisis resulted in the presence of IMF supervision by December 3, 1997 causing a shift in the political power. The new administration began to work for systemic reforms, which have been interrupted by the opposition in politics, entrenched Chaebols in economy, and labor unions in society.[1]

Despite the reform pressures from the people, the lack of driving forces reduced attracting direct foreign investment, which caused the stock index to fall from mid 500 in late February to low 300 by mid June 1998 coinciding with President Kim Dae Jung's (hereafter DJ) Washington visit. His party's victory in local elections and the promise of strong U.S. supports energized DJ to expedite reform programs. The progress may take longer than expected due to weakened political coalition, missed freshness of political appointees, unrelenting resistance of preoccupied interest groups, unbreakable old habits particularly in politics,[2] and unhealthy economic environment in the region including Japan and the countries experiencing the financial crisis.

Democracy and economic development have been interacting in the process of modernization in South Korea like most other Asian countries: authoritarian politics controlled the market while economic growth facilitated democratization. President Park Jung Hee launched a series of economic development plans (EDPs) in 1962, which enabled the government to allocate its resources by restricting political freedom in South Korea. The first three five-year EDPs proved to be very successful when the economy was small and inelastic. As the market grew, state intervention in the later period caused structural problems within the economy that eventually led to idle capacities and bottlenecks in the industries. With declined efficiency and competitiveness, President Park's early successes were becoming a fading memory by leaving oncoming structural problems.

The state intervention in the economy pursues either capitalistic efficiency or democratic equality, both which cannot be achieved simultaneously because of tradeoff

---

* Published by the *International Journal of Korean Studies* II (1) (Fall/Winter 1998): 69-99. Reprinted by the permission of the publisher. A Draft Paper was presented to the *Eighth International Economic Convention* held at the Korea University in Seoul, South Korea on August 18-19, 1998 sponsored by the Korean Economic Association.

between the two objectives. In fact, state intervention in lagged politics caused more problems than solutions in recovering market competition because of doing incorrectly or doing nothing for what the state should have done necessarily. Corrupted politicians collaborating with Chaebols can only result in the political-economic complex, which jeopardized the market function, forced economic decline and financial crisis requiring structural reforms with expensive costs. Since corrupt politics caused market failures and government failures, the theory of balanced development in politics with economy, rather than the Asian values, became persuasive in the age of globalization.[3]

The South Korean economy has been a role model of economic development. Newly faced with the financial crisis, it demanded a painful restructure of the entire system. So it is questioned whether the East Asian economic development model (EAM) is still alive. The Asian financial crisis was a happening in the process of economic development, where unresponsive politics ruined the economy. The EAM must be considered with a strong link to politics affecting its efficiency. Under the redefined EAM, the time span is extended to the advanced democracy stage. In this scenario, the three stages are considered for South Korea: first, economic takeoff under the authoritarian regime; second, conflicting interests between democracy and economic growth; and third, balanced development of subsystems in the age of internationalization.[4]

The economic experiences of South Korea provide valuable lessons for late coming transition economies particularly in North Korea. If North Korea pursues a systemic change towards the market economy, then Pyongyang needs to follow the course of openness that took place in China. The Chinese model teaches how to smooth out the freedom waves coming from economic openness and the South Korean model teaches how to maximize efficiency of resource allocation in the takeoff stage. The mixture of both experiences in China and South Korea will provide indispensable lessons for North Korea in the process of political and economic transformation when the DJ's engagement policy is realistic and mutually beneficial for inter-Korean economic cooperation.

The study sets three goals to be discussed in three main chapters. In the first, the study investigates the role of state in the South Korea economy in terms of market failures and government failures. Secondly, redefining the EAM with explaining that the model is not dead but alive under progress, the study discusses major issues on structural reforms arising in the final stage of South Korean economic development. Thirdly, it analyzes lessons learned from the South Korean economy to be applied to oncoming transitional woes of the North Korean economy. The study's findings will contribute to making policies for structural reforms in South Korea and to transforming the system of China, Vietnam, and North Korea by reducing trial and errors in efforts to escape from the poverty.

The Role of State in the South Korean Economy[5]

The welfare economic theorem states that a government cannot do any better than the market, and market efficiency is achieved by the Pareto optimal allocation of resources, which defines that no one could be better off by reallocating resources without making someone else worse off. Under this theorem, government intervention is justified to recover the efficiency in case of market failures due to imperfect competition, external effects, and public goods.[6] Imperfect competition is caused by uncertainty coming from inadequate information, increasing returns to scale, and entry barriers.[7] The government attacks imperfect competition and external effects to overcome *market failures* while it pursues public goods hurting more or less free competition in the market.[8]

A serious problem of state intervention in the market appears in conflict and tradeoff between capitalistic efficiency (dollars) and democratic equality (rights).[9] If a government favors efficiency measures to correct market failures by ignoring equality values, income distribution is worsened and social security is threatened. If a government favors equality measures to secure the social welfare by ignoring efficiency values, the market fails by losing free competition. The dilemma of state intervention, therefore, is an issue of political choice voting for a certain candidate among three categories: a conservative toward efficiency, a liberal toward equality, and an independent toward neutrality or compromise. The choice depends on the political climate though it always shifts from one to another by power dynamics between parties as well as government branches.

Government failures are another problem of the role of state in the economy raising social costs without achieving goals, caused by failures of commission and failures of omission.[10] The former comes from improper state intervention such as in public enterprises, budget allocation, and private sector control, while the latter comes from negligence of state intervention in matters necessary to be done such as in maintenance of infrastructure, foreign exchange rates, and interest rates. Government failures are caused by administrative incapability or interruption of government function due to the political-economic complex involved in corruption. The problems of developing countries are largely caused by both reasons, but those of South Korea belong to the latter.

The nature of power shows increasing returns to scale, so that incumbent political power is used to acquire economic power which makes it possible to acquire additional political power.[11] This kind of chain actions generates the monopoly power in politics and economy by creating the political-economic complex in the system. In the legislative branch, for example, candidates running for the office of National Assembly are not chosen by primary elections in each electoral district, but are nominated by a committee of the central party. This allows incumbent party bosses to strengthen the factional power in politics so that a failed candidate runs for the presidential race repeatedly. The lack of political competition interrupts new candidates to enter national politics, weakening democratic function of check and balance. So it is possible that President rules over the National Assembly while politicians are secured from legal charges, which is a starting point of government failures.[12] Similarly in both administrative and judicial branches, bureaucratic monopoly by regionalism and school faction jeopardizes societal fairness and reduces efficiency.

The rise of Chaebols is a byproduct of market failures and government failures. First, the government provided them with an easy access to financial institutions for loans and credits through cross-finance guarantees withheld from non-group companies. Their monopoly power terminated small businesses and created a series of subcontracts worsening quality of products as shown in the collapse of bridges and buildings. Secondly, Chaebols obtained most government contracts through disguised competition. It is a well-known secret that former presidents used to collect campaign funds from the presidential office, and endless scandals in government contracts were disclosed after power transfers. Thirdly, the export-led growth strategy provided import licensing, tax exemptions, and export subsidies to businesses for import substitution and export promotion without considering negative effects and regional fairness.[13] As a result, over expansion, heavy debts, bad investment, and high overhead costs from wastes caused a series of bankruptcies of South Korean firms.

Labor monopoly was another form of government failures. The labor union leaders have claimed that a large part of Chaebols' wealth should be shared with the workers since Chaebols accumulated wealth at the workers' cost by monopolistic profits, tax exemption, privileges and subsidies, and low wages by suppressing labor movement. The claim is justifiable, though the consensus to achieve the goal is difficult. When the labor movement became violent and politicized, the government collaborating with Chaebols sold some generosity of compromise to labor unions by prohibiting layoffs to secure jobs and allowed them a wrong routine of "no work and get paid" without improving the social security measures. The rigidity of labor market has forced domestic industries to move abroad and foreign firms to hesitate direct investment in South Korea.[14]

The relations between democracy and economic development have been inconsistent but positive signs resulted in many cases including South Korea.[15] Joseph Schumpeter viewed that there is no necessary relation between socialism and democracy since the one can exist without the other. At the same time he saw that there is no incompatibility between them since the socialist engine can be run on democratic principles in appropriate states of the social environment.[16] He emphasized democratic conditions including human material in politics, effective political decision, bureaucratic capability, democratic self-control, and effective leadership competition.[17]

The issue lies in whether the economic system is expected to be democratic. The fall of communism in 1991 evidenced that capitalism is a necessary, though not sufficient, condition for democracy, but democracy is not a precondition for capitalism though it is necessary for sustainable growth in the long run.[18]

Democracy is essential for sustainable growth since it facilitates check and balance in politics and promotes competition in the economy by minimizing corruption and maximizing efficiency. An efficient modernization of a nation requires coordinated efforts of the entire system by integrating vertical elements as well as horizontal elements of subsystems including politics, economy, national security, society, and others. If the economy moves quickly forward while politics remain lagged, the second class politics interrupt market competition, which distorts resource allocation. As a result, adjustment costs become expensive in the future, which the EAM has faced.

The theory of balanced development between politics and economy is controversial since the initial conditions are different in various countries including transition economies.[19] First, China chose *the autocratic path* in its modernization by pursuing economic growth first and moving gradually toward democracy later by adopting the South Korean model where political sacrifice was compensated by rising income for a while. Secondly, Russia chose *the democratic path* by pursuing democratization first and economic reforms later, resulting in regime's collapse since the economy could not support liberalized politics.[20] Thirdly, *the balanced path* is in simultaneous interactions between political opening and economic reforms in development.[21] Taking the autocratic path in the early stage, South Korea has been forced to choose the balanced path by pursuing simultaneous development of politics with economy since the financial crisis hit its economy.

China has survived while the USSR perished in the process of economic transformation. Economic reform proceeded political one in the former, while political reform proceeded economic one in the latter. The collapse of the USSR is explained by the fact that its failing economy could no longer support country's vast political-military system, and the bankrupt government could no longer guarantee law and order. In contrast, Deng Xiaoping adopted a gradually opening policy, attracting foreign capital, promoting exports, and pursuing economic transformation followed by political reform.[22] Deng achieved economic success, but he did not expect freedom waves from openness to hit a Beijing's square so fast and violently in 1989 similarly to that President Park saw the same in the major cities in South Korea, threatening survival of his regime.

The political-economic interactions are investigated by the two ways viewing from economy toward politics or vice versa. On the one hand, economic development facilitates democratization.[23] Firstly, economic growth is accompanied by trade expansion by taking comparative advantage of a country, which requires more education and training to produce better quality of products to win foreign competition. The knowledge gained from education and training awakens self-recognition respecting democratic values of freedom and equality, which refuse to accept the authoritarian rule ruining humanity in the society. Secondly, trade expansion raises the volume of transportation and communications through the border. The border traffics are controllable when the economy is small and simple, but it is too expensive to control when traffics are heavy. Expanded foreign trade with advanced technology expedites information flow and spreads western civilization, which stimulates liberalization. Thirdly, the rise of household income widens the band of economic middle class, which allows more people to receive education and to travel often to the world. The wider middle class demands more political power and strengthens the majority rule in the process of decision making by money power, which contributes to democratization. Finally, foreign trade expedites internalization recognizing the importance of reciprocity, which respects foreign values as much as own ones. The openness of local markets to foreign firms abolishes cultural barriers[24] and reduces self-determination of domestic politics due to increasing interdependence between nations of trade partners. The politics cannot remain closed in the market economy though the authoritarian regime tries to keep continuously their existing interests in politics and economy.[25]

On the other hand, democracy is necessary to maintain sustainable growth of capitalistic economies by maximizing efficiency. The South Korean economy remained efficient in the three five-year EDPs (1962-1976)[26] despite excessive intervention by the authoritarian regime because of following reasons. The economy was small and the market was inelastic, so government intervention was desirable until the market recovered competition. The EDPs were well prepared for resource allocation by forcing the economy to move from labor- towards capital- and technology-intensive industries with proper investment in infrastructure. The driving forces were aggressive like in the revolutionary period of Soviet Union by mobilizing available capital and labor. The export-led growth strategy and continuous policy adjustment to environmental changes were successful in moving from import substitution toward export promotion by accumulating capital and technology. Finally, the government coordinated properly with business and labor, which were motivated by hungry sprits with a pride of nation building in fatherland modernization.[27]

However, when the economy became complicated in the second half of 1970s, government intervention distorted resource allocation, which reduced efficiency and growth. The shipbuilding industry, for example, was expanded due to government subsidies when the world demand began to decline, so that the level of capacity utilization remained below 40% until mid-1980s, which lowered factor productivity and increased foreign debt.[28] Corrupt politics and bureaucrats sold monopoly power to favored businesses and labor unions by receiving bribes in returns, which caused market failures, government failures, financial crisis, and economic recession at the end. It is a reciprocal example to the former that corrupt politics have ruined the economy in South Korea.

What are the sources of corruption in details?[29] Firstly, corruption is accompanied by the lack of transparency and accountability in government and business. Corrupt public officials use their power for personal gains by receiving bribes, while private donors get what they want from the government. Secondly, policies and regulations having gaps between demand and supply invite corruption since businesses and individuals try to avoid red tapes by offering bribes to reduce costs and to save time. The thriving underground economies try not to evade tax as in rich economies, but mainly to dodge the red tape and the inevitable bribes in the formal sector.[30] Thirdly, if corrupt individuals are rarely detected and punished, or if expected returns of breaking laws are much higher than expected costs, or if social justice does not exist in the system, the system itself facilitates corruption. Finally, if the salary is low and job loss would not be a problem, it is easy to be corrupt since benefits are much higher than costs of punishment.

Then, what can be done about entrenched corruption in South Korea? The answer lies in the three categories: to enhance democratic function of check and balance in politics and government, to promote competition in economy and business, and to organize active citizens' groups for social interactions for consensus buildup by watching civil services and providing policy input.[31] The first category should focus on to reduce the discretionary power of government official, to enforce anticorruption laws, to reform the civil service, and to increase the accountability of government to citizens.[32] It is essential for the people to see and to believe that anyone who violates laws must pay the price sooner or later for one's wrong doing in the society without exception.

The East Asian Development Models Is Still Under Progress

The EAM, the rapid growth model of Japan, Taiwan, and South Korea, can be understood as a combination of both economic and non-economic factors. The former includes high investment ratios, small public sectors, export orientation, labor market competition, state intervention in the economy, large and efficient investments in human capital, and well-developed capacities to absorb new technologies. The latter includes ethnic and linguistic homogeneity, relatively compact geography, manageable population size, and Confucian tradition; which influence labor productivity, savings behavior, and other aspects of economic performance.[33] However, the Asian values became retarded and voices demanding to consider political elements are heard in defining the model.[34]

Economic growth sources are defined by both factor input mobilization and productivity growth, the shares of which vary according to country, period, and estimation method.[35] Dale Jorgenson estimated that the share of economic growth generated by capital and labor input is three quarters of total growth. In his study, U.S. economic growth from 1948-1979 was fostered by growth of capital input (45.6%), growth of labor input (30.7%), and productivity growth (24.7%).[36] The rise of savings affected by consumption behavior generates growth in capital input, while population growth generates increase in labor input which is affected by production behavior such as labor-leisure choices. Paul Krugman argues, by comparing the EAM to the Soviet Union in its early period of economic development, that East Asian growth is driven not by productivity growth in terms of efficiency gain, but rather by resource mobilization. He explains that input driven growth continuously and intensively supplies capital and labor consequently yielding diminished economic returns and a sharp deceleration of growth. Meanwhile, the diffusion of technology will place huge strains on Western society, so that no technological convergence between East and West is expected. He viewed that state intervention in the Asian economies would not make any visible difference.[37]

While Krugman presents sound arguments about problems of government intervention, he misconstrues important points on the EAM where investment is not a simple accumulation of fixed capital. In major equipment purchases from advanced countries, Seoul requires extensive transfer of technology. The transfer also naturally occurs through the learning-by-doing process on the jobs at joint-venture facilities. The World Bank estimated that the contributing share of total factor productivity to total growth was over 33% for Japan, Taiwan, and South Korea during the period of 1960-1989.[38] This number is much higher than Jorgenson's estimate of 24.7% for the United States. As long as the marginal return of capital exceeds its cost, the growth based on rapid capital accumulation would be highly desirable though its marginal productivity is likely to decline, not sharply as Krugman worried, but gradually as the capital stock deepens.

Due to the following short comings in its definition, the EAM needs to expand its scope to include the advanced stage of democracy. First, even though economists have disregarded the influence of political elements in the model, democratization has, in fact, largely affected economic development. It is fundamental to consider political elements in accurately defining the EAM from the view of political economy. Secondly, the time-line of the EAM considered only the two stages of economic takeoff and growth expansion. But the model must include the advanced stage of democracy to be built after structural adjustment since the financial crisis is a process of economic development. Thirdly, technological advancement in transportation and communications has made the world closer and faster than ever before. The trade relations largely affect foreign relations as recently seen between the United States and China. The globalization of the information age must be considered in defining the economic development model.

South Korean economic history is divided into three periods of major political changes. In the initial stage of *economic takeoff under the authoritarian regime (1962-1979)*, President Park controlled the one-half market economy by suppressing democracy. By crushing the opposing freedom movement, he fortified an authoritarian regime and allocated resources by launching a series of EDPs. An input-output analysis by this author indicated that the export-led growth strategy of South Korea was the best choice among available alternatives.[39] This strategy produced the largest GDP for the same level of aggregate final demand. Import substitution required a huge amount of physical and human capital which could be financed by export earnings, while export promotion required advanced technology which could be accumulated by import substitution; both were mutually supportive and complimentary. The movement of comparative advantage due to the shorter product-life cycle transformed the industrial structure absorbed by import substitution, and proper adjustment helped to maintain its competitiveness. Finally, a supportive strategy of domestic demand expansion was desirable only if market openness did not suppress consumption of domestic products in fair competition, though it proved to be wrong because of government failures.

The export-led growth strategy exploited economies of scale through foreign trade despite a narrow domestic market. Taking comparative advantage with favorite patterns of trade through efficient resource allocation, South Korea improved its products' competitiveness. Protection and subsidization allowed monopolistic profits to export industries rapidly promoting exports, and trade expansion widened the production possibility frontier in the economy. Though the overall economic returns from export promotion were larger than the cost, the incentives became a serious problem. As the economy grew, inefficiency developed due to poor allocation of resources, income inequality widened between favored and disfavored, and heavy social costs compounded from the suppression of democracy by the authoritarian regime.[40]

Thus, the government could achieve neither efficiency nor equality, and voices demanding freedom and democracy became louder. It was analyzed that "inefficiencies have been imbedded in the economy.....government-initiated investment activities as well as protective measures such as import restriction and monopolization, have weakened economic versatility and hindered proper functioning of the market mechanism.....the inequalities between income classes and regions were aggravated."[41] During the second half of 1970s the entire South Korean system declined in efficiency because political development lagged far behind economic growth. It was proven that government intervention caused market failures by the time of President Park's assassination.

In the second stage of *conflict between democracy and economy (1980-1997)*, President Chun and Roh relaxed control but politics remained only half-democratic as

Chaebols strengthened their monopolistic power. Seoul did not have westernized intellectuals to incite military revolution against President Park in early 1960s, but situations became changed when economic development expanded education.[42] In fact, anti-government sentiments began to evolve in 1972 when President Park revised the constitution to include his life long rule. The suppression forces of authoritarian regime were strong enough in 1970s when the driving forces for democratization was relatively week. The Park's assassination amidst social instability in 1979 temporarily reduced problems but little progress was made by his two successors.

President YS Kim allowed full freedom of expression not like his predecessors, but could not make any visible difference because system and people remained unchanged. As the first civilian president, he removed military culture from the government and pursued ambitious social reforms. However, his lack of professional knowledge and experience made him ignore the democratic process of decision making in the system, and his authoritarian leadership caused many trial and errors. After the Hanbo scandal he lost control of his presidency which was shared with DJ at his private home since elected. Conflicting political and economic interests plagued the period, and the confused leadership failed to integrate differing social interests. Seoul experienced government failures, and the external forces of the IMF took control its economy. The political situations, which should change in the third stage, was the major reason for this external supervision.

In the third stage of *balanced development of politics with economy (1998-2015)*,[43] the South Korean economy pursues a balanced development for its structural reforms, where followings must be considered. First of all, the market forces are not enough to remove the monopolistic power prevailing in the nation's entire system; the lack of driving forces slows reform. Only government intervention will promote efficient reform by rooting out resistance from the anti-reform groups including politicians and Chaebols. In order to avoid errors, the reform priorities should be fairly delineated through professional evaluation free from the persuasive pressures of political interest groups. Temporary state intervention will help to reconstruct fair competition in South Korea.

Secondly, the burdens caused by reforms should be shared fairly in a manner acceptable to each party. The political opposition, Chaebols, and labor unions do not want to lose any part of their interests, but no reform will succeed without downsizing and cutting costs. The leadership should force each party to share burdens coming from systemic reforms. The Tripartite Committee consisting of labor, business, and government should united constructively for the goal of recovering economic strength. If not, the South Korean people will pay the highest costs.

Thirdly, the initial conditions for fair competition should be seriously considered in reforms. The wealth of Chaebols came not from fair competition but from monopoly power, provided by the corrupt government, which devastated nearly all small businesses in the past. The revival of small and medium sized businesses is essential in reforms so that the government should bar Chaebols from participating in government contracts except in certain industries, which are not available for the small businesses, until the initial conditions are fully recovered. This kind of compensation for small businesses would correct distorted initial conditions that suppressed fair competition.

Fourthly, in banking reforms, it is essential to investigate the real demand of funds and to set available resources. Previous management should be brought to justice for their misconduct and replaced by fresh, new, efficiently operating management teams. The Bank Supervision Commission should be controlled not by the office of Prime Minister but by the Bank of Korea in order to assure its political neutrality. It is dangerous to amend the banking laws by allowing Chaebols to enter the banking business; such amendments oppose the direction of economic reforms.[44]

Fifthly, the Bank Supervision Commission should strictly force the bank to maintain each firm's debt-equity ratio below 200% through removal of cross finance guarantee. The Fair Trade Commission should closely watch internal transactions between group companies to root out monopolistic practices that violate antitrust laws. Consistent supervision increases efficiency and expedites structural reforms. It is neither reasonable nor helpful that Chaebols incite nationalistic sentiments in order to avoid foreign competition, and that labor unions reinforce workers' hatred against foreign investment to insure union cohesiveness. Particularly, the labor market jeopardizes economic reforms by expelling domestic firms to foreign countries and forcing foreign firms to hesitate in direct investment activities, which jeopardizes job creation in South Korea.[45]

Sixthly, in the course of economic recovery, Seoul should reduce the negative effect on the economy from excessive military expenditures. The U.S.-Korea security alliance deters external threats from the North, establishing a low-cost national defense. If DJ's engagement policy with the North yields a peace treaty and disarmament agreement as a preliminary step for unification, the two Koreas can divert military spending to future economic development. The leaderships of the two Koreas should use disarmament benefits by compromise as soon as possible.[46]

In sum, South Korean economic recovery is optimistic since it has highly educated labor forces, accumulated capital and technology through advanced industries, world-class management and marketing experience, and a mature and self-adjusting democratic leadership. When South Koreans pursue speedy reforms by equally sharing burdens for structural adjustment, the recovery will be successful, proving that the EAM is not dead but progressing, alive with continuously rapid growth. As mentioned in introduction, however, reforms and recovery can be significantly delayed if conflicting interests weaken the driving forces as seen in lagged politics.

We can consider the following three possible scenarios. (a) If the DJ leadership pursues speedy and aggressive structural reforms with the right direction, South Korea will regain its previous economic strength and growth rate within three years. (b) If the DJ leadership fails to integrate productive reform elements because of conflicting interests within the system, economic recovery will take more than a decade as was witnessed in Latin American countries. (c) If the DJ administration fails in promoting expeditious change but maintains a desirably focused reformative direction, the result will lie somewhere between these two extreme cases, taking five to seven years. However, it is too early to predict the economic recovery since there are various obstacles hindering structural reforms in South Korea such as political skirmish, Chaebol's resistance, and labor strikes. Swift success of system reforms depends on the people's ability to mobilize all possible resources, which will be honestly judged by the second generation in the history.

An Application of ROK Experiences to Transform DPRK

As discussed previously, South Korea experienced the political-economic relations while modernizing from authoritarian rule to the western standard of democracy. Democracy, reducing intervention costs through its feedback adjustment mechanism, is essential to maximize capitalistic efficiency. The balanced development of system minimizes costs induced by lagging subsystems. Government intervention in lagged politics causes market failures, and corruption from the political-economic complex results in government failures becoming a heavy burden of growth. The EDPs are efficient in the early stage of economic takeoff when the economy is small and inelastic. But in the later period when the economy becomes large and complicated, problems in efficiency and equality emerge due to misallocation of resources without competition in the market.

If South Korea had chosen a different strategy, the adjustment costs would have taken a different form. As long as the difference between integrated returns from the chosen growth strategy and those from other strategies are larger than reform costs, the costs must be the lowest price that South Korea has to pay for adjustment. If, from the beginning, Seoul had chosen a strategy that balanced economy with democracy, it would not have experienced today's frustration since no such a great performance could have appeared in its history of economic growth.[47] Once recovered, Seoul's economy will be stronger than ever before, having advanced democracy and market economy through structural reforms. Through this financial crisis with the help of external forces, South Korea matured towards political and economic internationalization.[48]

The South Korean experiences provide following lessons for transition economies of China, Vietnam, and North Korea. (a) Use a series of economic development plans in the early stage of economic takeoff by restricting political freedom. The aggressive driving forces will expedite the big push effect on the economy. The planning period must be less than fifteen years.[49] (b) Reduce government intervention gradually after ten years, and pursue the balanced path between politics and economy by leaning fair competition. It is necessary for the leadership to watch corruption closely. (c) Start from import substitution of labor-intensive products and move to export promotion of the same industries. Start to enter import substitution of capital- and technology-intensive products and move to export promotion of the same. (d) Supply proper capital by selling ownership except energy, transportation, communications, finance, and media businesses. Invest aggressively in education and training with research and development, but try to minimize protection of infant industries. (e) If politics remain unchanged, the economy loses efficiency and equality, which reduces exports, employment, and income. Then, the economy will have a problem in the balance of payments, which threatens continuous growth. Then, make sure that time is essential in this case to reduce adjustment costs for recovery. (f) Be aware that balanced growth of politics and economy is essential, and that other sectors are also important to reduce adjustment costs. Minimize defense budget not to hurt the economy. (g) The subsequent policy reforms for adjustment are necessary to make the economy efficient, reducing accumulated costs arising from state intervention. It is dangerous to maintain improper or outdated policies without correction, which raises unnecessary costs in the future.[50] The speedy policy adjustment is possible by making people work together with the system through the democratic process with qualified economists.

In the case of China, system transformation has faced obstacles in justifying its ideological shift, improving privatization and managerial efficiency, and struggling with corruption. "Building a socialist economy with Chinese characteristics means developing a market economy under socialism and constantly emancipating and developing productive forces....The party and the state have shifted the focus of their work from the practice of 'taking the class struggle as the key link' in the past to socialist modernization with economic construction as the core."[51] The party conservatives need excuses for transformation since they, who have enjoyed the old system of equality, are not used to the new system of efficiency.[52] China has set four goals for building its socialist economy through reform programs: to readjust its ownership structure, to improve its socialist market economy, to enhance its the system of income distribution based on the ownership of productive means, and to liberalize its domestic market to the world. Those are in pursuing efficiency with equality.

The starting point of economic transformation in China is allowing property rights and privatizing state-owned enterprises by introducing the price system into the market. This generally invites three major problems: bankruptcy due to poor corporate management, unemployment due to efficiency improvement, and inflation from high growth and poor financial policies.[53] A survey suggests that the authorities suspend production for unprofitable products, make calculations in light of real market conditions, and drop production plans that are not cost-effective.[54] Meanwhile, the unemployment rate in China has approached 20% in major cities such as Harbin and Shenyang. The government fears high unemployment causing social instability. Fortunately, the authorities could curb inflation, while the yuan values were appreciated due to fall of the Asian currency values.[55]

Corruption has been a persistent problem in China.[56] Properties in the socialist economies belong to the state, and the political power sets the privatization rules and distributes state owned properties to qualified individuals. The phenomenon of corruption has emerged along with the rise of private property and ownership, so China instigated the radical cure of corruption as follows.[57] Firstly, China maintains ideological guarantee, which opposes corruption and advocates cleanness by enhancing party building and education in ideology and ethics. Secondly, China provides better administration to remove the soil and conditions for rising corruption by formulating regulations and institutions. Thirdly, China launches a comprehensive project of system engineering for effective supervisory mechanisms to oppose corruption and to advocate cleanness. Since the initial political conditions were based on proletariat dictatorship and Marxist class struggle, political monopoly has caused corruption, and helped the second generation of bureaucrats to own privatized corporations. This would be the same in transforming the North Korean economy.

Military confrontation in the Korean peninsula has remained unchanged for half a century despite paying unnecessary prices: acceptance of authoritarian political rules, economic burdens from national security, and extreme dichotomy in societal values. Pyongyang has paid the price of confrontation directly and indirectly more than South Korea has because of the fall of the Soviet Union and its satellite countries. In applying other's lessons, it is necessary to revisit the reasons why the North Korean economy has hopelessly fallen similarly to the fall of communism.

The DPRK's problems are caused by the entire system.[58] The centrally planned economy with projected consumption and production by the state causes inefficiency by creating bottlenecks and idle capacities in industries. Marxist ideology does not allow personal property rights, and a small interest group holds the power under the name of proletariat dictatorship. Royalty, as opposed to performance-based compensation for workers, undermines motivation and reduces productivity. Heavy military spending from the dual economic system reduces investment in infrastructure and manufacturing facilities, raising overhead costs in the economy. Government censorship threatens communications, socialist brainwash interrupts creative ideas, and lack of education and training with research and development delays technological advancement, reducing productivity. Self-sanctioned autarkic economy makes it difficult for North Korea to exploit comparative advantage and to mobilize resources, and thus their production possibility frontier remains declined. North Korea misuses the resources by policing its own people, particularly intellectuals and political dissidents, in order to prevent internal uprising. The rigidity and inflexibility of centralized power interrupt self-adjustment, which reduces efficiency and productivity. While China is expediting economic transformation towards the market economy, Pyongyang wastes its golden time in playing fruitless games. It is the same as losing money or economy to ignore the value of time.

Pyongyang faces a dilemma: the openness threatens survival of the regime, but the economy cannot revive without openness. The only choice for the regime's survival is in the strategy of soft landing and multi-dimensional, simultaneous, and gradual transformation of the system. In multi-dimensional and simultaneous, all subsystems of North Korea including politics, security, economy, and society should be developed simultaneously with balance. Gradual transformation means that the reform starts partially in a specific region such as the Rajin-Sunbong area in the first step, and gradually expands to other locations such as Wonsan at the east coast and Nampo at the west coast, thus minimizing shocks from freedom waves. Then, openness can be applied to the entire area of North Korea after building confidence and immunity to external culture.[59]

Time is essential in economic development. Let's assume that Pyongyang wants to build a manufacturing plant for fertilizer in the suburban area of Wonsan. The first thing to be done is to build infrastructure including power stations, water and sewage lines, highways and byways, railways, sea ports, airports, and communications facilities, which may take at least five to seven years. The second step is to build the manufacturing plant itself including buildings and equipment, which may take at least three to five years without financial problems. The third step is to recruit and train employees and to assign jobs including overseas marketing, which is accompanied by operating plants and selling products to the world, that will take three to five more years. Pyongyang needs at least ten years in normalizing the plant without constraints. There is no time to waste.

The reality of North Korean economy is rather serious. Interviews with North Korean refugees suggest that "over 25% of population in many villages.....have died, with the height of the crisis occurring in fall 1996....even isolated instances of cannibalism are simply too widespread and too specific to be dismissed.....a major humanitarian disaster has already occurred with tens of thousands of people already dead from starvation and starvation-related illness."[60] The central government has been losing political influence over provincial and local authorities due to lack of grain power. The private market activities throughout the country are accepted, and the household responsibility system is selectively implemented. But no reforms have yet been observed.

North Korea has burdened China by demanding economic aids and producing influx refugees into the border provinces.[61] Meanwhile, South Korea has been a partner with China whose trade and investment to grow. Despite rhetoric of equidistance, China began to recognize that its economic interests in Seoul are more significant than its strategic interests in Pyongyang, and that unified Korea is not dangerous to China's security. As the Sino-American relations improve, China's economic interests become more important than its strategic one. So China may agree that the status quo seems not to be sustainable on the Korean peninsula.[62] It is true that the ball of North-South game is waiting for self-determination towards peace and prosperity of the Korean people.

A study from China maintains that a 'soft landing' is the most feasible strategy towards Korean unification.[63] Firstly, the risk of destruction caused by war is unacceptable to both sides and war does not correspond with the interests of the relevant parties when North and South both have serious economic problems. Secondly, China wants to strengthen traditional friendship with the North while to improve its economic relations with the South. The United States does not want heavy casualties by war, and Japan does not want the second Korean War threatening its national security. Finally, the achievements of quadripartite talks will help find a way towards a rational settlement of the Korean peninsula issue in terms of relaxation, cooperation, and consultations as a gradual process. This view represents the reality honestly judged by Chinese intellectuals.

The United States and South Korea pursue constructive engagement with North Korea, and the regional powers are supportive for peace and prosperity. The international community becomes closer through market openness by removing barriers towards globalization, so that it is the best way for Pyongyang to lean with the wind to avoid its disadvantages. South Korea wants to save military spending to recover the economy and to repay external debts. Further suppression of the North Korean economy pushes the regime towards collapse, which Seoul does not want. Possible returns from negotiations are limited and continuous demand for concessions from the North wastes time without gains. If the Pyongyang cannot make constructive relations with DJ, another five more years would be necessary to meet a next leadership who may not be as friendly as DJ.

DJ's engagement policy towards DPRK includes three principles: no allowance of armed offense from the North, no intention to harm or to absorb the North, and pursuance of conciliation and cooperation between North and South.[64] The theory is realistic and mutually beneficial; North Korea can transform its system without external risks while South Korea can minimize unification costs as a result of Northern self-generation. Both sides can save and divert resources from defense to economic purposes by signing a peace treaty with disarmament. It was not wise for the hard liners in the North to cause the submarine incident and armed infiltration when the two sides try to pursue cooperation. If DJ loses patience, Pyongyang becomes a loser by prolonging its difficulties.

The lessons from experiences of South Korean and Chinese reforms prove to be meaningful as North Korea faces difficulties of capital formation in its transformation. DPRK's capital comes from external loans, foreign direct investment, foreign assistance, war compensation, cooperation with Seoul, disarmament, domestic savings, sales of state properties, and labor exports. Its resource allocation should coordinate the structural balance with South Korea, invest early in agriculture, substitute imports of labor-intensive products, provide sufficient infrastructure, and educate human resources.[65] If Pyongyang hesitates to transform the system due to absorption phobia with DJ's engagement policy, it may permanently lose the chance of recovery.[66] Now is the time for the two Koreas to engage with each other for economic revival and peaceful reunification.

Summary and Conclusion

In summary, we viewed the role of state in the economy, survival of the EAM with reforms, and application of South Korean experiences to transform North Korea. First, the EDPs were efficient in the early development stage when the economy was small and inelastic. As the economy grew in scale and complexity, government intervention invariably caused market failures, and a corrupt political-economic complex led to government failures. Economic development facilitates democracy being essential for sustainable growth. In turn, democracy promotes check and balance in politics to minimize corruption while enhancing competition in the economy by maximizing efficiency. So the theory of balanced development between subsystems becomes persuasive while the Asian values have been controversial. The direction of structural reforms for South Korea points towards promotion of fair competition in the entire system of politics, economy, and society by removing the monopolistic power preoccupied by the old interest groups.[67]

Secondly, the financial crisis is a stage of economic development and the EAM is still valid and under progress. Krugman argued that the EAM is driven not by productivity growth but by resource mobilization, which we can reject since its contributing share of total factor productivity to growth proved to be over 33% during 1960-1989. The South Korean economy is optimistic owing to highly educated labor forces, accumulated capital and technology, world-class management and marketing experiences, and mature leadership and democracy with a self-adjustment function. If the DJ leadership pursues speedy and aggressive reforms, the economy will start to recover by the year 2000. The South Korean reforms require government intervention in restructure, appropriate burden sharing, equalized initial conditions, tight bank supervision, fair trade supervision, disarmament and resource conversion, and no leadership corruption.

Thirdly, the experiences of South Korea reveal to North Korea how to take off the land of vicious circle, while those of China teach them how to transform the system towards openness by smoothing out freedom waves. Since inter-Korean economic cooperation is fundamental for revival of the DPRK economy, Pyongyang may permanently lose the chance of recovery if it hesitates to change the system due to absorption phobia from the South. DJ's engagement policy is realistic and mutually beneficial since the North can transform the system without external risks, the South can minimize unification costs by Northern self-generation, and both sides can save costs by diverting resources from military to economic purpose. It is necessary in supplying and allocating resources for North Korea to consider industrial structure of unified Korea, to invest in the agricultural sector first for self-sufficiency, to substitute imports of labor-intensive products, to provide sufficient infrastructure for inexpensive overhead costs, and to educate and to train human resources.

This study concludes with three as policy recommendations: first for the South, second for the North, and the last for the world. ***Recommendations to Seoul:*** South Korea is now in the third stage of political and economic development approaching the western standard of democracy and market economy. The DJ leadership was successful in managing the financial crisis in the early stage, but the people began to question his capability and intention towards structural reforms. DJ must maintain speedy and aggressive driving forces with the consistent direction to recover fair competition within the system. In rooting out corruption, DJ must fairly investigate campaign fund scandals related to corrupt politicians and contributing businessmen who violated the laws; which is a starting point to make the system fair by bringing the wrong doers to justice. South Korean people should not confuse nationalism with patriotism. In domestic capital formation, it is better for South Korea to sell ownership to foreign investors than to borrow funds from foreign banks when domestic firms are weak in financial creditability and technological competitiveness. The nationalism is not patriotic since it hurts the economy in the age of globalization.

Recommendation to Pyongyang: The North Korean leadership pursues survival of its regime with economic recovery. As long as the Juche regime holds old principles, the economy will not fully recover the strength in the long run. Pyongyang must shift ideological orientation, as did China, from the equality of Marxist class struggle towards efficiency of classless competition by removing the monopolistic power of proletariat dictatorship in the system. The dual economic system separating military from the economy hurts integrated policy formulation. The independent military sector expedites arms buildup and reduces investment in infrastructure and capacity generation, jeopardizing productivity growth. Both peace treaty and disarmament agreement between the two Koreas is urgent to divert resources from military to commercial purpose. Inter-Korean economic cooperation is essential for recovery in the North. Be sure that the South is the most helpful partner for the North in the world. The DPRK must recognize that economic interests in the post cold war period became heavier than political-military interests due to nonexistence of external threats.

Recommendation to the World: The world should help the two Koreas to pursue balanced development of democracy with economy. The constructive engagement between the United States and China became visible since President Clinton's China visit in late June 1998. Since the powers want peace and stability in the region, they should cooperate to build a peaceful regime between the two Koreas. Particularly, China should do a better role in constructing a peaceful regime between Seoul and Pyongyang since unified Korea is more beneficial than divided one. Politically, China has been successful in transforming the system, so that the freedom waves from unified Korean would not be a threat. Economically, China's capital market is mature enough to absorb foreign capital so that a shift of South Korean capital from China to North Korea would not be a matter. China's trade with unified Korea would be much larger than that with divided one. Strategically, unified Korea could not be a threat to China since their economic relations will grow faster than expected, shadowing China's strategic worries as long as the balance of power exist in the region.

Endnotes

[1] Koh Young Jae, "Sunshine: Kim Dae Jung's Dilemma," *The Internet Hankyoreh*, July 14, 1998.

[2] Observed old habits: (a) The DJ administration placed the Commission of Bank Supervision under the control of the Office of Prime Minister. The Commission should be under the control of the Bank of Korea to keep political neutrality. (b) The Parliament stopped the Real Name System in financial transactions namely to promote flow of hidden funds, with which the DJ Party collaborated though it was criticized that the revision would help to avoid transparency of campaign funds. (c) The DJ party allows Chaebols to own banks, which was restricted in the previous administrations. "The Ruling Party Allows Bank Ownership to Chaebols," *Joongang Ilbo Internet*, June 8, 1998. (d) The five top Chaebols absorbed over 76% of total amount of corporate bond sales during the first five months in 1998, which is another type of corporate debts that should be reduced. Yoo Seung Ho, "Big Five Alone Ate All Funds, 27 Trillion Won by Selling Bonds," *Hankook Ilbo from Korea Link*, June 25, 1998.

[3] President Kim Dae Jung emphasized that balanced development of politics with economy is necessary in order to avoid the political-economic complex in his speech delivered to the invited guests of Korean-Americans at the Residence of ROK Ambassador to the United States in Washington, DC on June 9, 1998.

[4] For further reference, see WheeGook Kim, *Evolution of Democracy and Economic Development: A Case of Korea*, Washington, DC: East-West Research Institute (Monograph), February 1998, pp. 15-20. This was presented to the Philadelphia Symposium on Korea's Challenges Ahead held at the University of Pennsylvania on February 13, 1998.

[5] WheeGook Kim, *The South Korean Economy and The Cahebols*, Washington, DC: East-West Research Institute (Monograph), May 1998, pp. 3-8. This was presented to the 1998 Annual Conference on held at Adams Mark Hotel, Columbia, South Carolina on May 15-17, 1998 sponsored by the University of South Carolina.

[6] World Bank, *World Development Report 1997: The State in A Changing World*, New York:Oxford University Press, 1998, p. 27. The governments provide public goods for infrastructure, defense, law and order, education, public health, antipoverty programs, disaster relief, and so on as measures largely for equality.

[7] Amartya Sen, Nicholas Stern, and Joseph Stiglitz, "Roundtable Discussion, Development Strategies: The Roles of the State and the Private Sector," *Annual Conference on Development Economics 1990*, Washington, DC: World Bank, 1991, pp. 421-435.

[8] The exceptional cases can be seen in government investment for production capacity generation.

[9] Arthur M. Okun, *Equality and Efficiency: The Big Tradeoff*, Washington, DC: The Brookings Institution, 1975. P. 120. "In that sense, capitalism and democracy are really a most improbable mixture. Maybe that is why they need each other – to put some rationality into equality and some humanity into efficiency."

[10] Anne O. Krueger, "Government Failures in Development," *The Journal of Economic Perspective* 4(3) (Summer 1990): 9-23. Vito Tanzi and Hamid Davoodi, *Roads to Nowhere: How Corruption in Public Investment Hurts Growth*, Washington, DC: World Bank, 1998. Lack of infrastructure investment is a case of government failures.

[11] Adam Prezworski and et al, *Sustainable Democracy*, New York: Cambridge University Press, 1995, p. 40. The author quoted from Frederic C. Lane, *Profits from Power: Readings in Protection Rent and Violence Controlling Enterprises*, Albany, New York: State University of New York Press, 1979.

[12] WheeGook Kim, "Check and Balance: Watching Revival of Local Elections in South Korea," *Hankook Ilbo (Washington),* April 14-17, 1995. A series of three days article.

[13] Larry E. Westphal, "Industrial Policy in an Export-Propelled Economy: Lessons from South Korea's Experience," *Journal of Economic Perspectives* 4(3) (Summer 1990): 41-59. Mrinal Datta-Chaudhuri, "Market Failure and government Failure," *Journal of Economic Perspectives* 4(3) (Summer 1990): 25-39. Both viewed with positive results of state intervention because corruption effects were hidden under the surface at that time.

[14] Kevin Sullivan, "Thousands of Strikers Demonstrate in Seoul: Workers Protest New Labor Legislation," *The Washington Post*, December 12, 1996, p. A14. WheeGook Kim, "A Big Shake of Labor Laws in South Korea," *Hankook Ilbo* (Washington), January 4, 1997, p. 3. Unemployment measures have not been considered seriously.

[15] Adam Przeworski and Fernando Limongi, "Political Regimes and Economic Growth*," Journal of Economic Perspectives* 7(3) (Summer 1993): 51-69. Jacob De Hann and Clemens Siermann, "Political Instability, Freedom, and Development," *Economic Development and Cultural Change* 44(2) (January 1996): 339-350. Michael A. Nelson and Ram D. Singh, "Democracy, Economic Freedom, Fiscal Policy, and Growth in LDCs: A Fresh Look," *Economic Development and Cultural Change* 46(4) (July 1998): 677-696.

[16] Joseph Schumpeter, *Capitalism, Socialism, and Democracy*, London: Routledge, 1992, p. 284.

For the source of inefficiency under socialism, see Fredrich Hayek, *Knowledge, Evolution, and Society*, London: Buttler and Tanner, 1983. For Asian cases, see Robert A. Scalapino, *The Politics of Development: Perspectives on Twenties Century Asia*, Cambridge, MA: Harvard University Press, 1989. S. P. Huntington and J. M. Nelson, *No Easy Choice:Political Participation in Developing Countries*, Cambridge, Mass.: Harvard Univ. Press, 1976.

[17] *Ibid.*, pp. 289-296. Jongryn Mo and Chung-in Moon, "Democracy and ROK Economic Crisis," NAPSNet Forum Online, Berkeley, California: Nautilus Institute, March 18, 1998 discussed by Hugo Wheegook Kim and others on March 24, 1998. http://www.nautilus.org/napsnet/fora/index.html/.

[18] Peter L. Berger, "The Uncertain Triumph of Democratic Capitalism," in Larry Diamond and Marc F. Plattner, Ed., *Capitalism, Socialism, and Democracy Revisited*, Baltimore: Johns Hopkins University Press, 1993, p. 1-10.

[19] Minxin Pei, "The Puzzle of East Asian Exceptionalism," in Larry Diamond and Mark F. Plattner, Ed., *Economic Reform and Democratization*, Baltimore: Johns Hopkins University Press, 1995, pp. 112-125.

[20] Andres Aslund, "The Case for Radical Reform," in Larry Diamond and Marc F. Plattner... p. 74-85.

[21] Joan M. Nelson, "Linkages between Politics and Economics," in in Larry Diamond and Marc F. Plattner..... p. 45-58. Jusup Wanandi, "East Asian Domestic Policy and International Stability after the Currency Crisis," 1998 *Pacific Symposium on the Asian Financial Crisis: Security Risks and Opportunities* held at the U.S. National Defense University, Washington, DC on May 5-6, 1998.

[22] WheeGook Kim, "The Impact of Sino-American Relations on Korean Unification," *The Journal of East Asian Affairs* XI(1) (Winter/Spring 1997), p. 21. For further, see Paul Kennedy, *The Rise and Fall of the Great Powers: Economic Change and Military Conflict from 1500 to 2000*, New York: Vintage Book, 1989. William H. Overholt, *The Rise of China: How Economic Reform Is Creating A New Superpower*, New York: W. W. Norton, 1993.

[23] Francis Fukuyama, "Capitalism and Democracy: The Missing Link," in Larry Diamond and Marc F. Plattner, Ed., *Capitalism, Socialism, and Democracy Revisited*..... pp. 94-104.

[24] Adam Przeworski, "The Neoliberal Fallacy," in Larry Diamond and Marc F. Plattner, Ed., *Capitalism, Socialism, and Democracy Revisited*..... pp. 39-53.

[25] The transition economy such as in China has faced similar conflict between political conservatism and economic liberalism. In line with this, DPRK has hesitated to open the economy due to conflict between different interests of politics and economy. The engagement policy of DJ administration tries to compromise the differences by separating economy from politics despite transitional challenges from internal and external adversaries. The human rights movement in developing countries is considered as a similar process of democratization.

[26] Economic Planning Board, *The Fifth Five-year Economic and Social Development Plan 1982-1986*, Seoul: Government of Republic of Korea, 1982, p. 10.

[27] Pam Woodal, "Survey East Asian Economies," *The Economist*, March 7th-13th 1998, p. 12. The sources of Asian crisis include the virtue of high investment, small government, good government, flexibility, the virtues of long-term relationships, and education in the survey.

[28] WheeGook Kim and Moonsug Chang, *Mobilization and Industrial Potential for War: A Case Study of Republic of Korea*, Seoul: Korea National Defense University Press, 1987, p. 92. The government took over bankrupt firms by tax money and sold those businesses to a third party with low prices.

[29] The World Bank, World Bank Development Report 1997, pp. 99-109.

[30] Pranab Bardhan, "Corruption and Development: A Review of Issues*,*" *Journal of Economic Literature* XXXV(3) (September 1997): 1320-46, quoted from Francis T. Lui, "An Equilibrium Queuing Model of Bribery," *Journal of Political Economy* 93 (4) (August 1985): 760-81.
[31] Staff, "175 Assembly Members Signed Anti-corruption Law," *Digital Chosun Ilbo*, August 4, 1998.
[32] Sudan-Rose-Ackerman, "Corruption and Development," in Boris Pleskovic and Joseph E. Stiglitz, Ed., *Annual World Bank Conference on Development Economics 1997*, Washington, DC: The World Bank, 1998, pp. 35-57. Laws and programs breeding corruption rather than promoting competition must be eliminated, but deregulation and privatization should be carried out with care not to worsen the existing problems. Michael Johnson, "What Can Be Done about Entrenched Corruption?," in the same book, p. 82.
[33] Paul W. Kuznets, "An East Asian Model of Economic Development: Japan, Taiwan, and South Korea," *Economic Development and Cultural Change* 36(3) (April 1988): S11-S43. For further, see World Bank, *The East Asian Miracle: Economic Growth and Public Policy*," New York: Oxford University Press, 1993.
[34] For Asian values, Fareed Zakaria, "A Conversation with Lee Kuan Yew," *Foreign Affairs* 73(2) (March/April 1994): 109-126. Kim Dae Jung, "Is Culture Destiny? The Myth of Asia's Anti-Democratic Values," *Foreign Affairs* 73(6) (November /December 1994): 189-194. Staff, "Asian Values Revisited," *The Economist* July 25th-31st, 1998, pp. 23-28. "The attachment to the family becomes nepotism. The importance of personal relationships rather than formal legality becomes cronyism. Consensus becomes wheel-greasing and corrupt politics. Conservatism and respect for authority become rigidity and an inability to innovate. Much-vaunted educational achievements become rote-learning and a refusal to question those in authority."
[35] Herbert Giersch, Ed., *Towards an Explanation of Economic Growth*," J. C. B. More, Tubingen: Institut fur Weltwirtschaft an der Universitat Kiel, 1981. Jose Edgardo Campos and Hilton L. Root, *The Key to The Asian Miracle: Making Shared Growth Credible*, Washington, DC: The Brookings Institution, 1996.
[36] Dale W. Jorgenson, "Productivity and Postwar U.S. Economic Growth," in Dale W. Jorgenson, Ed., *Productivity Volume I: Postwar U.S. Economic Growth*, Cambridge, Mass: MIT Press, 1996, pp. 1-23. Dale W. Jorgenson and Zvi Griliches, "The Explanation of Productivity Change," in the same book, p 53 & 85. Robert M. Solow, "A Contribution to the Theory of Economic Growth," *Quarterly Journal of Economics*, in R. Becker and E Burmeister, Ed., *Growth Theory Volume I*, Brook Field, Vermont: Edward Elgar, pp. 2-32. Edward F. Denison, *Trends in American Economic Growth 1929-1982*, Washington, DC: Brookings Institution, 1985, pp. 28-30. For further references, William J. Baumol, Richard R. Nelson, and Edward N. Wolf, Ed., *Convergence of Productivity: Cross-National Studies and Historical Evidence*, New York: Oxford University Press, 1994. John Middleton, Adrian Ziderman, Arvil Van Adams, Ed., *Skills for Productivity: Vocational Education and Training in Developing Countries*, New York: Oxford University Press, 1993.
[37] Paul Krugman, "The Myth of Asia's Miracle," *Foreign Affairs* 73(6) (Nov./Dec. 1994): 62-78. The others view differently such as in Steven Radelet and Jeffrey Sachs, "Asia's Reemergence," *Foreign Affairs* 76(6) (Nov./Dec. 1997): 44-59. Asian corruption is equivalent to a tax on foreign firms of 20% or more, quoted from Shang-Jin Wei, "How Taxing is Corruption on International Investors?" *NBER Working Paper* No. 6030, 1997.
[38] World Bank, *The East Asian Miracle: Economic Growth and Public Policy*," New York: Oxford University Press, 1993, p. 58. Staff, "The Asian Miracle: Is It Over?" *The Economist*, March 1th–7th, 1997, pp. 23-25. Paul Krugman used Alwyn Young's estimates for 118 countries

over 1970, which were proved to be incorrect.

[39] WheeGook Kim, *An Alternative Growth Strategies of North Korea:Lessons from Experiences of South Korea and Taiwan*, Washington, DC: East-West Research Institute (Monograph), January 1996, p. 28. This was presented to 1996 Annual Conference of Allied Social Science Associations held in San Francisco, California on January 5-7, 1996.

[40] Since 1961, the authoritarian regimes faced difficulties due to the lack of legitimacy and political consensus. Political operations exhausted funds collected from Chaebols expecting corresponding returns. Since the judicial system was controlled by politics, social justice was seriously damaged. The weakness of check and balance caused corruption in personnel and financial affairs in every field of the society and provided special benefits to interest groups, deepening income inequality between rural and urban, East and West, owners and workers, and favored and disfavored. The flow of information was monopolized and controlled by the authorities to avoid antigovernment movement. The intelligence agencies and national police used huge funds to collect information to dry up student turmoil, and to destroy organized activities of opposition parties and human rights groups. The planned economy lost efficiency in resource allocation due to centralized decision-makings. Political instability and government inefficiency discouraged savings and foreign investment. The tenure system for university faculties was used by the government in order to force loyalty or at lease passive silence from intellectuals of the academic circle. The authorities made the office corps of armed forces not have time to read and to think in order to avoid military uprising against the regime. For further references, see Staff, "South Korea: A New Society," *The Economist*, April 15th-21th, 1989, pp. 23-26.

[41] Economic Planning Board, *The Fifth Five-Year Economic and Social Development Plan 1982-1986*, Government of the Republic of Korea, 1982, p. 10. The Korean Economy at the Turning Point. The South Korean government recognized that its intervention through economic plans caused serious problems in the period of *The Fourth Five-Year Economic Development Plan 1977-1981* in terms of high inflation, inefficiency, and inequality.

[42] WheeGook Kim, "Problems and Remedies of the North Korean Economy:A Strategic Approach," *The Korea Journal of Defense Analysis* VIII(2) (Winter 1996): 223-268. _____, *The Impact of Regional and Global Developments*, Washington, DC: East-West Research Institute (Monograph), September 1996, pp. 20-21. _____, "Openness, Coexistence, and Peaceful Unification, *Hankuk Ilbo (Washington)*, August 8, 1994, the third article of a six days series.

[43] The third stage is set until 2015, which is based on 18 years of the political cycle in the previous periods. The extension does not necessary mean the EAM to be successful. Whang In-Joung, *Economic Transformation of Korea 1945-1995: Issues and Responses*, Seoul: The Sejong Institute, 1997, pp. 9-40. This author divided the period into three segments including the nation-building stage 1945-1961 but excluding the period after 1995.

[44] The reasons why Chaebols should not own banks are as follows: (a) Chaebols may use the banking system for their own interests rather than for general public. Chaebols should not own infrastructure, financial institutions, and media. (b) The debt-equity ratio of top 30 Chaebols was 518.9% by the end of 1997 so that they should reduce the ratio to below 200% by selling existing bank stocks to keep their main industries. (c) The concept of a leading bank insisted by the Daewoo owner is no more than that of banking monopoly. Chaebols try to stimulate nationalism as a tactic in order to gain bank ownership, but the existence of a couple of foreign banks is beneficial for consumers to improve competition. (d) Since the funds for bank restructure come from taxes, the bank ownership should be transferred to the people not to Chaebols, which raises savings and improves income distribution. (e) Chaebol's participation in banking business helps

revival of old corruption coming from the political-economic complex.

[45] The Chaebol reforms have been often interrupted by politics due to campaign fund raise for coming elections as seen in June and July 1998 under DJ leadership. The next election for the National Assembly in the year 2000 may cause the same. If the DJ administration fails in reforms by that time, the driving forces towards reforms will be largely reduced and the regime may fail in reforms. If this is the case, the EAM loses hope for survival. Morton I. Abramowitz and James T. Laney, *Managing Change on the Korean Peninsula,: Task Force Report*, Washington, DC: The Council on Foreign Relations, Inc., 1998, p. 41. The Cost of Unification (quoted).

[46] Daryl M. Plunk, "A silver Lining in Korea's Crisis: New Pledges Signal Hope for Economic Recovery and Peaceful Reunification," *F.Y.I.* No. 169, Heritage Foundation, January 15, 1998. Selig Harrison, "A Dual Effects of Disarmament," *The Internet Hankyoreh*, January 14, 1998.

[47] Kim Sung Woo, "An Essay: Evolution of Democracy and Economic Development," *Hankook Ilbo from Korea Link*, January 9, 1998.

[48] Lee Jong Soo, "An Interview with Dr. Guy Surmont, A French Critic: The Korean Crisis Is A Development Process," *Hankook Ilbo from Korea Link*, January 21, 1998.

[49] The duration is based on the initial political-economic conditions of South Korea in 1962.

[50] Ching-yuan Lin, "East Asia and Latin America as Contrasting Models," *Economic Development and Cultural Changes* 36(3 Supplement) (April 1988), p. S156. "What set the experiences of Taiwan and South Korea apart from those of Chile and Argentina, therefore, were not the initial conditions and the incentive systems, which were largely similar, but the subsequent policy reforms, which were successful in Taiwan and South Korea, but not in..."

[51] Zeng Peiyan, "Develop Socialist Economy with Chinese Characteristics," Beijing Qiushi, October 16, 1997, No. 20, pp. 2-6, from *The World News Connection*, February 23, 1998, FBIS-CHI-98-030. Wei Shi, "Social Justice Plus Market Economy," Beijing Zhenli De Zhuiqiu, February 4, 1998, from *The World News Connection*, February 6, 1998, FBIS-CHI-98-035.

[52] An interview held on November 7, 1997 with Dr. Dyu In Yu, an immigrant from Moscow to New York, indicated that his most difficult problem after immigration was competition for survival in the free market to which he had not been used previously.

[53] Chi Feng, "China Finalizes Economic Principles for 1998," Hong Kong Kuang Chiao Ching, February 4, 1998, from *The World News Connection*, February 6, 1998, FBIS-CHI-98-035.

[54] Shi Xiaohong, "Strengthen Enterprise Management, Increase Competitive Power," Beijing Jingji Guanli, June 5, 1996, from *The World News Connection*, November 1, 1996, FBIS-CHI-96-212. For the case of Poland, see Jeffrey Sachs, *Poland's Jump to the Market Economy*, Cambridge, Mass: The MIT Press, 1993.

[55] Erik Eckholm, "On the Road to Capitalism, China Hits a Nasty Curve: Jobless," *The New York Time on the Web*, January 20, 1998. "Most of the state industries haven't yet laid off the workers they should, so the problem is still being hidden.....In the rural areas where a majority of China's 1.2 billion people still live, 130 million workers are already surplus, neither needed for farming nor employed by rural industries." Chen Yen, "Poll Shows Inflation Problem No Longer Sensitive; Unemployment Issue Becomes Focus of Popular Attention," *Hong Kong Ming Pao*, February 2, 1998, from *The World News Connection*, February 8, 1998, FBIS-CHI-98-033.

[56] Ye Tan, "Zhu Rongji Openly Said: "Leave No Route of Retreat," Hong Kong Ching Pao, July 7, 1998, from *The World News Connection*, July 8, 1998, FBIS-CHI-98-188. Staff, "Nationwide Anticorruption Campaign Begin," Beijing Xinhua, July 8, 1998, from *The World News Connection*, July 9, 1998, FBIS-CHI-98-189. Editorial, "Launch a Large-Scaled Struggle Against Smuggling," Beijing Xinhua Domestic Service, July 15, 1998, from *The World News*

Connection, July 16, 1998, FBIS-CHI-98-196.

[57]Ruan Chongwu, "Perfecting Mechanisms, Opposing Corruption, Advocating Hosesty and Cleanness," *Beijing Renmin Ribao*, May 16, 1996, from *The World News Connection*, June 20, 1996, FBIS-CHI-96-120. Zheng Hongfan and Cui Shixin, "The Test of Time--Account on the Building of Clean and Honest Party Style in the New Period," *Beijing Renmin Ribao*, June 27, 1996, from *The World News Connection*, Aug. 8, 1996, FBIS-CHI-96-153.

[58] WheeGook Kim, "Problems and Remedies of the North Korean Economy," pp. 234-240. See *Northeast Asia Peace and Security Network Daily Report*, July 12, 1996, Discussions by the same author.

[59] This is the Chinese model, which is in line with the DJ's engagement policy.

[60] USIP, Special Report: North Korea's Decline and China's Strategic Dilemmas, Washington, DC: U.S. Institute for Peace, October 1997, p. 2. See further Chen Jian, The China Challenge in the Twenty-First Century: Implications for U.S. Foreign Policy, Washington, DC: United States Institute of Peace, 1998, Peaceworks No. 21., Conclusion: Living Peacefully with China in the 21st Century, p. 24.

[61] Staff, "The Grain Dependency of North Korea to Chian Rose Largely," Digital Chosun Ilbo, March 2, 1998. North Korea imported 1.135 million tons of grains (US$194 Million) including corn, wheat, and rice from China in 1997, that is over two times higher than 1996 imports from the same country which was 0.497 million tons.

[62] Robert Scalapino, "An Interview: Two Korea Relations, Advancement or Stalemate," *Hankuk Ilbo from Korea Link*, January 30, 1998. He believes that China would not give up its interests in North Korea. However, we can consider the time when economic interests become larger than strategic interests between the United States and China.

[63] Su Guiyou and Liu Yusheng, "An Analytical Report on the 1997-1998 International Situation," *Beijing Zhongguo Xinwen She*, January 26, 1998, from *The World News Connection*, January 29, 1998, FBIS-CHI-98-026.

[64] "Inaugural Address of 15th President," *Digital Chosun Ilbo*, February 25, 1998.

[65] WheeGook Kim, "Problems and Remedies of North Korean Economy….., p.249.

[66] USIP, Special Report: Challenges of Building a Korean Peace Process," Washington, DC: USIP, June 1998.

[67] WheeGook Kim, "The Initial Conditions in Competition," *The Professors Newspaper*, July 13, 1998, p. 3. A Korean version published in Seoul.

Chapter V
Did South Korea Choose the Best Growth Strategy and Can North Korea Follow the Lessons from the South?*

Introduction

It has been reported that the popularity of former President Park Jung Hee (1961-1979) is rising to its highest as the 2002 presidential election year approaches in South Korea. It is very disappointing that general public can forget the painful past so easily that demagogues misguide history using erroneous explanations for their personal interests. It is desirable to evaluate whether President Park chose the best economic growth strategy for South Korea and his authoritarian presidency was necessary for efficient economic development assuming that the former was the case. Some people believe that the military government can do better than a civilian one in the early stages of economic development, which is questionable. Additionally, considering that current political and economic situations of North Korea are worse than those of South Korea in 1960s, it is meaningful to examine whether Chairman Kim Jung Il of North Korea can follow the lessons from the South in its successful economic growth.

It was a miracle that South Korea experienced rapid economic development on a land devastated by a three-year civil war that destroyed the entire industrial capacity of the peninsula. The Korean War mobilized the rural manpower into the army and the expansion of the armed forces led to military coup in South Korea in May 1961. After that, President Park launched a series of five-year economic development plans. When the economy was small and inelastic in the early 1960s, state intervention was successful in mobilizing resources for labor-intensive industries by pursuing the export-led growth strategy. As the market grew, however, state intervention in the later period caused structural problems by creating bottlenecks and idle capacities in industries, which reduced economic efficiency and market competitiveness. A half century after the Korean War, the world moved toward globalization owing to technological advancement and the borderless flow of information, but the history remains there as was.

State intervention is able to cause both market and government failures. State intervention in the market pursues either capitalistic efficiency (dollars) or democratic equality (rights), which is impossible to achieve simultaneously because of necessary tradeoffs between the two objectives. Due to the lack of checks-and-balances in the system, state intervention is able to encourage monopoly in the market, which distorts resource allocation, reduces economic efficiency, and finally results in market failure. State intervention is also able to cause government failure from doing nothing for what

* Published by *The Journal of the Korean Economy* 3(1) (Spring 2002): 19-57. Reprinted by the permission of the publisher.

to be done and or doing something for what not to be done. Either government incapability or interruption of government function by the political-economic complex causes government failure. Both market and government failures expedited the financial crisis in Asian countries in 1997. The theory of balanced development between politics and economy became more persuasive than the role of Asian values after the 1997 financial crisis. In fact, democratization contributes to free competition in politics by removing absolute power, which increases the economic and social efficiency of the entire system by reducing unnecessary costs for adjustment in the long run.

The authoritarian leaders eagerly pursue economic development but often forget that economic growth facilitates democratization while authoritarian politics control the market. Economic growth with foreign trade expands education and training of workers to compete with foreign products. The foreign trade through multinational firms expedites information flow through borders due to increasing transactions of goods and services. Nation states can no longer monopolize information because of the availability of the Internet, wireless telephones, satellite televisions, fax machines, digital video disks, printers and copiers, and many others. The expanded knowledge through education and business contacts awakens self-consciousness toward democracy pursuing freedom and equality. The rise of household income widens the middle class, which demands more political power. The industrialization in the urban area raises the number of workers, expediting unionization for more economic gains from the capitalists. Both middle and working classes have largely contributed to democratization in South Korea.[1] The international pressures from the trade partners are so influential that the authoritarian states gradually lose their grip restraining freedom waves from foreign countries.

The Sunshine Policy of President Kim Dae Jung and inter-Korean Summit in June 2000 have reduced tension between the two Koreas. But North Korea has faced serious conflict between two strategic goals of politics and economy. Its socialist system reduces economic efficiency while economic growth challenges its totalitarian regime. Even its diplomatic normalization with Washington and Tokyo would not guarantee economic growth equipped with factor mobilization, productivity growth, and demand creation. But if it opens its door, Pyongyang can apply the lessons from South Korean experiences. The two Koreas might coordinate with each other in resource allocation, inter-Korean trade, direct investment, and financial and humanitarian aid. But the limit of economic cooperation lies in the absence of a peace treaty, non-existence of reciprocity and transparency, and technical problems disrupting trade and investment. Moreover, placement of its name on the list of terrorist states by the United States is a paramount obstacle for North Korea to pursue economic ties with other countries.[2]

The purpose of present study is to investigate whether President Park Jung Hee chose the best growth strategy for South Korea, whether his authoritarian presidency was necessary for economic development, and whether Chairman Kim Jung Il of North

Korea can follow the lessons from the experiences of South Korea. This study consists of three main sections. The first section reviews theoretical background of export-led growth strategies for South Korea: balanced growth with import substitution or unbalanced growth with export promotion. The second section investigates whether President Park chose the best economic growth strategy by formulating an input-output model and analyzing estimated results of four growth strategies. The third section examines how to apply the South Korean experiences in transforming its system toward the market economy drawing upon current problems of the North Korean economy, exploring issues of economic development and democratization. This study will contribute to policy development for both Korean governments and help others to analyze the political and economic development on the Korean peninsula.

Theoretical Background of Growth Strategies[3]

The economy of South Korea, like Taiwan, Singapore and Hong Kong, has been developed by an export-led growth strategy with consecutive economic development plans controlled by the central government. In the early stage of industrial development, a surplus in the primary sector raises demand for manufactured products, so gains from exports in this sector made imports of nondurable and labor-intensive consumer goods possible.[4] As investable funds are generated by primary exports, technological potential improves by education and training, demand for imports rises continuously, and the economy begins to substitute for labor-intensive imports by protection and subsidization. As a result of successful import substitution, the labor-intensive industries, such as textiles and clothing, expand their exports by exploiting low-wage labor. This stimulates more import demand for consumer and producer durable, and accelerates more education and training, capital accumulation, and technology transfer. But this is challenged by the movement of comparative advantage and protectionist threats against those labor-intensive imports in foreign countries.

Balanced Growth and Import Substitution

New ideas on the mechanism of economic development in traditional societies have evolved over the past five decades. Rosenstein-Rodan introduced the theory of the 'Big Push' explaining that a minimum quantum of investment is necessary to initiate self-sustaining growth, a little like taking an airplane off the ground.[5] However, an isolated and small amount of investment does not provide a sufficient impact on growth. It is only the beginning of a departure from the concept of traditional static equilibrium owing to increasing returns, technological external economies, and market imperfection in the less developing countries (LDCs).[6]

Annexed to this big push, Ragnar Nurkse introduced a concept of balanced growth in limited markets and areas of mass poverty.[7] According to Nurkse, balanced growth is an increase in production over a wide range of consumables, according to consumers' preferences with self-generated demand met with a given labor force, techniques, and natural resources, and only through the use of more capital. “In the absence of a meaningful rise of world export demand for primary products, a pattern of mutually supportive investment in different lines of production can enlarge the size of the market and help to fill the vacuum in the domestic economy of low income areas."[8] This means balanced investment between agriculture and manufacturing and horizontal diversification in manufacturing. Nurkse believed that international trade would not increase rapidly due to the slow expansion of primary exports, supply and demand constraints of manufacturing exports in LDCs, and protectionist trends against labor-intensive exports in developed countries (DCs). This implied that growth through foreign trade is hardly expected to narrow income differences between DCs and LDCs.[9]

Raul Presbisch argued that most Latin American countries faced a decline of primary exports due to their low demand elasticities and protectionist policies in DCs, and the difficulty of manufacturing exports due to the lack of industrial infrastructure in LDCs. He suggested that "import substitution stimulated by a moderate and selective protection policy was an economically sound way to achieve certain desirable effects."[10] His theory of center-periphery system meant that developed countries (center) organize the economy for their interests by using technological advantages, while developing countries (periphery) supply raw materials demanded by the center.[11] Thus, the strategy of import substitution by protection diverts primary resources to industrial products without export constraints. This expedites technology penetration, domestic job creation, and structural change of manufacturing despite massive demand for investment.

The growth through import substitution is linked to balanced growth, but the two approaches differ from each other. Balanced growth is based on a balanced allocation of resources, but import substitution (IS) has some limitations. IS involves in a strategy of improving the balance of payments by restricting tariffs, quotas, and an overvalued exchange rate, all of which penalize exports. IS requires protection and subsidization for a country's scarce factor that increases costs of production and also consumption, distorts resource allocation, and worsens income distribution in labor-surplus LDCs by increasing returns to capital. Capital formation is massively financed by domestic savings, which reduce consumption. It is difficult to increase savings because domestic producers supply enough consumer goods with lower prices, income distribution shifts from importers to income recipients of new industries, more imports are required for industries to produce consumer goods, and inefficiency of substituted industries lowers profits and savings.[12] When domestic market is small, growth through import substitution is constrained by lacks of economies of scale in production and the limit of domestic consumption resulting in higher capital costs and lower efficiency. In fact, the growth strategy of import substitution maintains sellers' markets dominated by monopolists or oligopolists, and no incentives are provided to improve productivity, which raises inefficiency and worsens income distribution as experienced in South America.

Unbalanced Growth and Export Promotion

Albert Hirschman stressed the unbalanced growth theory, holding that investment concentrated in leading sectors of the economy generates more output, employment, and income through forward and backward linkages. He emphasized decision-making for investment to economize scarce resources. The incentives such as business profits (in private) and social welfare (in public) attract investment which brings disequilibrium. When the economy is moving ahead, growth policy tries to maintain a previous disequilibrium, which generates additional disequilibrium requiring a movement toward continuous growth.[13]

Hirschman considered two types of investment: substitution and postponement choices. He favored the latter involving in decisions regarding the sequence of several projects. He suggested social overhead capital (SOC) must precede or at least be kept in balance with directly productive activities (DPA). If SOC is expanded, for example, existing DPA becomes less costly, which attracts further DPA. If DPA is expanded first, production costs will rise so that demand for SOC will also rise. When investment motivations are deficient, it is safer to rely on development via shortage of investment rather than via excess capacity, while the opposite is true if motivations are sufficient. The balance between SOC and DPA is equally dangerous because there will be no incentive to induce investment.[14] Hirschman stressed that a development policy must pursue linkage effects to maximize induced investment decision. He hypothesized that countries having assigned the higher priority to high-linkage industries would have higher rates of growth than would countries that have assigned lower priority to them.[15] The theoretical contribution of this idea is a pioneering concept connecting interindustrial linkages to economic development.

Hirschman introduced the concept of antagonistic growth from his experience in Argentina. The income receivers of one of the two sectors are gaining at the expense of those of the other sector at each stage in the sequential growth process. A concentration of resources may neglect other crucial objectives, which comes to public attention. This brings a new concentration for them, creating a new neglect to existing beneficiaries. It reflects the interaction of politics and economy in LDCs,[16] explaining that unbalanced growth depends on resource allocation by the government. The growth through export promotion is combined with the concept of unbalanced growth. The specialization based on a country's comparative advantages increases competitiveness in foreign markets. This competitiveness is reinforced by tax exemptions, duty exemptions, lower interest rates, domestic currency devaluation, and lower utility rates. Due to protection and subsidization, the intensive allocation of limited resources to export industries pulls the economy more than the balanced one. Thus, growth through export expansion is analogous to unbalanced growth due to different demand for industrial products from foreign markets and different allocation of resources to meet those demands.

It is necessary to clarify the relationships between growth strategies of import substitution and export promotion. The former, as Raul Prebisch insisted, concentrates on domestic market demand by restricting imports and focusing less on exports, while the latter gives equal weight to import substitution and export promotion. Export promotion requires a certain degree of domestic technologies accumulated by import substitution particularly in manufacturing. Meanwhile, earnings from exports can finance import substitution, so the strategy of export promotion is not an exclusive, but a supportive and complementary to import substitution for the economy.

However, the growth strategy of export promotion (EP) has certain limitations. EP via unbalanced resource allocation introduces conflicts between private profits and public services. Excess capacities in leading sectors cause an efficiency problem, and bottlenecks in other sectors spread inflationary pressures throughout the economy. The crucial question is not whether to create the unbalance,[17] but what the optimum degree of unbalance is, and where and how much the economy should accelerate growth. In contrast, EP via unbalanced growth provides intensive investment to key sectors with large linkage effects, and generates more growth than balanced investment. But linkage effects are neutralized by intermediate imports, underutilized production capacities,[18] capital-intensiveness of products, trade patterns,[19] and ignorance of linkages in plans.[20] The costs of protection and subsidization for export-led growth are paid in terms of additional costs of production, consumption, allocation, and distribution. Furthermore, EP faces difficulties from increasing factor costs and technology gap in production, foreign protectionism, pressures from market liberalization and currency appreciation.

Pros and Cons of Growth Strategies

Balanced and unbalanced growth is on the same plane of economic development in the long run. If unbalanced investment (ex ante) arrives at a certain saturated point (ex post), it becomes an equilibrium point of the economy with a balance which remains unchanged until new demand induces additional unbalanced investment stimulating the economy. The balanced allocation (ex ante) does not necessarily invite economy-wide balanced growth (ex post) due to the following reasons: (a) technological changes stimulate the change of industrial linkages, value added per dollar output, and imported intermediates in the long run; (b) the change of relative prices causes the substitution of inputs in the production process and even causes the substitution of imports, which makes existing linkages vary; (c) new products and change of product-mix affect factor intensity, which alters the original stimulus of final demand; (d) underutilization of production capacities rooted by constraints of input supply and output demand neutralizes linkage effects; and (e) economies of scale caused by an increase in demand for a particular sector affect linkage relations. Ex ante investment creates ex post structure of industries, which is different from ex ante structure. In sum, the balanced allocation does not allow a country to remain unchanged in the industrial structure in the long run.[21]

Table II-1. Sticky Import Substitution and Export Promotion

<table>
<tr><td>Time Period</td><td>1</td><td>2</td><td>3</td><td>4</td><td>5</td></tr>
<tr><td>Import Substitution (IS)</td><td colspan="2">Labor-Intensive</td><td colspan="2">Capital-Intensive</td><td>------------</td></tr>
<tr><td>Export Promotion (EP)</td><td>-----------</td><td colspan="2">Labor-Intensive</td><td colspan="2">Capital-Intensive</td></tr>
</table>

Note: "Labor-Intensive" or "Capital Intensive" indicates labor-intensive manufacturing or capital-intensive manufacturing for import substitution or export promotion.

Since import substitution or export promotion is sticky, IS continues even after EP begins. As shown in Table II-1, suppose the economy begins with labor-intensive IS at time 1, and finishes major substitution at time 2; and begin with capital-intensive IS at time 3 and finishes major substitutions at time 4. However, additional IS for labor-intensive products continue after time 2, and additional IS for capital-intensive products continue after time 4. The labor-intensive EP starts at time 2 when its major IS ends, but continues until time 4 when capital-intensive IS ends and its EP starts. Thus, IS and EP arise together during time 2 for labor-intensive, during time 3 for capital-intensive of IS with labor-intensive of EP, and during time 4 for capital-intensive products.

The efficient allocation of resources provides favorable patterns of trade for export promotion based on comparative advantage, while factor inputs and productivity growth are crucial for competitiveness, basically owing to technology and labor quality. Research and development is essential to keep a leading edge of technology among suppliers, provided by funds, manpower, and management,[22] and diffusion of technology invites high returns of investment.[23] Paul Krugman argues that East Asian growth is driven not by productivity growth but by resource mobilization. He believes that input-driven growth requires continuous and intensive supply of capital and labor, consequently yielding diminished economic returns and a sharp deceleration of growth. Meanwhile, Western society will strain the diffusion of technology, so no technological convergence between East and West is expected. He considers that state intervention in the Asian economies would not make any discernible difference.[24] However, the World Bank estimated that the contributing share of total factor productivity to total growth was over 33 percent for Japan, Taiwan, and South Korean during the period 1960 to 1989,[25] which was higher than U.S. productivity growth of 24.7 percent during the period 1948 to 1979.[26]

Rational Expectations and the Role of Government in Growth

In the short-run adjustment, the effectiveness issue of public policies has been examined in the literature of rational expectations. Sargent and Wallace argued that government policies are not effective because people expect the policy impact and behave or adjust to the policy at the same time with perfect foresight.[27] However, policy effectiveness can be justified by following reasons: (a) people's expectations are applied not only to economic agents but also to policy makers so that future decisions expected by economic agents influence policy makers, (b) the equilibrium conditions in developing countries is remarkably vulnerable because of demand constraints, uncertainty, and inconsistency depending largely on both internal and external economic environments, and (c) the flow of transborder information is interrupted in developing countries though the control of information becomes difficult as the economy grows through foreign trade and foreign investment and information technology advances and diffuses widely.

In the long-run economic planning, market imperfections in LDCs often fail in the efficient allocation of resources, so that state intervention improves its efficiency.[28] Since the market prices do not represent the opportunity cost of the use of factors or certain commodities to society, the free market cannot provide optimum resource allocation.[29] In that case, economic planning is justified to fill the gap between private and social interests. Since the market function in LDCs cannot provide rapid structural change, the government coordinates massive investment and invites rapid structural reform.[30] In turn, the major argument against planning is costs of intervention. The optimum degree of government intervention is based on necessity and sufficiency. The necessity of intervention is predictable, but its sufficiency for successful industrialization can not be easily quantified as LDCs' planners intend or desire to achieve.[31] The positive impact of government intervention has shown in the economic miracle from East Asian countries before the financial crisis in 1997.[32]

However, government intervention often creates more problems than remedies in the short as well as long run. The nature of power shows increasing returns to scale, so that incumbent political power is used to acquire economic power, which makes it possible to acquire additional political power.[33] This chain of actions generates monopoly power in politics and economy by creating the political-economic complex, jeopardizing its fundamental goals of efficiency and equality as illustrated by the Asian financial crisis in 1997. The relationship between politics and economy has been inconsistent worldwide, but positive achievements have occurred in many cases. Democracy is essential for sustainable growth since it facilitates checks and balances in politics and promotes competition in the economy by minimizing corruption and maximizes efficiency throughout the entire system. The theory of balanced development between subsystems (politics and economy) is controversial since the initial conditions are different in various countries including transition economies.[34] If the economy moves quickly forward when politics lags behind, the market may lose the function of fair competition by political pressures, which disturbs efficient resource allocation. As a result, the adjustment costs will be expensive in the future as shown in the restructuring of banking industry and conglomerates in South Korea. Since economic development is a function of time costs in the long run, a balanced development between politics and economy will maximize economic efficiency and political equality.

Did South Korea Choose the Best Growth Strategy?

Four Growth Strategies in South Korea: An Input-Output Model

The performances of four projected growth strategies can be compared with each other by applying an input-output method. It is assumed that the initial base year is 1975 and the terminal year is 1985 in this model, so both 1975 and 1985 IO tables are used.

(a) *Export Promotion without Import Substitution* (Strategy I): Assuming that the export structure remains unchanged at the 1975 structure but export volumes rise by actual amounts in 1985, no further import substitution is expected during the period of 1975-1985 and the technology remains unchanged at the level of 1975, and the domestic demand structure is not different from the actual market so that imports may rise because of absence of import substitution. The column vectors of both output and value added generated by 1985 exports, $X_i[Exp(1985)]$ and $VA_i[Exp(1985)]$, are obtained.

(3.A.1) $X_i[Exp(1985)] = [I\text{-}Ad(1975)]^{-1}*[Exp(1975)]$ and

(3.A.2) $VA_i[Exp(1985)] = Av(1975)* [I\text{-}Ad(1975)]^{-1}*[Exp(1975)]$

where $[I\text{-}Ad(1975)]^{-1}$ indicates the Leontief inverse matrix (domestic model) for 1975, Av(1975) represents a diagonal matrix of value added for 1975, [Exp(1975)] denotes the column vector of 1975 exports, and * means multiplication of two vectors.

(b) *Export Promotion with Import Substitution* (Strategy II): This is the actual growth strategy which South Korea has pursued and achieved great performance in the past. Output and value added generated by 1985 exports can be obtained by:

(3.B.1) $X_i[Exp(1985)] = [I\text{-}Ad(1985)]^{-1}*[Exp(1985)]$ and

(3.B.2) $VA_i[Exp(1985)] = Av(1985)* [I\text{-}Ad(1985)]^{-1}*[Exp(1985)]$

where all variables are obtained by the real input-output tables in 1985 because the export structure is actually based on unmodified 1985 transactions.

(c) *Import Substitution without Export Promotion* (Strategy III): Assuming that export volumes in 1985 stay at the 1975 level, and the rising proportion of 1985 exports from 1975 is allocated for import substitution. The 1985 import vector is modified by non-existence of import substitution for agriculture and mining. The representative vector for this strategy, ImpSub(1985), is obtained by a proportional mix of both 1975 export vector and adjusted 1985 import vector:

(3.C.1) $ImpSub(1985) = g*[Exp(1975)] + h*[ImpMod(1985)]$

where "g" indicates the proportion of 1975 exports amount in 1985 exports, "h" denotes the rising proportion of 1985 exports from 1975, and [ImpMod(1985)] represents the modified import vector based on 1985 imports:

(3.C.2) $X_i[ImpSub(1985)] = [I\text{-}Av(1985)]^{-1}*[ImpSub(1985)]$ and
(3.C.3) $VA_i[ImpSub(1985)] = Av(1985)*[I\text{-}Ad(1985)]^{-1}*[ImpSub(1985)]$

where Xi[ImpSub(1985)] and Xi[ImpSub(1985)] indicate the column vectors of output and value added generated by this growth strategy.

(d) *Domestic Demand Expansion* (Strategy IV): If there are no constraints in domestic demand and supply[35], the expansion of domestic demand can be a supportive growth strategy. If this strategy is applied independently, it is linked closely to the theory of balanced growth. The private consumption vector is assumed as a representative of final demand for this strategy.[36] The resources are converted and reallocated from exports to consumption by the consumption vector at time t, [Con(t)]:

(3.D.1) $X_i[Con(t)*EXP(t)] = [I\text{-}Ad(t)]^{-1}*[Con(t)]*EXP(t)$
(3.D.2) $VA_i[Con(t)*EXP(t)] = Av(t)*[I\text{-}Ad(t)]^{-1}*[Con(t)]*EXP(t)$

where $X_i[Con(t)*EXP(t)]$ indicates output demand generated by domestic consumption reallocated from exports at time t, and EXP(t) denotes the converted amount of exports at time t. The change of value added generated by export promotion is compared to that generated by domestic demand expansion during a certain period:

(3.D.3)
$$\begin{aligned} & dVA_i[EXP(t)] - dVA_i[Con(t)*EXP(t)] \\ & = Av(t)*[I\text{-}Ad(t)]^{-1}*\{[EXP(t)] - [Con(t)*EXP(t)]\} \\ & \quad - \quad Av(t\text{-}1)*[I\text{-}Ad(t\text{-}1)]^{-1}*\{[EXP(t\text{-}1)] - [Con(t\text{-}1)*EXP(t\text{-}1)]\}. \end{aligned}$$

The positive value of the equation (3.D.3) implies that export promotion with import substitution generates more value added than domestic demand expansion. But the strategy of domestic demand expansion was not applicable to an economy with lack of capital and technology at the takeoff stage, such as South Korea in this period.

Estimated Results and Analyses

The input-output exercises based on four alternative growth strategies, as shown in Table III-1, prove that South Korea chose the best growth strategy – Export Promotion with Import Substitution (Strategy II). First, this strategy generates the largest GDP (multiplier: 0.646908) for the same amount of aggregate final demand, except the strategy IV, which was not viable for South Korea. Second, import substitution requires a huge amount of physical and human capital, which can be financed by export earnings. Export promotion requires advanced technology accumulated by import substitution. Both EP and IS are mutually supportive and complementary. Third, export promotion is accompanied by increasing demand for imports so that profits generated by exports may decline significantly without import substitution. Fourth, the movement of comparative advantage due to the product-life cycle theory requires structural changes from time to time, which is adjusted by import substitution to maintain international competitiveness of domestic products.

Table III-1. Projected GDP Multipliers Generated by Growth Strategies
South Korea from Base Year 1975 to Terminal Year 1985

Five Sectors	GDP-Strategy 1	GDP-Strategy 2	GDP-Strategy 3	GDP-Strategy 4
Agriculture	0.067774	0.031247	0.028710	0.166032
Mining	0.012210	0.009273	0.010487	0.004639
Manufacturing	0.315508	0.346476	0.338431	0.177510
Social Overhd	0.010904	0.032845	0.032022	0.034541
Service	0.235267	0.227067	0.175112	0.415231
The Economy	*0.641663*	***0.646908***	*0.584762*	*0.797953*

Sources: Above estimates are based on both 1975 and 1985 Input-Output Tables published by Seoul: Bank of Korea, 1978 and 1988.

Export Promotion without Import Substitution (Strategy I) requires less amount of capital formation with external finance, which may reduce the outstanding foreign debt in South Korea. But increasing import demand for consumer and producer goods may cause a balance of payments problem. Considering that the share of labor-intensive exports declines gradually due to loss of foreign competitiveness, this strategy may face demand constraint in the foreign markets. Import Substitution without Export Promotion (Strategy III) requires manpower for research and development, capital formation, and advanced technology. Intensive import substitution without export promotion invites inefficiency and economic decline. The resource conversion from export promotion to import substitution breaks mutually supportive relationships between them. The lack of advanced technology and qualified manpower heavily disturbs proper import substitution. Domestic Demand Expansion (Strategy IV) is desirable if domestic investment can be fully financed by domestic savings, rapid decline of exports creates excess capacities, the domestic market has enough potential to absorb its supply, and the trade balance does not create a balance of payments problem. This was not viable strategy for South Korea.

Domestic Capital Formation: Sources and Allocation

The economic conditions of South Korea in the 1950s were dismal given a land devastated by a three-year civil war after decades of Japanese colonial exploitation. The proportion of GDP in the secondary sector was 10.1% in 1953 and 15.9% in 1960, and its employment was 5.0% and 26.0% respectively while the primary sector hired 75.0% and 66.0% correspondingly. The 47.4% of workers received an elementary level education, but 42.8% received no education by 1960 due to colonial suppression, war, and poverty.

The proportion of fixed capital formation in GDP was 21.0% from the 1962-1971 period but increased to 33.6% in the 1982-1991 period, while average domestic savings increased from 11.7% to 32.0% respectively. The average share of domestic savings to investment rose from 55.7% to 95.4% in the same periods shown in Table III-2. The sources of external capital was borrowing, foreign direct investment, and foreign aid, mainly from the United States, as shown in Table III-3. Borrowing from foreign countries was $3.4 billion during the first and second five-year plan periods, rising to nearly $20 billion in the third and fourth plan periods, and declining slight to $18.8 billion in the third ten-year period. As economic conditions became attractive, foreign direct investment rose from $96 million in the period of 1962-1971 to $7.4 billion in the period of 1982-1991. Foreign aid reached almost $1.3 billion in the first ten years, but declined rapidly in the 1970s as its economy moved to the capital-intensive industries.

Table III-2. Fixed Capital Formation: South Korea
Selected Years, Average Percent at Current Prices

Period	1962-1971	1972-1981	1982-1991
Investment/GDP	21.0	28.9	33.6
Saving/GDP	11.7	21.6	32.0
Savings/Invest	55.7	74.7	95.4

Sources: The Bank of Korea, Economic Statistics Yearbook, various years.

Table III-3. Sources of External Capital: South Korea
Selected Years, Current U.S. Million Dollars

Types of Sources	1962-1971	1972-1981	1982-1991
Borrowing	3,419	19,939	18,774
Foreign Dir Invest	96	1,153	7,431
Foreign Aid	1,284	13	0

Sources: The Bank of Korea, Economic Statistics Yearbook, various years.

The share of capital formation in agriculture was 8.4% during the first and second five-year economic development plan period and maintained that level during the three decades. The average investment share in manufacturing was 21.2% in the first and second five-year plan periods, 18.7% in the third and fourth plan periods, and 23.9% in the third ten years. A share of public utilities including electricity, gas and water, was maintained at the level of 8.0 to 9.0%, while that of transportation and communications was 22.9%, 22.6%, and 13.9% during the three ten-year periods defined in Table III-2 and 3. The average investment share in dwelling was 10.8% in the period of 1962-1971, but rose to 17.3% in the third ten year period as household income rose. As a result of capital formation, the industrial structure was transformed in terms of shares of GDP and employment in the primary, secondary, and tertiary sectors.

Factor Productivity and GDP Sensitivity to Export Growth

The ratio of incremental GDP to domestic fixed capital formation (dGDP/dK), a proxy of capital productivity, was 0.386 in the period of 1961-1970, 0.232 in 1971-

1980, and 0.230 in 1981-1990 (an average of 0.283 for 1961-1990). Underutilization of production capacities reduces capital productivity. An export incentive policy such as protection and subsidization attracts more investment to the targeted industries than needed which creates over capacities. Idle capacities in one industry create bottlenecks in the other which causes inflation due to supply constraints. The problems of bottlenecks and idle capacities induce industrial inefficiency and economic decline.

The average annual growth rate of labor productivity in South Korea was 11.82% in the period of 1975-1984, and declined to 9.48% in the period of 1985-1994.[37] The high growth of labor productivity was attributable to education and training, research and development, and technology transfer efforts, in addition to modernization of production facilities. South Korean conglomerates have been in better conditions for research and development than small- and medium-sized businesses, which contribute to productivity growth if other things are equal.[38]

Model I in Table III-4 explains that GDP growth is positively related to the proportion of investment to GDP and employment growth. Ways to raise production without additional capital lie in utilizing idle capacities, substituting labor for capital, and increasing productivity. Model II explains that the proportional change of GDP is positively related to the incremental change of exports. Its sensitivity depends on the share of imported intermediate inputs and labor-intensive products in exports.

Table III-4. The Sensitivity of GDP to Export Growth
South Korea, 1953-1986, Two Regression Models

(dY/dt)/Y	Constant	(dK/dt)/Y	(dL/dt)/L	(dX/dt)/X	R-Square
Model I	0.01307	0.16192*	1.00307*		0.27068
(t-Statistic)	(0.66934)	(2.48754)	(2.45393)	--------------	DW=2.219
Model II	0.01109	0.15942*	0.57450	0.07804*	0.36059
(t-Statistic)	(0.59515)	(2.57116)	(1.29574)	(2.01940)	DW=2.015

Sources: The Bank of Korea. DY/dt indicates the change of GDP, dK/dt denotes fixed capital formation, dL/dt represents the change of employment, and dX/dt means the change of exports. * indicates the significance at the level of 95%.

Patterns of Export Promotion and Import Substitution

Patterns of Export Promotion (1975-1985): (a) The share of exports in South Korea shifted from labor-intensive industries in 1970s to capital- and technology-intensive industries in 1980s. The export share of textiles and clothing in South Korea rose from 19.4% in 1966 to 30.4% in 1975, but declined to 21.7% in 1985, while that of electronics and communication equipment rose continuously from 1.38% in 1966 to 11.2% in 1985. (b) The export expansion rate[39] during the period of 1975-1985 was higher in petroleum and coal products (10.2%), iron and steel products (16.9%), other metal products (14.9%), electrical appliances and equipment (14.8%), and transportation equipment (19.4%). (c) One dollar of aggregate exports created 64.16

cents in 1975 and 64.69 cents in 1985 (rose by 0.52 cents) during the period of 1975-1985 in terms of direct and indirect effects. This was caused by the change of export share in the economy, technological transformation, different shares of imported intermediate input, and change of factor costs. (d) The GDP share generated by exports in South Korea rose from 18.6% in 1975 to 22.7% in 1985 while the output share generated by exports rose from 24.8% to 28.3%, correspondingly.

Patterns of Import Substitution (1975-1985): (a) The import index (1966=100) in Korea rose to 493 in 1975 and 1,291 in 1985. The import share declined rapidly in processed food products from 17.5% in 1966 to 3.1% in 1985, basic chemicals and their products from 23.2% to 11.0%, industrial machinery from 20.2% to 10.2%, and transportation equipment from 17.3% to 3.3% correspondingly. (b) The import substitution rate[40] was 3.47% in South Korea during the period of 1975-1985. Higher import substitution appeared in chemical products, iron and steel, machinery, and transportation equipment. (c) Import demand for $1.00 exports in South Korea rose from 35.8 cents in 1975 to 37.2 cents in 1985. Higher import demand for exports was in the categories of textiles and clothing, chemicals, iron and steel, and electronics. (d) The import substitution rate for exports was negligible due to raw materials, producer durables, sophisticate intermediates, and a lack of technological expertise in specific items. Major import substitution for intermediates in South Korea was in chemical products, iron and steel, and other metals in the period.

Can North Korea Follow the Lessons from the South?

The previous section suggests that export promotion with import substitution was the best growth strategy chosen by South Korea in the early stages of economic development in the 1960s. Although President Park pursued continuous economic development with his growth strategy, South Korea paid heavy costs directly or indirectly originated by his authoritarian rule suppressing democratic movement to retain political power. It is ironic that South Koreans admire an opponent of democracy even though his authoritarian presidency was not necessary for efficient economic growth in the long run.

Authoritarian Rule by President Park (1961-1979)

In politics and government, Park's authoritarian regime faced many difficulties due to a lack of legitimacy. Park tortured, jailed, and expelled his opponents to foreign countries to secure his political power base. Police and intelligence officers closely watched daily activities of military officers, politicians, and business people to minimize threat from internal uprising. They falsely created conspiracy cases by providing fake evidence of links to North Korea, intimidating political oppositions. The political party nominated candidates to run for the National Assembly, and its members could not vote their consciences, but took orders from the Blue House. The National Assembly did not represent the people but simply became a rubber stamp extension of the Blue House. He fortified his power by appointing loyal persons from his home province to key positions in his administration. They were career officers but their roles were similar to political appointees. The judicial branch fell under the control of President Park who appointed judges who were personally loyal to him. As a result, the function of checks-and-balances disappeared and the King-President controlled the entire government.

In economy and business, President Park launched a series of five-year Economic Development Plans (EDPs) in an attempt to control the economy by industrial policy. The Economic Planning Board (EPB) allocated available resources and managed overall development affairs, while the Korea Development Institute (KDI) supplied policies to the government, becoming the dominant think tank in Seoul. In the first and second EDPs (1962-1971), export promotion with import substitution was successful for labor-intensive industries. The subsequent third and fourth EDPs (1972-1981) invested in heavy and chemical industries because of self-defense pressures, decreasing competitiveness of labor-intensive exports, and long term prospects of capital-intensive exports.[41] However, intensive investment in major industries during the short period of time created huge idle capacities while other industries faced bottlenecks, which reduced factor productivity and economic efficiency. Thus, poor allocation of resources distorted the industrial structure, and protection and subsidization for export industries generated monopolistic profits to favored business groups at the expense of consumers. The conglomerates were able to access to loans with favorable interest rates, which were then invested in real estate for huge capital gains. As a result, income disparity widened between rural and urban, east and west, owners and workers, and favored and unfavored, which created serious social resentments against Park's regime.

In society and labor, President Park prohibited formation of labor unions to prevent their political mobilization and to secure the economic interests of conglomerates which supplied funds for further political operations. As a result, workers suffered from low wages, while the conglomerates enjoyed business profits which they shared with politicians. The share of employee compensation in GDP in manufacturing industries for South Korea and Taiwan was 31.8% and 44.3% in 1974, 41.8% and 47.1% in 1980, and 42.6% and 50% in 1986 respectively. This implies that employees of South Korea received wages less than those of Taiwan by 8.3% of GDP in average in the same period.[42] President Park destroyed judicial independence by politicizing the judicial system and forcing intellectuals support his regime or at least keep silent by threatening their job security. President Park needed a reliable power base supporting his regime. He fortified his power by surrounding himself with loyal military officers from his home province, creating an informal organization having a more influential than formal chain of command. He gave them special favors in education, assignments, and promotions. Similar favors were given to career officials in other ministries, so that persons selected from his home province or those close to them filled major positions in his entire regime. They formed the mainstream of the regime while others remained in supporting roles, which intensified regionalism in South Korea. Regionalism favored loyalty to capability, which reduced efficiency and expedited antagonism against his regime by the unfavored.

The Cost of Authoritarian Politics in South Korea

Generally speaking, economic development facilitates democratization owing to self-recognition by increasing education and training, information flow through borders by increasing trade and technological advancement, formation of the middle class demanding more political participation, and internationalization demanding reciprocity and equal opportunities between nation states. At the time of military coup in 1961, South Korea was at a low stage of educational and industrial development because of Japanese exploitation and destruction from the Korean War. But a decade of trade and investment generated more income and improved the quality of life. President Park wanted to make a nation free from starvation and achieved rapid economic growth which expedited democratization, although he hoped to keep political power in his life. History shows a similar ironic case in China. Chairman Deng Xiaoping opened the five special economic zones in 1978 and allowed free trade and investment, keeping its socialist system while exploiting capitalistic profits. China also sent many bright students to the United States and Europe to learn advanced science and technology. Increasing openness through education and trade made China face democratic movements in major cities, leading to the Tiananmen Incident in 1989. It was similar to the Pusan-Masan Incident in South Korea in 1972. President Park and Chairman Deng understood democratic impulses emanated from foreign countries, but underestimated those generated by individual conscience and values. They brought economies alive at the takeoff stage, but failed to keep efficiency because of corruption from the political-economic complex.

The financial crisis in South Korea in 1997 came from corrupt politics, over-expanded businesses, and uncompromising labor unions. First, the government had been a main source of corruption to protect interests of Chaebols due to the lack of check-and-balance in the National Assembly, bureaucratic monopoly in the administration, and non-existence of social justice in the judicial system. Second, Chaebols had over-expanded and their monopoly power caused problems: misallocation of resources, heavy debt-financed structure, cross-finance guaranteeing system, lack of transparency, and others. Third, the labor unions had been powerful in wage negotiations with business owners since 1988, so that the workers gained more compensation than productivity growth in average. Fourth, the value of Korean Won vis-à-vis U.S. Dollars remained high and strong value of Korean Won raised prices of its exports. Moody's credit rating on South Korea declined which raised costs of foreign loans when financial scandals of Hanbo and Kia appeared on the horizon. Thus, major exports from South Korea began to lose their competitiveness in the world market, resulting in a huge trade deficit. Meanwhile, rapid outflow of foreign capital expedited problems of the balance of payments in South Korea. The financial authorities knew the perilous situations of foreign exchanges in March 1997, but failed to provide remedies to avoid embarrassing the presidential candidate from the ruling party. The Bank of Korea used up foreign exchange reserves to protect the Won from falling although currency devaluation was necessary and realistic.

When President Kim Dae Jung took over the power, his administration pursued reform policies focusing on financial institutions, corporate management, state-owned enterprises, and labor relations. However, his reform policies faced continuous resistance from existing interest groups in politics, economy, and society. Additionally, corruption of the ruling party itself created another problem. As a result, the administration spent a huge amount of tax money to restructure the system, but its performance was far behind general expectations. Those adjustment costs were the prices to be paid for authoritarian politics beginning from President Park in 1961. Park could mobilize available resources intensively and aggressively, but the civilian government led by Chang Myun could do the same through the democratic process. Considering that the armed forces were better trained than civilian manpower due to the Korean War, we can imagine that the degree of performance could be better in the military regime than a civilian in the 1960s. However, as we noted above, authoritarian politics strengthens the economic power by creating a political-economic complex, which interrupts competition in the market, distorts resource allocation, and reduces capitalistic efficiency. After the 1997 financial crisis, South Korea paid a high adjustment cost to fix the problems. If South Korea pursued gradual development strategies under a democratic government in the 1960s, the adjustment costs would not have been so expensive.

Political development is essential in pursuing sustainable growth because the check-and-balance system in politics promotes competition in economy, and the self-adjustment function of the democratic system reduces corruption. The modernization of a nation-state requires coordinated and integrated efforts of its subsystems, including politics, economy, security, and others. If the economy moves fast forward while politics in lag, the system creates problems of corruption reducing efficiency so that adjustment costs impose a heavy burden on economic growth over the long run. The current leadership of South Korea recognized that balanced development between politics and economy is necessary to escape from the economic crisis. However, the reality of politics is different from ideal. The political monopoly in South Korea came from the nominating system for party candidates running for the National Assembly. Candidates who wanted to be a National Assembly member had to demonstrate loyalty to a party boss in order to get the nomination. If a member of National Assembly voted against the party line, he could not get nominated in the next election. Therefore, the nominating system should be removed and primary elections need to be introduced. This is the most urgent and important reform, but both ruling and opposition parties do not want to revise the election law in order to maintain their existing interests. Since the party candidates running for the Assembly seats in each electoral district become delegates to vote for the presidential candidate of each party, the nominating system guarantees the presidential candidacy of the party chairman, while the primary election system requires open competition.

Lessons from South Korean Experiences

We are able to draw followings from the South Korean experiences. First, when the market was not competitive and the economy was primitive, government intervention with plans and policies were necessary to expedite economic takeoff by providing efficient resource allocation. The efficiency gain could remain until the economy was simple and easily controllable in labor-intensive industries pursuing import substitution. Second, when the economy became increasingly complex by moving towards capital- and technology-intensive industries pursuing export promotion, government intervention caused market failures by creating bottlenecks and idle capacities. Therefore, reduced state intervention was necessary by depending on market function. Third, the favored groups of the political-economic complex such as politicians-bureaucrats-judges with powerful business interests have enjoyed monopolistic benefits, jeopardizing market efficiency and inviting economic decline, which culminating in the financial crisis of 1997. Inefficiency coming from corruption could have been corrected by removing entrenched monopoly power in politics, economy, and society through democratization. In other words, balanced development between politics and economy reduces adjustment costs in the long run to fix problems caused by the political-economic complex.

The South Korean experience provides several lessons for transition economies such as China, Vietnam, and North Korea, as noted in this author's previous studies:[43] (a) a series of economic development plans should be used in early stages of economic takeoff, even if political freedom is restricted, as the aggressive driving forces expedite a big push effect on the economy; (b) government intervention should be gradually reduced after ten years from the initial point, and a balanced path should be pursued between politics and economics based on fair competition with the leadership watching corruption closely; (c) economic expansion should start from import substitution of labor-intensive products and move to export promotion of the same industries, and import substitution of capital- and technology-intensive products should be emphasized at the start, moving to export promotion of the same products; (d) proper capital could be supplied by selling ownership (except in energy, transportation, communications, finance, and media industries), and aggressive investments should be made in education and training and research and development, but with an effort to minimize protection of infant industries; (e) if politics remain unchanged, the economy will lose efficiency and equality, which threatens continuous growth, thus time is important in this case to reduce adjustment costs for recovery; (f) balanced growth between politics and economy is essential, and other sectors are also important to reduce adjustment costs, and the defense budget should be minimized to economize limited resources; and (g) subsequent policy reforms for adjustment are necessary to make the economy efficient, reducing accumulated costs arising from state intervention. Since outdated policies induce unnecessary costs, speedy policy adjustment is essential through the democratic process. Self-adjustment function of democratic decision-making system should be respected because it is a source of economic efficiency in the long run.

Can North Korea Learn from the South Korean Lesson?

The economic problems of North Korea stem from its socialist system. The planned or projected consumption and production by the government causes inefficiency by bottlenecks and idle capacities in industries. Marxist ideology does not allow personal property rights, and a small group holds political power under the name of proletariat dictatorship. Loyalty-based compensation for workers lessens motivation and reduces productivity. The heavy burden of military expenditure reduces investment for infrastructure and manufacturing facilities, which raises overhead costs in the entire economy. Heavy censorship threatens borderless communications, and brainwashing interrupts creative ideas, and lack of education and training and research and development disturbs technological improvement. A self-sanctioned autarkic economy makes North Korea unable to exploit its comparative advantage in the economy so that the production possibility frontier remains unexpanded. It is also difficult for North Korea to mobilize resources to increase input factors for additional production. Pyongyang has used much of its resources to prevent internal uprising by policing intellectuals and political dissidents, a waste of resources making the economy inefficient. The rigidity without flexibility by centralizing power interrupts self-adjustment, which reduces efficiency and productivity. The leadership of North Korea must understand the importance of time-cost considering that Pyongyang has wasted time by delaying many opportunities for meager gains.

Unfortunately, Pyongyang faces a dilemma: openness threatens the survival of the regime, but the economy cannot revive without openness. The only available option is clear: "to open its door by taking a risk and provide a peace treaty with Seoul." It is essential that North Korea should give up development and proliferation of weapons of mass destruction. If Pyongyang follows this option, the international community will become closer and friendlier through pursuing trade and investment by removing barriers toward globalization for mutual prosperity. However, as long as North Korea pursues the development of weapons of mass destruction and maintains the forward deployment of conventional weapons near the DMZ area, the United States, Japan and South Korea must prepare militarily against this threat. Additional investment of North Korea in its national security further jeopardizes its economic growth. If North Korea wants to realize economic growth, it must open the market and remove the military threat. This is the only way Pyongyang can survive. It is obvious that the Sunshine Policy of President Kim Dae Jung is unable to exist without reciprocity and transparency. If Chairman Kim Jung Il wants to remove North Korea's name from the U.S. List of terrorist states and to get support from the international community, the only option to take is to make North Korea *a normal nation* which can apply the lessons from South Korean experiences for its own economic development. This has been the course pursued by many Eastern European countries. Every dictator throughout history wanted to keep their political power, but failed because they did not listen to outside advisors to address and resolve both existing and coming problems.

Summary and Conclusion

We have examined that the export-led growth strategy with import substitution under President Park Jung Hee and determined that it was the best choice at the takeoff stage of the South Korean economy in the 1960s. Despite his early success in economic development by the intensive mobilization of factor input, his achievements are tarnished for several reasons that were not necessary for economic development. First, Park took political power by force and did not hesitate to torture, jail, and expel his opponents ruthlessly. Police watched over dissidents continuously, and his administration disrupted their employment opportunities. Humanism must be respected as part of values for economic development. Second, his authoritarian politics suppressed democratization by force. The political power was used to acquire economic power, which led to additional political power. Corruption from the political-economic complex caused both market and government failures. Third, President Park intensified regionalism in South Korea by designating a faction from his home province as the mainstream of his administration, providing special favors in personnel management. He created additional seats in the National Assembly providing a proportional representative system with no electoral districts in order to collect political campaign funds illegally and to expand his influence in politics. Fourth, the military coup brought military culture into society so that an undemocratic way of thinking prevailed, leading to a friend-or-foe mentality with no middle ground. Finally, because none of these measures was essential to economic growth, a civilian government could have achieved the same degree of performance as Park did for economic development. Even assuming that his economic performance was better than a civilian government, the cost of unbalanced development between politics and economy was much more expensive than short-term gains from his early success.

Like China, North Korea can follow the South Korean model of economic growth considering that current situations of the North Korean economy are not better than that of South Korea in the early 1960s. In the early stages of economic development, capital formation is essential to expand production capabilities. North Korea can borrow from external savings, attract foreign direct investment, and receive foreign aid if the leadership has an intention to reform its politics and economy. Additional sources include World War II compensation from Japan, a peace dividend from signing a peace treaty with South Korea and the resulting disarmament, privatization of state-held assets, export of the labor force, and domestic savings from export earnings. Resource allocation can be based on unbalanced growth strategy and coordinated industrial structure with South Korea, early investment in agriculture, export promotion with import substitution starting from labor-intensive industries, investment in infrastructure, and the formation of human capital. The government must reduce its intervention as soon as the economy diversifies. The experiences of South Korea well illustrate that authoritarian politics disrupt competition in the market, inducing both market and government failures. The transformation of socialism into a market system requires recognition of personal property rights, introduction of a price system, privatization of state-owned enterprises, and provision of efficiency measures. In the process of economic transformation, Russia experienced that people did not easily change their old habits in terms of the way of thinking and their way of life. Both Russia and China fighting against corruption have been well documented. North Korea would experience the same if it opens its markets. Thus, North Korea can utilize the lessons from the South Korean experience to minimize the cost of unnecessary adjustment.

Then, will North Korea follow the lessons from South Korean experiences? The answer is not so simple. First, socialist ideology and domestic politics in North Korea are critical factors. Chairman Kim Jung Il has monopolized information by isolating the people from the outside world in order to hide domestic problems. If it opens the door to the world, its people will know the reality of its totalitarian regime, which suppressed them in order to retain political power despite poor economic conditions. This may cause an internal uprising threatening the survival of its regime. Second, trade expands the production possibility frontiers for trading partners by taking comparative advantage for exports, while an autarkic economy having a fixed market cannot expand this frontier. Thus, North Korea cannot survive without foreign trade and investment over the long run. Third, North Korea has maintained its over-expanded armed forces and developed weapons of mass destruction, which it has tried to use a leverage in negotiations with South Korea and the United States, although these expenditures reduced investment in infrastructure causing economic decline. Unfortunately, the development of weapons of mass destruction and the forward deployment of conventional forces have created problems in international relations, leading U.S. President George W. Bush to call North Korea part of the "Axis of Evil" along with Iraq and Iran in his 2002 state of the union address. North Korea has to make a critical decision whether it will stay in the "Axis of Evil" or move away from it because the United States has made it clear that it is willing to destroy the evils together with their terrorist associates to protect its national security.

Policy Recommendations to North Korea: First, North Korea should open its door to the world as soon as possible, and liberalize its politics in line with economic development by taking risks. Otherwise, North Korea will perish without economic transformation through foreign trade and investment. Higher risks will give high returns although openness itself does not guarantee economic success. Second, because inter-Korean economic cooperation is not sustainable due to the lack of reciprocity and transparency, North Korea must provide a political-economic environment that capitalizes foreign aid for its economic takeoff, while South Korea needs to enhance its capabilities by improving efficiency with competition in politics and economy. Third, North Korea should change the concept of national security. Based on realism, North

Korea may seek cheating from partners and better achievement of gains, which is impossible in the age of globalization. But liberalism suggests that basic determinants of state preferences are representation and rent-seeking in government, market incentives in business, and social identity and values in society. It means that military strength is not the only measure of national security considering that no countries in Northeast Asia intend to attack North Korea as long as it remains as a normal state. Finally, there are some reasons why North Korea remains on the U.S. list of terrorist states. As long as the name is not removed from that list, economic survival of North Korea would be difficult. The majority of South Korean people do not support the Sunshine Policy if North Korea avoids reciprocal and transparent actions for "southern hospitality." The current U.S. position toward North Korea is realistic and reasonable, even though the South Korean government believes that it negatively affects inter-Korean relations. The ball is in North Korea's court.

Endnotes

---

[1] Edward N. Muller "Economic Determinants of Democracy," in *Inequality, Democracy and Economic Development*, ed. Manus I. Midlarsky, New York: Cambridge University Press, 1997, 137. "capitalist economic development also initially heightens income inequality in a country, and this is expected to have a negative impact on democratization because a high level of income equality radicalizes the working class, enhances class polarization, and reduces the tolerance of the bourgeoisie for political participation by the lower classes." Therefore, the rise of working class can negatively contribute to democracy.

[2] Reuters, "Iran, Iraq and North Korea Dismiss Bush Accusations," *The New York Times on the Web*, January 30, 2002. President called Iraq, Iran, and North Korea as an "Axis of Evil." Michael O'Halon, "Choosing the Right Enemies," *The New York Times on the Web*, February 6, 2002.

[3] WheeGook Kim, "Alternative Growth Strategies of North Korea: Lessons from Experiences of South Korea and Taiwan" presented to the 1996 Annual Convention of the Allied Social Science Associations held at San Francisco Hilton Towers, San Francisco, California on January 5-7, 1996.

[4] Bela Balassa, *The Newly Industrializing Countries in the World Economy*, New York: Pergamon Press, 1981, 4-6.

[5] Paul N. Rosenstein-Rodan, "Problems of industrialization of Eastern and South-Eastern Europe," Economic Journal_53 (June-September 1943): 202-11. _____, "Notes on the Theory of the 'Big Push'," reprinted in *Economic Development for Latin America*, ed. Howard S. Ellis and H. C. Wasllich, New York: St. Martin's Press, 1961.

[6] _____, "Natura Facit Saltum: Analysis of the Disequilibrium Growth Process," in *Pioneers in Development*, ed. Gerald M. Meier and Dudley Seers, New York: Oxford University Press for World Bank, 1984, 207-21.

[7] Ragnar Nurkse, *Problems of Capital Formation in Underdeveloped Countries*, New York: Oxford University Press, 1953, 12. W. Arthur Lewis,_*The Theory of Economic Growth*, London: Allen & Unwin, 1955, 274-83. Tibor Scitovsky, "Two Concepts of External Economies,"

Journal of Political Economy 62 (April 1954), 143-52. Rodan and Nurkse stress the balance in demand (markets), but Lewis and Scitovsky emphasize the balance in supply (investment).

[8] Ragnar Nurkse, "Balanced and Unbalanced Growth," in *Equilibrium and Growth in the World Economy*, ed. Gottfried Haberler and Robert M. Stern, Cambridge, Mass.: Harvard University Press, 1961, 241-59.

[9] _____, "International Economy and the Problem of Growth," in *Equilibrium and Growth in the World Economy*, pp. 304-24.

[10] Raul Prebisch, "Five Stages in My Thinking on Development," in *Pioneers in Development*, p. 179. He concerned about the disparities of income and wealth in the periphery as well as between center and periphery countries. The disparities in the periphery were explained by the concentration of land, protection, and inflation; but those between countries were considered by technological advantages.

[11] _____, *The Economic Development of Latin America and Its Principal Problems*, New York: United Nations, 1950. _____, *Economic Survey of Latin America*, New York: United Nations, 1950.

[12] John H. Power, "Import Substitution as an Industrialization Strategy," *The Philippine Economic Journal* 5(2) (1966): 169-74 and 191-9. John H. Power, "Import Substitution as an Industrialization Strategy," *The Philippine Economic Journal* 5(2) (1966): 169-74 and 191-9.

[13] Albert O. Hirschman, *The Strategy of Economic Development*, New Heaven: Yale University Press, 1958. Chapter 4. Arguments about Unbalanced Growth. He argues that balanced growth may not stimulate the economy in the absence of sufficient resources such as capital, entrepreneurs, and decision-makers because of lack of big pushing powerAlbert O. Hirschman, *The Strategy of Economic Development*, New Heaven: Yale University Press, 1958. Chapter 4. Arguments about Unbalanced Growth. He argues that balanced growth may not stimulate the economy in the absence of sufficient resources such as capital, entrepreneurs, and decision-makers because of lack of big pushing power.

[14] Ibid., Chapter 5. Investment Choices and Strategies.

[15] Ibid., p. 112 and 116 in Chapter 6. Interdependence. The backward linkages utilize significant amounts of intermediate inputs from other activities, while the forward linkages provides inputs to the other activities, generating further impact on domestic demand and supply.

[16] Albert Hirschman, "A Dissenter's Confession: 'The Strategy of Economic Development' Revisited," in *Pioneers in Development*, 108-9. This explains the politico-economic complex in LDCs.

[17] A. P. Thirlwall, *Growth and Development*, London: McMillan Press, 1978, 181-6. Ashok Mathur, "Balanced versus Unbalanced Growth," *Oxford Economic Papers* 18 (July 1966): 137-57. Paul P. Streeten, "Balanced versus Unbalanced Growth," *The Economic Weekly* (April 20, 1963), 669-71, reprinted by Gerald M. Meier, *Leading Issues in Economic Development*, 642.

[18] V. Bulmer-Thomas, *Input-Output Analysis in Developing Countries*, New York: John Wiley & Sons, 1982, 183-97. V. R. Panchamukhi, "Linkages in Industrialization: A Study of Selected Developing Countries in Asia," *Journal of Development Planning* 8 (1975): 121-65. The correlation coefficients between linkages and capacity underutilization were positive, and the relationship between output and income multiplier was negative in Indian experiences.

[19] Exporters exploit a country's comparative advantage, which does not necessarily represents larger industrial linkages.

[20] Hollis B. Chenery and T. Watanabe, "International Comparisons of the Structure of Production," *Econometrica* 26(4) (October 1958): 487-521. Pan Yotopoulos and Jeffrey Nugent, "A Balanced Growth Version of the Linkage Hypothesis," *Quarterly Journal of Economics* 87(2) (1973): 157-71. Prem S. Laumas, "Key Sectors in Some Underdeveloped

Countries," *Kyklos* 27(1) (1975): 62-79. Leroy P. Jones, "The Measurement of Hirschmanian Linkages," *Quarterly Journal of Economics* 90(2) (May 1976): 330. James Riedel, "Factor Proportions, Linkages and the Open Developing Economy," *The Review of Economics and Statistics* 57(4) (1975): 487-94. Victor Vulmer-Thomas, "Trade, Structure and Linkages in Costa Rica," *Journal of Development Economics* 5 (1978): 73-86. Guido Cella, "On the Input-Output Measurement of Interindustry Linkages," *Oxford Bulletin of Economics and Statistics* 46(1) (1984): 73-84. James W. McGilvray, "Linkages, Key Sectors and Development Strategy," in *Structure, System, and Economic Policy*, ed. Wassily Leontief, New York: Cambridge Univ Press, 1977, 49-65. Geoffrey Hewings, "The Empirical Identification of Key Sectors in An Economy," *Developing Economies* 20(2) (June 9182): 173-95.

[21] Ronald E. Miller and Peter D. Blair, *Input-Output Analysis: Foundations and Extensions*, Englewood Cliff, N.J.: Prentice-Hall, 1985, 266-73. Victor Vulmer-Thomas, *Input-Output Analysis in Developing Countries*, 194-7.

[22] Eric A. Hanushek, "Expenditures, Efficiency, and Equity in Education: The Federal Government's Role," *American Economic Review* 79(2) (May 1989): 46-51. _____, "Economics of Schooling: Production and Efficiency in Public Schools," *Journal of Economic Literatures* 24 (September 1986): 1141-77. George Psacharopolous and Maureen Woodhall, *Education for Development: An analysis of Investment Choices*, New York: Oxford University Press, 1985.

[23] Richard Levin and others, "Appropriating the Returns from industrial Research and Development," *Brookings Papers on Economic Activity*, Washington, DC: Brookings Institution, 1987, 783-820. Richard R. Nelson, "Government Stimulus of Technological Progress: Lessons from American History," in *Government and Technical Progress*, New York: Pergamon Press, 1982, 451-82. Richard M. Cyert and David C. Mowery, ed., *Technology and Employment: Innovation and Growth in the U.S. Economy*, Washington, DC: National Academy, 1987.

[24] Paul Krugman, "The Myth of Asia's Miracle," *Foreign Affairs* 73, 6 (November/December 1994): 2-78. Others have different views. See Steven Radelet and Jeffrey Sachs, "Asia's Reemergence," *Foreign Affairs* 76,6 (November 1997): 44-59.

[25] World Bank, *The East Asian Miracle: Economic Growth and Public Policy*, New York: Oxford University Press, 1993, p. 58. Also see "The Asian Miracle: Is It Over?," *The Economist*, March 1-7, 1997, pp. 23-25. Paul Krugman used Alwyn Young's estimates for 118 countries over 1970, which proved to be incorrect.

[26] Dale W. Jorgenson, "Productivity and Postwar U.S. Economic Growth," in Dale W. Jorgenson, ed., *Productivity, Volume 1: Postwar U.S. Economic Growth*, Cambridge, MA: MIT Press, 1995, 1-23.

[27] Thomas J Sargent and Neil Wallace, "Rational Expectations and the Theory of Economic Policy," *Rational Expectations and Econometric Practice*, ed. Robert E. Lucas, Jr. and Thomas J. Sargent, Minneapolis: University of Minnesota Press, 1981, 199-213.

[28] Subrata Ghatak, *An Introduction to Development Economics*, London: Allen & Unwin, 1986, 309.

[29] A. P. Thirlwall, *Growth and Development*, 212-4. Bela Balassa, "The Lessons of East Asian Developments: An Overview," *Economic Development and Cultural Change* 36 (3 Supplement) (April 1988): S273-90. The role of government is to create a modern infrastructure, to provide a incentive system, and to help export expansion.

[30] Martin Fransman, "International Competitiveness, Technical Change and the State: The Machine Tool Industry in Taiwan and Japan," *World Development* 14(12) (1986): 1375-96. Joseph E. Stiglitz, "Technological Change, Sunk Costs, and Competition," *Brookings Papers on Economic Activities: Social Issue on Microeconomics*, Washington, DC: Brookings Institution, 1987, 883-939. Martin Fransman, "International Competitiveness, Technical Change and the

State: The Machine Tool Industry in Taiwan and Japan," *World Development* 14(12) (1986): 1375-96. Joseph E. Stiglitz, "Technological Change, Sunk Costs, and Competition," *Brookings Papers on Economic Activities: Social Issue on Microeconomics*, Washington, DC: Brookings Institution, 1987, 883-939.

[31] Ronald Findlay, "Trade, Development, and the State," in *The State of Development Economics: Progress and Perspectives*, ed. Gustav Ranis and T. Paul Schultz, New York: Basil Blackwell, 1988, 78-95. World Bank, World Development Report 1987, New York: Oxford University Press, 58-77. The priorities are given to high technology; infrastructure including transportation, communications, and power; welfare improvement without resource abuses.

[32] Gustav Ranis, "Another Look at the East Asian Miracle," *The World Bank Economic Review* 9(3) (September 1995): 509-534. He pointed out that East Asian governments clearly understood the importance of human capital. World Bank, *The East Asian Miracle: Economic Growth and Public Policy*, New York: Oxford University Press, 1993, 79-103.

[33] Adam Przeworski et al., *Sustainable Democracy*, New York: Cambridge University Press, 1995, p. 40.

[34] Minxin Pei, "The Puzzle of East Asian Exceptionalism," in Larry Diamond and Marc F. Plattner, eds., *Economic Reform and Democratization*, Baltimore, MD: Hohns Hopkins University Press, 1995, 112-25.

[35] If domestic savings exceed demand for capital formation and the economy keeps trade surplus, and if production capacities are underutilized because of unexpected fall of exports, a part of resources to be allocated to exports is purely reallocated to domestic demand without any frictional costs.

[36] The private consumption is chosen as a representative-vector because: (a) Government expenditures, either consumption or investment, are planned by the central authorities. (b) Fixed capital formation, either private or public, is focused on construction, machinery, transportation and communication equipment. (c) Fixed capital formation means investment for both exports and domestic demand, which is not limited to domestic demand only. (d) The final demand vector of government consumption in the input-output tables lies in one sector, government services and defense, in South Korea showing limit of data limitations.

[37] Ministry of Labor, *Yearbook of Labor Statistics*, Seoul: ROK Government, various years.

[38] Eui Hang Shin and Moon-Ki Suh, "An Analysis of Structural Determinants of Organizational Effectiveness: The Case of Business Firms in South Korea," *International Journal of Korean Studies* III(1) (Spring/Summer 1999): 163-189.

[39] The export expansion rate is defined by a changing ratio of export-generated output to total domestic output for an industry during a certain period [(dOUT*EXP/dt)/OUT].

[40] The import substitution rate is defined by a changing ratio of total imports among total output for an industry [dIMP/dt)/OUT].

[41] Dong-Se Cha and Kwang Suk Kim, eds., The Half Century of the Korean Economy: Historical Evaluation and Vision for 21st Century," (Seoul: KDI, 1995), p. 50.

[42] The Bank of Korea, *Input-Output Tables*, Seoul, Korea: ROK Government, various years. National Statistical Office, *Major Statistics of Korean Economy*, Seoul, ROK Government, various years. Council on Economic Planning and Development, *Input-Output Tables*, Taipei, Taiwan: Executive Yuan, various years. _____, *Taiwan Statical Data Book*, Taipei, Taiwan: ROC Government, various year. Considering depreciation, taxes, and labor intensity in both economies in comparing the statistics, the difference may be reduced to around 5.0% of GDP.

[43] Wheegook Kim, "Democracy and Economic Development in South Korea and Its Application," International Journal of Korean Studies, Vol. 2, No. 2 (Fall/Winter 1998), p. 83-84.